ECONOMICS AS SCIENCE

This book provides a critical approach to the study of economic thought – from neoclassical economics, to Marxian economics, and to Keynesian economics – through the lens of science and the scientific method.

It examines the collection of ideas that constitute the core of economic thought in the five basic fields of economics: growth theory, income distribution, macro-economics, price theory and international trade. In each of these, the analysis is chronological, detailing the various events and developments that led scholars to inquire into the underlying mechanics of the phenomena in question. This is followed by a critical examination of the various scholarly contributions, including those of Nobel Prize laureates, in terms of their scientific merit. Each of the five core chapters begins with a listing of chapter objectives and ends with a summary, as well as discussion questions to encourage debate. Short excerpts from the key works are provided to allow the reader firsthand exposure to primary sources.

Reinforcing the idea that economics is a scientific endeavor, *Economics as Science: A Critical History of Economic Thought* sets out to demonstrate the relevance of the tools and techniques students of economics acquire during their studies in understanding economic phenomena throughout the ages. It will be an invaluable resource for students of the history of economic thought and economics more generally.

Bernard C. Beaudreau is Professor of Economics, Université Laval, Canada.

ECONOMICS AS SCIENCE

A Critical History of Economic Thought

Bernard C. Beaudreau

Routledge
Taylor & Francis Group
LONDON AND NEW YORK

Designed cover image: wynnter/Getty Images

First published 2025
by Routledge
4 Park Square, Milton Park, Abingdon, Oxon OX14 4RN

and by Routledge
605 Third Avenue, New York, NY 10158

Routledge is an imprint of the Taylor & Francis Group, an informa business

British Library Cataloguing-in-Publication Data
A catalogue record for this book is available from the British Library

Library of Congress Cataloging-in-Publication Data
Names: Beaudreau, Bernard C., 1955– author.
Title: Economics as science: a critical history of economic thought / Bernard C. Beaudreau.
Description: Abingdon, Oxon; New York, NY: Routledge, 2025. | Includes bibliographical references and index.
Identifiers: LCCN 2024053704 (print) | LCCN 2024053705 (ebook) | ISBN 9781032863337 (hardback) | ISBN 9781032863306 (paperback) | ISBN 9781003527060 (ebook)
Subjects: LCSH: Economics—History.
Classification: LCC HB75 .B35 2025 (print) | LCC HB75 (ebook) | DDC 330.09—dc23/eng/20250219
LC record available at https://lccn.loc.gov/2024053704
LC ebook record available at https://lccn.loc.gov/2024053705

ISBN: 978-1-032-86333-7 (hbk)
ISBN: 978-1-032-86330-6 (pbk)
ISBN: 978-1-003-52706-0 (ebk)

DOI: 10.4324/9781003527060

Typeset in Times New Roman
by codeMantra

CONTENTS

TABLES

PREFACE

This book grew out of the belief that the history of scientific thought, whether it be in/of physics, biology, psychology or economics, should be as thought provoking as it is informative, as useful to the undergraduate student attempting to understand the evolution of a discipline as it is to the graduate student conducting leading-edge research in a specific field, and lastly as entertaining as it is critical. It is with this in mind that I set out to write a critical history of economic thought, one that is as thought provoking as it is controversial. *Economics as Science: A Critical History of Economic Thought* examines the history of the five fundamental fields in economics through the prism of science and the scientific method. They are growth theory, income distribution, macroeconomics, price theory and international trade theory.

The material contained in this book originated in years of lecture notes from my undergraduate and graduate history of economic thought courses. I would like to thank the generations of economics students at Université Laval, both at the undergraduate and graduate level, for their many comments and criticisms.

1
INTRODUCTION

After nearly a quarter century of success (1945–1975), economics now finds itself once again in a state of crisis. The Productivity Slowdown of the 1970s and the inability of policy to restore growth, the stock market crashes of 1987 and 2008, the Financial Meltdown of 2008, the Great Recession, the Debt Crisis in Europe and the failure of free-trade to bring prosperity to the world's poor have all contributed to increasing cynicism. Questions abound. How did we get it so wrong? How did a discipline that goes back centuries find itself incapable of explaining these events, let alone preventing them? Even the former Queen of England, Elizabeth II, weighed in, asking London School of Economics' professors why they failed to predict the Financial Meltdown of 2008?

These developments raise a number of questions, not the least of which is why? Why have we, despite over two centuries of structured thought, failed to understand the workings of highly advanced, highly complex systems of wealth creation? Put differently, why has the body of knowledge commonly known as economics come up short? Where did we go wrong?

To answer this question, we turn our attention to history, to the events that shaped economic thought and to the economic thought proper. Take for example, growth theory. Why is it that despite decades (1980–2020) of what can only be described as an all-out attempt to understand the underlying causes, we have yet to understand growth as evidenced by the still-unresolved Productivity Slowdown and the West's inability to return to pre-1970s growth rates. Add to this the fact that we have failed in our attempt at understanding and hence solving the problem of economic development. Clearly, something is amiss.

Similar narratives can be told in nearly all fields in economics, from income distribution to price theory to international trade. Take for example the theory of

DOI: 10.4324/9781003527060-1

the firm, the cornerstone of the theory of growth as well as a key element in all fields. According to classical, radical and neoclassical thought, material wealth is increasing in labor and capital. Yet, according to elementary physics, both modern-day labor and capital are organizational factor inputs and, as such, not physically productive as neither is a source of what is considered by material scientists to be the only physically productive factor input, namely force or energy. In short, production theory stands in violation of basic physics. Another example is consumer theory where it is typically argued that *Homo œconomicus* maximizes utility by choosing goods and services subject to a budget constraint, a view that constitutes the profession's vision of *Homo sapiens*, namely as an avaricious goods and services accumulator and effort minimizer. Interestingly, this profile of the raison d'être of our species has not migrated outside of economics (i.e. to the fields of sociology, psychology or business administration). This is not particularly surprising, given that it is orthogonal to all that we know about the human condition, about human motivation and about human behavior.

More examples will be provided throughout the book. Together, they raise what we believe is the most fundamental question of the history of economic thought and of economics in general, namely why? Why the lack of scientific laws? Why the disregard for the findings of the tributary fields of physics and psychology? Why does economic theory appear to stand apart from science in general?

This book points to a single cause, namely its origins as a branch or offshoot of moral philosophy. Despite being a subject matter dealing primarily with material processes (i.e. energy-based processes), it remained a fundamentally moral field of inquiry, developing principles and laws whenever necessary that were and continue to be, for the most part, orthogonal to those found in natural philosophy.

It will be argued that throughout its two-and-one-half-century history, it was unable to shed its cloak of moral philosophy. Perhaps the best example is the birth of neoclassical economics which came on the heels of the increasing radicalization of European society in the mid-19th century, largely as the result of the rise of radical thought (Friedrich Engels and Karl Marx). The radical school maintained, in the classical tradition, that because labor was in fact the only physically productive factor input, then it – and it alone – was entitled to all of the resulting income/wealth so to speak. Wanting to uphold the existing social and economic order and prevent a return to a planned/state-controlled economy, classical economics including Alfred Marshall and William Stanley Jevons responded by simply decreeing *ex-cathedra* that capital was physically productive, violating the laws of classical mechanics according to which tools, not being a source of force/work, are not physically productive. In this instance, moral philosophy-based ideology, not science, won the day.

In fact, it could be argued that if science had been invoked, then the classical economists at the time, including the radicals, would have come to understand that in an industrial economy, neither labor (machine operatives) nor capital (tools) is physically productive, but that both are organizational inputs, providing the framework/organization for the force/energy that powered the industrial revolution and industry today. In hindsight, the resulting non-scientific ideology and its associated propaganda made matters worse as today, material processes as modeled in economics and engineering are orthogonal to one another, having little in common.

To further illustrate this point, compare economics and thermodynamics, two fields that were in large measure born of the steam engine, and hence are of roughly the same age. As Adam Smith made clear in the title of his 1776 magnum opus, *An Inquiry into the Nature and Causes of the Wealth of Nations*, the purpose of political economy was to understand the nature, but more importantly, the causes of the wealth of nations. Similarly, the purpose of thermodynamics was to understand steam/heat, specifically as a force, the force powering the industrial revolution. Two hundred years later, the latter characterizes to the point of defining physics (Laws of Thermodynamics), while economics finds itself in a state of recurrent crises and paradoxes, the Leontief paradox, the information paradox and the Productivity Slowdown being just a few.

Clearly, the time is nigh. For economics to move forward, it must shed the cloak of ideology and embrace science, whatever the outcome.[1] It is with this in mind that this book sets out to critically examine the history of what are considered to be the five fundamental fields of modern-day economics, namely the theory of growth, income distribution, macroeconomics, price theory and international trade. The approach is simple, consisting of separating fact from fiction, science from ideology.

The book is organized as follows. To begin with, a series of core principles that will be used throughout the ensuing chapters will be presented and developed. These include (i) the fundamental physics of material processes, (ii) the fundamentals of information and coordination strategies and (iii) the fundamentals of exchange activity in an industrial context (i.e. the *Industrial Exchange Sequence*), and are presented in Chapter 2. Subsequent chapters are organized around the five key fields, namely economic growth, income distribution, macroeconomics, price theory and international trade. Each chapter will be organized as follows. To begin with, historical regularities will be presented through the prism of the core principles. For example, economic growth in 19th-century Great Britain will be examined using the basic elements of process engineering. This will then be followed by a historical narrative of the corresponding economic thought with an emphasis on its scientific underpinnings. Hypotheses and theories that either were not tested or were tested and unsupported, but which continue to be part of the literature (i.e. be taught), will be considered to be ideology.[2] The last chapter summarizes our findings in table form, identifying which theories and ideas are truly scientific in nature, and which can best be described as a form of ideology. A concluding chapter closes the book.

Notes

1. It is important to distinguish science from the scientific method, the latter being an approach to understanding and the former, the body of scientific knowledge.
2. While we realize that ideology has a pejorative connotation, this is not the meaning ascribed to it here. Rather, it should be understood as a set of unproven ideas, hypotheses and concepts. Ideology can become science if it (i) does not violate the laws of the physical world and (ii) has been tested repeatedly and found to be true.

2

CORE PRINCIPLES

Unlike energy and matter, knowledge is unique in that while it too cannot be destroyed, it can be created. Put differently, the stock of knowledge is "non-decreasing" over time – that is, over time knowledge either remains constant or increases. And, of course, it is bounded above by what shall be referred to as the truth. Once something is understood, is tested, is proven, then it cannot be undone. In short, case closed, summarily speaking.

In this vein, it stands to reason that the endeavor which began over two century and a half ago by the French Physiocrats as a quest to understand wealth will have yielded and will yield a non-decreasing stock of knowledge – that is, a stock that is either constant an increasing function of time. With every generation, new knowledge, new information and new findings will increase (or not decrease) the stock of knowledge with the result that today, after manifold generations, we "know" more than yesterday, and a lot more than a century ago.

This is important as we set about the task of examining the history of economic thought. Those who came before us endeavored to understand that which we take for granted today. As Isaac Newton once pointed out, we know more than those that came before us for the simple reason that we are standing on their shoulders. It is with this in mind that we now turn and examine the core principles in the science of wealth. That is, the set of principles that have evolved over time and today stand as a tribute to science in general and economics in particular. First and foremost is wealth, more specifically, the equations of motion of wealth. What is wealth and how is it created? Here, we borrow from applied physics and formalize wealth in terms of material processes. As one of an infinite number of material processes in the known universe, wealth follows a set of rules, notably those taken from classical mechanics and thermodynamics. In doing so, we are implicitly stating the

DOI: 10.4324/9781003527060-2

obvious, namely that economics like all other material sciences cannot violate the laws of physics. Put differently, there cannot be a set of rules for the known universe and another for economics.

Among the other core principles presented in this chapter are (i) a theory of economic institutions (i.e. markets versus hierarchies), known as the information and coordination strategies approach to economic institutions and (ii) the industrial exchange sequence approach to understanding industrial-era transactions technologies.

Specific Objectives

At the end of this chapter, you should:

- Understand the physical underpinnings of material processes in general and those that underlie the creation of wealth.
- Understand the distinction between physically productive and non-physically productive factor inputs.
- Understand the physical limits to productivity growth.
- Understand the role of capital, labor, supervision and information in material processes.
- Understand the role of machine speed and speed in general in the unprecedented increase in wealth over the past two centuries.
- Understand the problem of information and coordination, both within firms and in the economy in general.
- Understand the various strategies firms and societies have used and continue to use in order to solve their respective information and coordination problems and their relative strengths and weaknesses.
- Understand the temporal nature of the production process and the need for coordination.
- Understand the role of money (credit, fiat money) in the production process.
- Understand the role of entrepreneurial expectations in the creation of wealth.

Core Principle I: Wealth, Value Chains/Bushes and Material Processes

Economics is the study of material wealth, the latter being defined as goods and services. Goods are defined as transformed raw materials and are material in nature. By contrast, services are defined simply as one or a series of transformations performed on an object. Think of a haircut, or a bus ride. A hair cut transforms your scalp, while a bus ride transforms your physical position in space, bringing you from point A to point B. For the sake of exposition, goods will be defined in terms of value chains. A value chain is a formal representation of the myriad material processes involved in the production of a good.

Value Chains and Bushes

Value chains and bushes are conceptual representations of the various processes and sub-processes which together define the overall production of a good. Value chains are a chronological series of stages or links, while value bushes are simply disaggregated value chains, with multiple, parallel raw material, manufacturing and marketing links. Take, for example, the value bush for an iPhone. Each of the components can be seen as a branch and thus a value chain, produced in different plants, oftentimes in different countries. The final products (components) of each of these value chains are then brought together at the assembly link to produce the final product, that is, iPhone *per se*, after which additional value added is provided by the transport, marketing and sales links.

It is assumed that each stage/link in the value chain creates or adds value. Hence, the title, value chain. And the value process is synonymous with material processes. That is, each value process is also a material process. In other words, adding value is an example of a material process, and as such analogous with other such processes in the natural world including photosynthesis.

Visions-Augmented Value Chains

A more complete representation of the various processes and sub-processes that define goods and services are the visions-augmented value chain (VAVC) and bushes (VAVB), which as their name implies include an initial, pre-production entrepreneurial-visions link. The entrepreneurial-visions link corresponds to the stage at which a good and/or process is conceived of. In the case of the iPhone, it consists of the entrepreneurs/managers/R&D laboratory that came up with the idea of a telephone that combined the features of an MP3 player, a computer and myriad other applications. Sequentially, the visions link precedes the resulting value chain per se and finds itself at the apex.

The role of the visions stage/link is, as such, to conceive of goods and services as well as the associated value chain and/or bush. For example, most observers agree that one of Steven Jobs' greatest managerial attributes was his concern for detail in so far as the Apple VAVCs were concerned. New product releases were near perfect in so far as communication and coordination was concerned. If a product was scheduled for launch on March 1, worldwide, then on the morning of March 1st, all Apple suppliers would have it on hand.

TABLE 2.1 Vision-Augmented Value Chain

Stage 1	Vision of Product/Process
Stage 2	Raw materials and intermediate inputs
Stage 3	Manufacturing
Stage 4	Marketing

The visions-augmented value chain is an important analytical construct in growth, macroeconomics, microeconomics and international trade.

The Conglomeratization of Industry

Not only are most producers integrated vertically (i.e. the links in a value/supply chain), but many are also conglomeratized, by which it should be understood operating in myriad different (and sometimes related) markets, both nationally and internationally. For example, ten large food conglomerates control more than half of the world's food supply. Companies like General Electric of the United States and Lever of Great Britain are highly diversified (across products) and multinational.

The point here is that the bulk of world GDP and trade is carried out by a few hundred large multiplant, multiproduct, multicountry conglomerates, not by a large number of small-atomistic, single-product, single-plant companies. It goes without saying that deciphering their behavior is a daunting and complex task, one that cannot be accomplished using simple mundane abstractions. Interestingly, Matthew Boulton, Adam Smith' muse, produced a number of goods (known at the time as toys) at his Soho manufactory in Birmingham.

Material Processes

As wealth consists of, by definition, the set of goods and services produced in a given time period, and that goods and services are themselves the result of multiple sequential and parallel value-adding material processes and sub-processes, it stands to reason that by transitivity, wealth consists ultimately of the value of all material processes in an economy. Hence, it follows that to understand wealth, one must begin by understanding the workings of the individual material processes and sub-processes.

The Science behind Material Processes

Material processes are not exclusively found in economics but are ubiquitous in nature. Planetary motion, photosynthesis, chemical reactions and human existence itself are all examples of material processes. It therefore stands to reason that because of their universality, any and all formalizations should, at the very least, be consistent across disciplines. In other words, the general rules or laws that govern material processes should be the same across disciplines. This is a property known as consilience.

> The central idea of the consilience world view is that all tangible phenomena, from the birth of stars to the workings of social institutions, are based on material processes that are ultimately reducible, however long and tortuous the sequences, to the laws of physics.
>
> *(Wilson 2012, 291)*

Definition: Consilience

In science and history, consilience (also convergence of evidence or concordance of evidence) refers to the principle that evidence from independent, unrelated sources can "converge" to strong conclusions. That is, when multiple sources of evidence are in agreement, the conclusion can be very strong even when none of the individual sources of evidence are very strong on their own. Most established scientific knowledge is supported by a convergence of evidence: if not, the evidence is comparatively weak, and there will not likely be a strong scientific consensus.

This principle is based on the unity of knowledge; measuring the same result by several different methods should lead to the same answer. For example, it should not matter whether one measures the distance between the Great Pyramids of Giza by laser range finding, by satellite imaging, or with a meter stick – in all three cases, the answer should be approximately the same. For the same reason, different dating methods in geochronology should concur, a result in chemistry should not contradict a result in geology etc.

The word consilience was originally coined as the phrase "consilience of inductions" by William Whewell ("consilience" refers to a "jumping together" of knowledge). Another way of looking at consilience is in terms of overall objectives or intent. For example, in the case that concerns us (wealth-related material processes), economists are not the only ones interested in the workings of the economy. Process engineers share similar objectives, namely understanding the equations of motion of material processes. Engineers, however, do so with the intention of improving overall technological efficiency, while economists do so with the goal of better understanding the process of wealth creation and ultimately, of allocative efficiency.

This being said, it stands to reason that in the name of consilience or universality, the basic underlying model of material processes in both disciplines should be similar, if not identical. Otherwise, problems will arise, not the least of which will be lack of equivalence. There cannot be two realities, each equally true. Put differently, there cannot be a set of immutable laws in physics and engineering, and another in economics. In what follows, a consilient model of material processes known as the Energy-Organization (EO) approach to modeling material processes is presented an approach which bridges these two disciplines.

The Energy-Organization Approach to Modeling Material Processes

Whereas most models of production focus almost exclusively on capital and labor, the focus here is on the two "universal" factor inputs, namely broadly defined energy and broadly based organization. Broadly defined energy includes both animate and inanimate forms of energy. By animate energy, it should be understood muscular (human and animal) power; by inanimate energy, it should be understood wind, fossil fuel-based, hydraulic and nuclear power. All production processes/material processes involve the consumption of energy of one type or another.[1] Organization will be defined as the conception/design of, and the overseeing (i.e. supervision) of energy-consuming (i.e. entropic) production processes. The development of the steam engine by Papin, Savary, Newcommen and Watt in the 17th and 18th centuries is an example of the former, while its day-to-day operation is an example of the latter. In the nature, the design of and supervision of energy-consuming processes is governed by forces which are not, at least yet, fully understood. These will be referred to as naturally occurring or spontaneous entropic processes. What differentiates these from man-made (i.e. anthropomorphic) entropic processes is the exact form of organization, broadly defined. From the Paleolithic era to the present, *Homo sapiens* have designed and redesigned man-made entropic processes (i.e. anthropic entropic processes). For example, the development of stone tools in the *Paleolithic* period altered the very nature of work. By reducing waste (i.e. increasing efficiency), primitive tools such as hammers and knives increased the amount of work that could be accomplished for a given quantity of muscular energy. In fact, the development and improvement of man-made entropic processes is what defines various pre-historical and historical eras (e.g. the stone age, the bronze age, the machine age).

The core of the EO approach to modeling production processes (Beaudreau 1998) is Issac Newton's second law of motion, namely $F = ma$, where F = force, m = mass, and a = acceleration. Put differently, $a = F/m$. That is, acceleration is simply force divided by mass. The corresponding definition of work is $W = fd$, where W = work, f = force, and d = distance: work equals force times distance. Thus, the greater is f, *ceteris paribus*, the greater is W. The greater is d, *ceteris paribus*, the greater is W. In short, the more force exerted and the longer the distance (or time period) over which the force in question is exerted, the more work performed. Redefining work as output permits us to write the basic axiom of the EO approach, namely that for any given, well-defined man-made entropic process, output is an increasing function of energy consumption.

Contrast this with the standard definition of work found in political economy, namely that work is an increasing function of capital and labor (i.e. $W = f(K, L)$). Capital and labor, it is argued, produce output (value added). Both are assumed to be productive. Just what it is that capital and labor do in production processes is unspecified. Terms such as capital productivity and labor productivity, however, connote the idea that both somehow work. Inanimate forms of energy such as oil, gas and electricity consumption are assumed to be intermediate inputs, and, hence, are not productive in the conventional sense. Put differently, they are not factors of production (value adding). Rather, capital and labor are assumed to add value to energy and other raw materials. Broadly defined organization is also ignored. Production processes are assumed to exist, and management issues are, in general, ignored.

The Physics-Economics Divide

Clearly, the physical and economic definitions of work and hence, value are orthogonal. For three centuries, physicists have focused on force and energy as the basis of work; economists, on the other hand, have focused on capital and labor. In physics, tools and machines (i.e. capital) modify and transmit force and energy, but are not, as such, a source of energy – and thus, work. In political economy, energy (inanimate energy forms) is viewed as an intermediate good, and, thus, is not productive in the traditional sense (value-adding).

A Physical Model of Production

Here, the analysis begins by examining the purely physical aspects of production, namely the relationship between work and energy. To this end, production is defined in terms of the following functional relationship between work (i.e. output) and the force (i.e. energy) expended in the process.

$$W(t) = F[E(t)] \tag{2.1}$$

where $W(t)$ = work in period t; and $E(t)$ = energy (i.e. force) in period t.

Animate and Inanimate Forms of Energy

In general, energy can be disaggregated into two categories, namely $E_a(t)$, animate (i.e. muscular) energy, and E_i(t), inanimate energy ($E(t) = E_a(t)+E_i(t)$). Examples of animate energy include human and animal (i.e. muscular force, force brawn), while examples of inanimate energy include internal combustion, steam power, wind power, hydraulic power and electrical power. Work will be modeled as an increasing function of animate and inanimate force/energy.

The Role of Tools/Machines

From the Paleolithic era (i.e. the Stone Age) on, work as defined here has invariably involved the use of tools/machines. These include axes, adzes, levers, presses, drills, screws, hammers, screwdrivers, saws *etcetera*. This raises the question what is the role of tools in broadly defined work? Are they a source of energy? Are they productive in the classical sense? A similar question was raised by Nobel Prize laureate (Chemistry) turned economist Frederick Soddy in the 1920s. Who or what, he asked, was ultimately responsible for producing goods and services? As the following allegory indicates, in Soddy's mind, there was no doubt: energy was the primary factor.

> At the risk of being redundant, let me illustrate what I mean by the question How do men live? by asking what makes a railroad train go. In one sense or another, credit for the achievement may be claimed by the so-called engine-driver, the guard, the signalman, the manager, the capitalist, the share-holder—or, again, by the scientific pioneers who discovered the nature of fire, by the inventors who harnessed it, by labour which built the railroad and the train. The fact remains

> that all of them by their collective effort could not drive the train. The real engine-driver is the coal. So, in the present state of science, the answer to the question how men live, or how anything lives, or how inanimate nature lives, in the sense in which we speak of the life of a waterfall or of any other manifestation of continued liveliness, is, with few and unimportant exceptions, By sunshine. Switch off the sun and a world would result lifeless, not only in the sense of animate life, but also in respect of by far the greater part of the life of inanimate nature.
>
> *(Soddy 1924, 4)*

Accordingly, because tools are not a source of energy, they are not productive in the physical sense. That is, they do not work. Nowhere is this better illustrated than in the applied physicist's definition of a machine which consists of an instrument used to transmit or modify force/energy.

> Machinery is used to change the magnitude, direction and point of application of required forces in order to make tasks easier. The output of useful work from any machine, however, can never exceed the total input of work and energy.
>
> *(Betts 1989, 172)*

Arthur Beiser, in Modern Technical Physics, provides a similar definition:

> A machine is a device which transmits force or torque to accomplish a definite purpose.
>
> *(Beiser 1983, 208)*

By using primitive hammers and knives, early man (i.e. Paleolithic and Neolithic man) was able to better direct and apply his force. Formally speaking, however, while tools allowed him to minimize energy loss (i.e. wasted energy), they did not allow him to increase the total amount of work beyond the initial level of force. That is, they were not a source of additional energy.[2] Implicit here is the basic notion of thermodynamic efficiency, defined as work out versus work in. By better transmitting muscular force, tools improved early man's thermodynamic efficiency. With the same amount of energy, more work could be done.

The Problem of Defining and Measuring Productivity

This raises the key question of the scientifically-accurate measure of tool/capital productivity. Specifically, how should the productivity of tools/machines (i.e. capital) be defined and measured? The answer is self-evident. Since tools/machines/capital are not a source of energy, they cannot be regarded as productive in the classical sense (i.e. performing work/working). Rather, capital productivity must be measured in terms of its ability to transform force/energy into useful work, a concept known as second-law efficiency. As such, the notion of capital productivity is qualitative (i.e. a scalar), and not quantitative in nature. Increasing the amount of capital, *ceteris paribus*, will not increase output. However, increasing the quality of capital, say by improving thermodynamic efficiency, will increase output. For example, James Watt's improved steam engine, by reducing the heat loss of the Savary and Newcommen steam engines via an external condenser, increased the overall efficiency (i.e. exergy) of what at the time was known as "fire power." One important fact remains, namely that it was not and is not an energy source.

This allows us to rewrite Equation 2.1 as follows:

$$W(t) = \eta(t)E(t) \tag{2.2}$$

where $\eta(t)$ is defined as second-law efficiency.[3]

Equation 2.2 implicitly defines the EO approach to production processes. $W(t)$, output/work is an increasing function of $E(t)$, energy/force, and $\eta(t)$, thermodynamic efficiency, the latter being defined by the organization of the material process in question. Increasing $\eta(t)$, thermodynamic efficiency, *ceteris paribus*, leads to higher output/work. Increasing energy, *ceteris paribus*, leads to higher work/output. $\eta(t)$ is tool-specific. Better, more efficient tools will have higher $\eta(t)$'s, and vice versa.

A Tool/Machine Taxonomy

According to classical mechanics, there are three basic tools/machines: the lever, the inclined plane and hydraulic press.[4] Each directs and applies a specific form of energy. Table 2.2 lists the three basic tools/machines as well as the associated composite tools, which are combinations of basic tools. For example, the lever is the basic tool/machine, which transforms force in the case of a crane, a wheel barrow, and various pulleys. All tools/machines, it therefore follows, can and should be viewed as combinations of the three basic tools: the lever, the inclined plane and the hydraulic press (see Betts (1989), Beiser (1983)).

TABLE 2.2 A Tool Taxonomy

Basic Tool	*Composite Tool*
Lever	Scissor, Plier, Wheel barrow
Hydraulic Press	Hydraulic Jack
Inclined Plane	Wedge, Jack, Screw

Source: Beaudreau (1998), 22.

A Specific Functional Form: The Kinetics-Based EO Production Function

The EO approach to modeling material processes can be further refined in a number of useful ways. For example, alternative functional forms can be introduced. One such function form is the kinetics-based production function where the exact relationship between energy use $E(t)$ and output $W(t)$ is set in terms of the laws of kinetics. This is illustrated in Equation 2.3 where output is increasing in $s(t)$, machine speed, which, itself, is increasing in energy, $E(t)$ according to $E(t) = 1/2m(t)s(t)^2$, where $m(t)$ is mass. The latter is the simple law of transitional kinetics. In other words, machine speed $s(t)$ is increasing in the square-root of energy $E(t)$.

$$W(t) = s(t)T(t) \text{ s.t. } E(t) = 1/2m(t)s(t)^2 \quad (2.3)$$

This functional form is extremely useful in understanding productivity growth in the 19th and 20th centuries as it focuses on the role of machine/process speed as the key factor in increasing levels of wealth. For example, both the steam engine and the electro-magnetic motor contributed to raising the standard of living by raising throughput rates of existing, sometimes archaic material processes.[5]

CAPSULE: SPEED AND ACCELERATION AS THE KEY FACTORS IN INDUSTRIALIZATION AND GROWTH

While the growing energy use throughout the 19th and 20th centuries was the key to the process of industrialization and today's wealth levels, it manifested itself in the form of ongoing acceleration and greater and greater process speeds. Charles Babbage, the 19th-century polymath, referred to velocity (of industrial processes) as the defining factor of the industrial revolution, and 20th-century business historian Alfred D. Chandler described the second industrial revolution in the following terms:

> In modern mass production, as in modern mass distribution and modern transportation and communications, economies resulted more from speed than from size. It was not the size of the manufacturing establishment in terms of number of workers and the amount and value of productive equipment, but the velocity of throughput and the resulting increase in volume that permitted economies that lowered costs and increases output per worker and per machine.
>
> (Chandler 1977, 244)

The General Electric Company, in a video released in 1937, referred to acceleration as "the magic hand of speed" in reference to the productivity gains from electric unit drive.

> Our transportation systems, our industrial processes, our factory machinery – all of these have felt the magic hand of speed – controlled speed that has given us more things to enjoy and more time in which to enjoy them: that has produced more goods, for more people at less cost, and that has created a better standard of living for the average man. These are the benefits of every-increasing speed and accurate control.
>
> (General Electric Company 1937)

A General Model of Material Processes: The Energy-Organization Framework

Our discussion of the role of tools in material processes brings us to the second universal factor input, namely, organization. Machines define the framework in which force/energy is transformed into work. In physics as in economics, it is implicitly assumed that (i) well-defined work (read: material) processes exist (i.e. Equation 2.2) and (ii) that they are self-regulating. In this section, the broader question of organization – specifically, the organization of the use of broadly defined energy to accomplish specific goals, in this case, the creation of wealth, is examined. The discussion begins with a definition of what shall be referred to as man-made entropic processes – that is, anthropomorphic energy-using processes. This is then followed by two issues, namely (i) the design of and (ii) the supervision of man-made energy-consuming processes. Together with tools, these constitute broadly defined organization.

Naturally Occurring Entropic Processes

This section begins with a discussion of entropic processes in general. Entropic processes can be defined as environments in which energy is transferred from one system to another or others in the form of work. For the sake of discussion, define two basic types of entropic processes: natural entropic processes which occur spontaneously in nature, and anthropomorphic entropic processes, which, as their name implies, are conceived of and overseen by human-beings (i.e. managed, supervised). For example, solar radiation, the wind, the tides, river currents, unicellular and multicellular organisms are examples of natural spontaneously occurring entropic processes based on solar energy, and its derivatives. The production of food, tools, shelter and culture, however, are examples of anthropomorphic entropic processes. What distinguishes these two sets of processes is the nature of the relevant set of instructions. In the former, it evolved randomly (or so it appears) over the course of the last 15 billion years, while in the latter, it evolved over the course of the last 2,000,000 years. In the case of anthropomorphic entropic processes, *Homo sapiens sapiens* designs and supervises (i.e. oversees) the work process. Take, for example, the simple windmill, which converts a temperature gradient (i.e. the wind) into work. The human body, however, is an example of a natural entropic process whose blueprint is the result of millions of years of evolution/mutation (i.e. the human genome), and whose supervision is auto-regulated (autonomic nervous system, paleopallium).

Man-Made Entropic Processes

Clearly, tools are the defining element in man-made entropic processes. They are to production processes what the human body is the process of life. They transmit and/or modify force/energy. Given the presence of friction, it follows that the better are the tools (i.e. the less friction), the higher the efficiency, and the greater the work.

The presence of energy and tools, however, is not a sufficient condition for work as both occur spontaneously in nature. Also required is an activity which shall be referred to as the overseeing of or supervising of material processes. For example, take the case of a simple gasoline engine-powered water pump. With an endless supply of refined hydrocarbons (gasoline), it can work continuously *ad infinitum*. Suppose, however, that, for some reason, the pump arm spontaneously dislodges itself from the drive shaft. Clearly, in this case, the energy provided by the engine will be lost ($\eta(t) = 0$), unless of course the problem is rectified. Supervision, as this example illustrates, is an important aspect of organization. Man-made entropic processes are subject to breakdown. Supervision, one could argue, minimizes the resulting energy loss. Nineteenth-century political economist Alfred Marshall described the role of supervision in manufacturing in the following terms:

> New machinery, when just invented, generally requires a great deal of care and attention. But the work of its attendant is always being sifted; that which is uniform and monotonous is gradually taken over by the machine, which thus becomes steadily more and more automatic and self-acting; till at last, there is nothing for the hand to do, but to supply the material at certain intervals and to take away the work when it is finished. There still remains the responsibility for seeing that the machinery is in good order and working smoothly; but even this task is often made light by the introduction of automatic movement, which brings the machine to a stop the instant something goes wrong.
>
> *(Marshall 1890, 218)*

To capture the role of tools and supervision in production processes, Equation 2.2 was rewritten as follows:

$$W(t) = \eta[S(t), T(t)]E(t) \tag{2.4}$$

where $S(t)$ and $T(t)$ correspond to the level of supervision at time t and tools at time t, respectively. For the time being, it is simply assumed that second-law efficiency is an increasing function of tools and supervision. Thus, for a given quantum of energy, the more/better tools and supervision, the greater is second-law efficiency (i.e. $\eta(t)$), and hence, the greater is output (i.e. $W(t)$). Capital and supervision, it therefore follows, are not directly productive; rather, they contribute to work via their effect on second-law efficiency.

Here, the analysis stops short of explicitly modeling supervisory activity, except to point out the obvious, namely that, historically, it has been carried out by individuals (animate supervision), and secondly, has been organized hierarchically with conventionally defined workers (lower-level supervisors) at the bottom, line supervisors above and senior managers (e.g. CEOs, CFOs and the board of directors) at the top. It is clear that while not a source of energy, the supervisory input is nonetheless a sine quo non of virtually all production processes. Without supervisors, output becomes probabilistic (including the null set). Tools and machines break down, resulting in a loss of energy and output.

CAPSULE: AGRICULTURE THROUGH THE PRISM OF THE EO MODEL

Agriculture is a key sector in virtually all countries in the past, in the present and undoubtedly, in the future. How then are we to understand this essential sector scientifically, beyond the standard labor and capital? Beginning with plant-based agriculture, photosynthesis is the material process whereby energy, specifically solar radiation, transforms carbon dioxide, water and chlorophyl into glucose or sugars – in short, transforming light energy into chemical energy. The actual work is not that of the farmer, nor that of the fossil fuel powered tractor, but that of solar radiation. Take away the sun, and the whole process ends.

For animal-based agriculture, the starches, glucose and sugar generated by plant-based agriculture are transformed into various proteins, which are then consumed, fueling life in general.

Ultimately, solar radiation is what powers both plant-based and animal-based agriculture. The carbon dioxide, the water and the chlorophyl are necessary but are not what does the actual work – that is, what is being physically productive. It therefore stands to reason that farmers don't de facto produce, rather they metaphorically set the table for the sun to do its job, so to speak. Similarly, tractors don't produce crops, rather they too set the table so to speak. The latter, however, is also a material process, powered today by fossil fuels. Plowing, harrowing, planting, tilling and harvesting are all material processes. However, neither is actually productive in the sense that it yields glucose and sugars – in short, food.

Upper-Level Managers: Leibenstein's Taxonomy

Upper-level managers/supervisors can be further classified according to their function. For example, in his work on economic development, Harvey Leibenstein identified two types of managers, namely routine and innovative. Put differently, some upper-level supervisors/managers are concerned with the day-to-day workings of the firm, while others are concerned with altering either the production process or some part thereof, or the product itself (value added) – what Leo Alting refers to the *hardness, state, or information content.*

> I may distinguish two broad types of entrepreneurial activity: at one pole, there is routine entrepreneurship, which is really a type of management, and for the rest of the spectrum we have Schumpeterian or new type entrepreneurship. (We shall refer to the latter as N-entrepreneurship.) By routine entrepreneurship we mean the activities involved in coordination and carrying on a well-established, going concern in which the parts of the production function in use (and likely alternatives to current use) are well known and which operates in well-established and clearly defined markets. By N-entrepreneurs, we mean activities necessary to create or carry on an enterprise where not all markets are well established or clearly defined and/or in which the relevant parts of the production function are not completely known.
>
> *(Leibenstein 1968, 72)*

The former are the equivalents of the supervisors referred to above, while the latter are the equivalent of the designers/conceivers, those who conceive of or improve upon existing entropic processes or products. Put differently, progress requires dynamic innovative managers; otherwise, upper- and lower-level supervisors will be condemned to manage the existing set of anthropomorphic entropic processes *ad infinitum*. Recall that anthropomorphic entropic processes, unlike natural entropic processes, are man-made, subject to change if and only if changed.

The Generalized Energy-Organization Production Function

This simple two-factor model (energy and organization), based on the laws of classical mechanics, thermodynamics, kinetics and the principles of organization (i.e. design and supervision), describes virtually all production processes, past, present and future. Take, for example, tree harvesting. Prior to the advent of the mechanical saw, animate energy was transmitted and applied by tools such as axes and saws to fall trees. The required supervision was typically provided by the owners of animate energy (i.e. lumberjacks). With the advent of the chain saw, animate energy (i.e. the internal combustion engine) was combined with inanimate energy, with essentially the same tools and supervision (i.e. saw teeth), to accomplish the task. More recently, with the advent of the mechanical harvester, inanimate energy alone is used in conjunction with tools to accomplish the task. The requisite supervision is provided by the operator. As this case clearly demonstrates, technological change has resulted in a case in which labor goes from providing energy and organization to providing only organization.

Another telling example is weaving. In the Paleolithic era, fibers or reeds were woven together to produce clothing, baskets and sieves using one's hands (i.e. animate, muscular energy). With the advent of the loom (i.e. tools), human force was better transmitted and applied, resulting in higher output. Primitive looms, it therefore follows, are examples of man-made or anthropomorphic entropic processes. The application of water, steam, and electric power to the hand- and foot-operated loom led to the power loom where human energy was replaced by water, steam and ultimately electric power, transforming labor's role from that of inanimate energy source and supervisor (i.e. overseer) to that of simple supervisor with the result that today, little to no human energy is deployed in the weaving process. In the following passage, 19th-century British economist Alfred Marshall describes just such a change:

> *We may now pass to the effects which machinery has in relieving that excessive muscular strain which a few generations ago was the common lot of more than half the working men even in such a country as England ... in other trades, machinery has lightened man's labours. The house carpenters, for instance, make things of the same kind as those used by our forefathers, with much less toil for themselves .... Nothing could be more narrow or monotonous than the occupation of a weaver of plain stuffs in the old time. But now, one woman will manage four or more looms, each of which does many times as much work in the course of a day as the old hand loom did; and her work is much less monotonous and calls for much more judgment than his did.*
>
> *(Marshall 1890, 218)*

The operative word here is "manage." Analytically speaking, factory workers in the 19th century no longer worked; rather, they managed. Simon Newcomb, the 19th-century physicist and economist, described the far-reaching change in labor's role in production brought about by steam-powered machinery as follows:

> *We may readily apply the principle here illustrated to the actual historical facts. The introduction of machinery during the last hundred years has to a certain extent changed the directions of man's occupations. Instead of making things with their own hands, as they formally had to do, they are now managing machines or assisting in various ways in working them. The pin-makers are no longer at work; a few of them are feeding pin-making machines, but the majority of them have learned other employments. A large class of carpenters no longer push the plane; a portion of them feed the planning machines, and*

the remainder are fully occupied in executing work that increased refinement which demand has encouraged. The same thing may be traced all through the channels of industry.

(Newcomb 1886, 390)

This was a recurrent theme in the 19th century, extending beyond political economy into such fields as engineering and mechanics. For example, James Martineau, a professional engineer, in a lecture to the Liverpool Mechanics Institute, spoke of "machinery rapidly supplanting human labour and rendering mere muscular force…worthless… That natural machine, the human body, is depreciated in the market. But if the body have lost its value, the mind must get into business without delay" (Tylecote 1957, 262).

The depreciation of human muscle-based power continued in the early 20th century with the introduction of electric power. More flexible than steam power, it resulted in the mechanization of sectors of the economy that had resisted earlier mechanization. Consider, for example, the following quote describing the effects of electric-powered materials-handling equipment on the nature of work in the mining industry, taken from David Nye's work on the electrification of America (Nye 1990):

Thus, for some, electrification meant unemployment as a few skilled jobs replaced unskilled labor. At Green Ridge Colliery, for example, a station engineer, motorman, and helper could run an electric locomotive that replaced six mule drivers, four boy helpers, and seventeen mules. At New York and Scranton Coal, three men and a locomotive replaced seven boys and fourteen mules. Down in the mines other electrical machines replaced hand labor, increasing productivity but reducing the need for artisanal skill. Such innovations were contributory factors in the United Mine Workers strikes of 1900, 1902, and 1912. A similar kind of labor replacement disturbed the steel workers, as General Electric designed a set of electrical motors and controls for rolling mills. The corporation proudly announced, One man surrounded by a dozen or more operating levers controls every motion of steel from the ingot furnace to the completed rail…. Every motor replaced a man, but the work is done better and more quickly than formerly. In many mills, a motor [was] installed on a charging and drawing machine, arranged so as to automatically grip and withdraw the hot bloom from the furnace, and release it when clear of the furnace door. The motorman has simply to start and stop the motor.

(Nye 1990, 206)

Substitutes or Complements

The resulting two-factor (energy and organization) model of production processes provides a rich framework in which to study production-related questions. For example, it provides a theoretical basis for studying the role of conventionally defined energy, capital, labor and organization in production. To what extent are energy and organization substitutable? Can managers be substituted for energy, and can labor be substituted for capital? Further, it provides the necessary framework to study technological change and its effects on the various factor inputs over time. For example, has second-law efficiency (i.e. η) increased or decreased over time?

Another relevant question, especially in light of the energy crisis in the 1970s and 1980s, is whether tools (i.e. capital) and broadly defined energy are substitutes or complements? Most analysts felt that they were substitutes (Solow 1974; Berndt and Wood 1975). Hence, the accepted view at the time held that companies would simply substitute away from energy over to capital and labor. The EO approach to production analysis provides an altogether different view on this issue. The answer is a qualified no. Theoretically, for a given value of $\eta(t)$, an increase in capital (i.e. tools) cannot make up for a loss of energy. Referring to Equation 2.4, the only way in which more capital could compensate for less energy is if the result was higher second-law efficiency. That is, only if the additional capital increases $\eta(t)$ will output increase. As pointed out earlier, because machines and tools are not a source of energy, but rather, apply and transmit energy, it follows that, *ceteris paribus*, quantities of capital and energy cannot possibly be substitutes, but rather, have been and will always be complementary inputs. Tools and machines cannot create energy. More tools for a given level of energy cannot and will not result in more work.

This leaves the possibility of second-law efficiency-increasing investment. In this case, the level of second-law efficiency, is assumed to be increasing in broadly defined capital, as measured by the value of tools and machines. That is, the more capital, the higher is $\eta(t)$. Were this to hold empirically, then capital and energy would be substitutes in the sense that more capital, by providing for higher $\eta(t)$ values, reduces the amount of energy required to perform a fixed, given amount of work. The point is that capital and energy can only be considered substitutes if and only if the former is heterogeneous in nature. More efficient capital can, at least theoretically, compensate for less energy; otherwise, they are complementary.

CAPSULE: THE PHYSIOCRATS, THE FIRST SCIENTIFIC ECONOMISTS?

France under Louis XIV was awash with government largesse and spending, the French state having exploded size-wise. A group of encyclopedists, known as "les économistes," or "physiocrates" turned their attention to wealth and its creation, providing an alternative to British mercantilism which was in full swing.[6] *In short, they maintained that agriculture was the source of all wealth, public administration and manufacturing being essentially sterile activities.*

This was and remains a controversial position, to say the least. After all, the French state had ballooned, and Britain was in the early years of the industrial revolution. This raises the question, is there any truth to this view. Can it be justified? The answer is yes and here's why.

In pre-industrial societies, the overall energy constraint is defined by the available food supply. Workers, be they in manufacturing or government, are powered, so to speak, by their calorie intake. The same holds for beasts of burden. Hence, it therefore follows that agriculture and the resulting food supply define a pre-industrial society's energy constraint and, consequently, its wealth constraint.[7]

This, of course, was no longer the case with industrialization that witnessed the use of fossil fuels to drive manufacturing, mining, transportation and virtually all other human activities/material processes. This goes a long way in understanding the prominence of sun gods in ancient civilizations, the sun (i.e. solar radiation) being the source of all life and wealth.

Energy-Organization Productivity Measures

The EO approach to modeling production processes provides important insights into both the definition, the construction and the use of productivity measures. Typically, productivity is measured as the ratio of output (value added) to one or many inputs. For example, in the past, political economists have defined and measured labor and capital productivity. Labor productivity is the ratio of output (value added) to labor input; capital productivity is the ratio of output (value added) to capital input. As pointed out above, implicit in these notions is the fact that both capital and labor are physically productive, raising an important question. Does the fact that an input is physically present in plants necessarily imply that it is physically productive? Take, for example, the case of managers. Are managers physically productive? If so, then how should their productivity be measured? After all, managers are a sine quo non of production. The point is that productivity measures differ both with regard to their content and, of course, with regard to their meaning. Those which refer to energy and force ought to be viewed as physically productive, while those which refer to organization ought to be viewed as organizationally productive. The fact that conventionally measured labor productivity increases does not imply that labor is responsible for the increase. As argued above, the only physically consistent measure of productivity is the ratio of output to total energy.

Energy Productivity Measures

Three energy-related productivity measures follow. Referring to Table 2.3, the first is the ratio of output to animate energy (i.e. $W(t)/E_a(t)$), commonly known as labor productivity. For this ratio to be meaningful (i.e. in terms of thermodynamics), it must be the case that the labor in question is a source of energy. Otherwise, labor

TABLE 2.3 EO Energy Productivity Measures

Productivity Measure	*Definition*
$W(t)/E_a(t)$	Ratio of work to animate energy
$W(t)/E_i(t)$	Ratio of work to inanimate energy
$W(t)/E(t)$	Ratio of work to total energy

Source: Beaudreau (1998), 29.

productivity as conventionally defined is devoid of any meaning. As argued here, labor in modern production processes is more appropriately viewed as a form of lower-level organization (i.e. supervisor).

The second productivity measure is the ratio of output to inanimate energy (i.e. $W(t)/E_i(t)$), $E_i(t)$ being broadly defined to include electrical, thermo-mechanical, and all other inanimate forms of energy. By virtue of Equation 2.2, this measure explicitly defines $\eta(t)$, thermodynamic efficiency. Lastly, the third law of thermodynamics provides us with a third measure of productivity, namely the ratio of output to total energy (i.e. $E(t)$). This measures the relationship between output and the broadly defined energy input. Clearly, energy-conversion tables (i.e. labor-BTU, electric power-BTU) are required to render this measure operational. However, for production processes requiring no animate energy (i.e. $E_a(t)$), this ratio is equivalent to the output-inanimate energy ratio.

Organization Productivity Measures

As pointed out, continued energy-deepening throughout the 19th and 20th centuries altered fundamentally the supervisory input (i.e. $S(t)$). In the pre-industrial revolution period, the organizational input (i.e. $S(t)$) and the source of energy (i.e. $E(t)$) were one-in-the-same namely conventionally defined worker. Weavers, stonecutters, shoemakers and artisans in general provided both energy and organization. In time, as inanimate energy replaced animate energy (i.e. high-speed steam engines), the organizational aspect of production changed. A new class of production-related personnel came into being, namely managers. Together with workers who had been relieved of the physical demands of work, managers supervised these highly productive production processes. With this was born the fully functional organization hierarchy, with workers (lower-level supervisors) at the base, and senior managers (upper-level supervisors) at the apex. To capture the developments in supervision technology, two sub-classes of supervisors are defined: $S_l(t)$, lower-level supervisors (i.e. workers) and $S_u(t)$, upper-level supervisors, where $S(t) = S_l(t) + S_u(t)$. The former find themselves at the base of the organizational hierarchy, while the latter find themselves at the apex.

Table 2.4 defines the resulting three organization-related productivity measures, namely the ratio of work to total supervisors, the ratio of work to lower-level supervisors, the ratio of work to upper-level supervisors, and lastly, the ratio of work to

TABLE 2.4 EO Organization Productivity Measures

Productivity Measure	*Definition*
$W(t)/S(t)$	Ratio of work to supervisors
$W(t)/S_l(t)$	Ratio of work to lower-level supervisors
$W(t)/S_u(t)$	Ratio of work to upper-level supervisors
$W(t)/T(t)$	Ratio of work to tools and machines

Source: Beaudreau (1998), 30.

tools and machines. The second is typically referred to as labor productivity, the third as managerial productivity and the last, as capital productivity.

Core Principle I: Summary and Conclusion

In 1924, Nobel Prize-winning chemist Frederick Soddy asked and answered the rhetorical question, how do men live?

> *At the risk of being redundant, let me illustrate what I mean by the question "How do men live?" by asking what makes a railroad train go. In one sense or another, credit for the achievement may be claimed by the so-called "engine-driver," the guard, the signalman, the manager, the capitalist, the share-holder, -or, again, by the scientific pioneers who discovered the nature of fire, by the inventors who harnessed it, by labour which built the railroad and the train. The fact remains that all of them by their collective effort could not drive the train. The real engine-driver is the coal. So, in the present state of science, the answer to the question how men live, or how anything lives, or how inanimate nature lives, in the sense in which we speak of the life of a waterfall or of any other manifestation of continued liveliness, is, with few and unimportant exceptions, "By sunshine." Switch off the sun and a world would result lifeless, not only in the sense of animate life, but also in respect of by far the greater part of the life of inanimate nature.*
>
> *(Soddy 1924, 4)*

Three years later, Frederick G. Tryon of *The Institute of Economics*, writing in the *Journal of the American Statistical Association*, went further, arguing:

> *Anything as important in industrial life as power deserves more attention than it has yet received by economists. The industrial position of a nation may be gauged by its use of power. The great advance in material standards of life in the last century was made possible by an enormous increase in the consumption of energy, and the prospect of repeating the achievement in the next century turns perhaps more than on anything else on making energy cheaper and more abundant. A theory of production that will really explain how wealth is produced must analyze the contribution of this element of energy.*
>
> *(Tryon 1927, 281)*

Core Principle I: Applications

We cannot overstate the importance of *Core Principle I* to the study of economics and hence to the history of economic thought. As economics has been, is, and will forever be the science of wealth, it stands to reason that unless wealth is truly understood, all that follows will be moot, not to mention incorrect. Put differently, if our understanding of wealth is wrong, then nothing – absolutely nothing – can be right. It's not unlike building a house. Without a solid foundation, the rest of the house will crumble; however, well-built it happens to be. The EO approach provides just such a foundation, one that is grounded in the physics of material processes.

Its applications are as unlimited as the science of wealth itself. It is the basis for all work in the fields of economic growth, of income distribution, and of price theory, to mention just a few. Its appeal is universal as it is consistent with similar work on material processes in other fields (biology, process engineering, astronomy).

Physical Productivity and Rents

Perhaps one of the most important applications of the EO approach to modeling material processes is in the field of income distribution. Income distribution is the study of the rules and/or processes that determine the distribution of wealth (transformation, value added, output). As shall be argued later (Chapter 4), the problem of income distribution stands as one of the most important and influential in the history of economic thought, having been at the root of most if not all of the controversies (micro and macro) of the 19th century.

The problem of income distribution is analogous to the problem of assigning ownership or property rights (i.e. to wealth), one of the cornerstones of modern-day liberal democracies. In other words, who gets what? Or, put differently, how does society divvy up the income/wealth pie among the various factor inputs? As shown above, material processes require numerous factor inputs, from energy to supervision, to tools, and to management. The currently accepted apportionment criterion (neoclassical) is based on physical productivity. That is, each factor is remunerated according to its physical – and thus measurable – contribution.

The EO approach to modeling material processes, however, casts a long shadow of a doubt on such a standard, owing in large measure to the laws of classical mechanics. Specifically, according to the latter, tools (capital) are not physically productive. Add to this the fact that modern labor is a supervisory input and hence not physically productive and you get an energy standard, namely that because energy is the only physically productive input, it stands to reason that it would be, from a legal point of view, entitled to all of the value/wealth.

This has important implications for income distribution. If a physical productivity standard is the accepted criterion, then unless the price of the energy input is equal to the value of its output, energy rents will result, defined as the difference between the value of energy's productivity and its cost.[8] Historically, these rents were divvied up among the other, non-physically productive, organization-based factor inputs, resulting in the current distribution of income where labor and capital lay claim to the lion's share of these rents.

As will become evident in Chapter 4, the creation of these rents, largely the result of the rising energy consumption that accelerated material processes, and their distribution among the owners of labor and capital were at the root of a number of debates in the history of economic thought, including 19th-century Owenism, Marxism and 20th-century Technocracy.

Role of Energy in the History of Economic Thought

Given its role in material processes, one would surmise that it played an important role in the history of economic thought. In *Energy and the Rise and Fall of Political Economy*, published in 1998 (Westport, CT: Greenwood Press), it was argued that political economy or the study of material wealth was born of an energy-related innovation in the form of the steam engine and the resulting acceleration of material processes. While prior to the 19th century, world GDP had been relatively constant. The steam engine, by increasing energy use/consumption, ushered in the industrial era, an era marked by unprecedented increases in energy use, manifesting itself in greater process speeds (due to acceleration) as well as unprecedented increases in material wealth – in short, the high, sustained levels of growth of the 19th and 20th centuries.

As shall be shown (and argued in *Energy and the Rise and Fall of Political Economy*), despite its fundamental role in material processes, energy and speed were and continue to be the forgotten factor input in modern political economy. Early political economists (Adam Smith, David Ricardo, Jean-Baptiste Say) had considerable difficulty conceptualizing the role of the steam engine and its role in material processes. Adam Smith referred to it simply as machinery, which is labor productivity-increasing, a practice that continued throughout the 19th century.[9] However in their defense, it is important to keep in mind that the science of heat/steam as a force, thermodynamics, was also in its infancy.

Core Principle II: Information and Coordination Strategies

Core Principle II relates to the problem of coordination, specifically the coordination in complex systems. Modern industrial economies are examples of highly complex systems, with thousands, if not millions of value chains/bushes, and millions of economic agents. Economic specialization has, over the course of the past two centuries, increased at a spectacular rate, begging the question: How do societies solve the corresponding coordination problem, defined as what, when and how to produce? In other words, what are the various strategies used that allow for the high degree of specialization and exchange that characterizes modern economies?

Core Principle II has to do with information and coordination strategies (ICSs). More specifically, it consists of the set of ICS for specialization and exchange to emerge. An ISC has two objectives, namely to inform agents, and to coordinate their behavior. Among these are hierarchical ICSs (e.g. command economies) and decentralized ICSs (e.g. market economies). Information and coordination are provided by the state in the former, and by the price mechanism in the latter.[10] First, some history.

In the Paleolithic era, economic activity was organized around the tribe/clan with varying degrees of specialization and exchange. Men hunted, defended the tribe/clan from attack, and crafted tools, while women collected seeds and berries, reared children, and prepared meals/clothing. Roles were defined by a number of factors, including genetics and tradition. With the coming of the first civilizations (e.g. Mesopotamia) came a new form of social and economic organization, one based on a greater degree of specialization, namely organized exchange. For example, in Mesopotamia, wealth creation and exchange were organized by the local temple priests. Goods and services were stored and traded within the confines of the temple. The result was a more complex form of social and economic organization similar to modern-day market-based economies, with specialized producers, and specialized traders, the latter operating the equivalent of modern-day stores. With this shift came an important increase in economic complexity, defined as "the order resulting from the interactions of many heterogeneous agents" (Durlauf 1997). Producers became specialized, and complex exchange emerged in the form of temple-based exchange. This raises a number of interesting, and until now, unanswered questions, namely, why and how did this happen? What prompted the emergence of this form of economic complexity? Was it spontaneous in nature, or was some specific form of information and coordination required? If so, what form did it take?

Another significant increase in economic complexity occurred in the 19th century with the coming of industrialization (Berg 1980; Beaudreau 1999). Tasks that had until then had been performed on a small-scale (i.e. putting-out) were now performed on a large-scale in factories (i.e. pulling-in). Material processes were accelerated and overall output increased manifold as a result. With this shift came a new ICS in the form of rules-based laisser-faire, replacing what until then had been discretion-based, hierarchical ICSs. This raises another set of questions, namely were the two related, and if so, how? Was the shift to a rule-based ICS a cause or an effect? Could the first industrial revolution have occurred within a discretion-based, hierarchical ICS (i.e. mercantilism)?

These questions are important for a number of reasons. For one, they are important historically. What prompted these paradigm, epoch-defining (i.e. industrialization) increases in economic complexity, and what role did ISCs play? What were the corresponding institutions? How did they emerge and evolve? Second, they are important theoretically. Can economic complexity increase spontaneously – that is, in a Nash sense – as is commonly believed. Or, is it more appropriately modeled as based on coordination? Third, they are important from a practical point of view. For example, what lessons does the past have to offer to countries that are presently attempting to move to more complex forms of economic organization? In addition, one could argue that a better theoretical and historical understanding of the emergence of complexity and subsequent innovations in complexity is an invaluable input in the current debate over development and growth strategies [Glaeser et al. 2004; La Porta et al. 1998].

Core Principle II addresses these questions. Specifically, it examines the emergence and evolution of economic complexity, defined as large-scale specialization and exchange (LSSE). This consists of an account of the first and second industrial revolutions, both of which witnessed a marked increase in economic complexity. Given the role of rules-based ICSs, specifically of laisser-faire, in industrialization, we examine various aspects of what Karl Polanyi referred to as the "Great Transformation." We conclude with a discussion of our results, and a summary of our findings.

Production Process Complexity and Economic Complexity

The study of economic complexity is as old as economics itself, dating back in time to the French Physiocrats, and to Adam Smith's *An Inquiry into the Nature and Causes of the Wealth of Nations*. According to Smith, complexity, while being the result of new technologies, notably the steam engine, was determined by the extent of the market. The greater the extent of the market, the greater the overall level of specialization (division of labor) in the economy and, consequently, the greater the level of wealth. Economic complexity, as such, was technology-driven, but market determined. Specialization at the firm level according to Smith required coordination. The latter was the responsibility of the entrepreneur, whose task it was to coordinate parallel and sequential high-throughput, Boulton-Watts rotary-drive powered production sub-processes within the firm. Specialization and mechanization, he argued, were key determinants of productivity growth, as evidenced by the following passage taken from Chapter 1 of *An Inquiry into the Nature and Causes of The Wealth of Nations*.

> *The great increase in the quantity of work which, in consequence of the division of labour, the same number of people are capable of performing, is owing to three different circumstances; first, to the increase in dexterity in every particular workman; secondly, to the saving of the time which is commonly lost in passing from one species of work to another; and lastly, to the invention of a great number of machines which facilitate and abridge labour, and enable one man to do the work of many.*
>
> *(Smith 1776, 7)*

According to the Classical and Neoclassical political economists, coordination within the firm was the task of the entrepreneur. Beyond him/her, coordination would be carried out by markets. Just where in-firm coordination ended, and markets began was not-well demarcated. Clearly, production sub-processes within the firm were coordinated by the entrepreneur. Anything beyond, it was usually assumed, was left to the market.

The early 20th century witnessed a shift in this frontier, with an increase in hierarchical, internal coordination in the form of highly vertically and horizontally integrated firms (Sobel 1972; Chandler 1977). Increasingly, the invisible hand of the market was being replaced by the visible hand of large, vertically and horizontally-integrated management hierarchies.

CAPSULE: THE ICS HAND: VISIBLE, INVISIBLE, VANISHING?

The hand metaphor has been and continues to be a key part of the economics mainstream, providing insights into the underpinnings of various ICS – that is, communication and coordination strategies.[11] *Adam Smith, the proverbial father of the metaphor, assumed that the 18th-century hand was visible in the form of mercantilism when the bulk of economic activity was controlled by the state. Charters were required to do business and prices were often set by royal edict.*[12]

The free market, as outlined by Smith, would replace hierarchy with the price mechanism. In short, prices would communicate useful information and, in so doing, coordinate economic activity.

The emergence of large-scale, vertically integrated producers in the late 19th/early 20th century witnessed the rise of managerial capitalism (as opposed to market capitalism) where hierarchy in the form of complex management structures replaced markets (especially in value chains and bushes).

By the end of the century, the visible hand of managerial capitalism began to vanish with the rise of outsourcing, leading to the concept of vanishing hand, by which it should be understood that markets appeared to be making a come-back.

This raised a number of fundamental questions, questions the profession continues to study to this very day. What happened? Why the sudden reversal of fortunes? After all, according to basic theory, markets were assumed to dominate to hierarchies, or so it was thought. Ronald Coase (1937) reframed the question in terms of transactions costs, arguing that when transactions costs are high, firms internalize what would otherwise be arms-length transactions. Others, including Oliver Williamson, examined various alternative communication and coordination strategies, the result of which was a taxonomy of organizational structures consisting of: market governance, bilateral governance, trilateral governance and unified governance [Williamson (1985)]. Market governance is the preferred arrangement in the case of recurrent and non-specific transactions, whereas trilateral governance is used for occasional and medium specific transactions. Unified governance is preferred for recurrent and highly specific transactions.

Further Discussion

Historically, the shift from a discretionary ICS (mercantilism) to a rules-based ICS (free markets), and back to what essentially were local hierarchies in the form of large, highly integrated, multiplant firms and multiproduct, we maintain, was motivated by what can be referred to as "coordination of complexity" efficiency rather than by basic allocative efficiency considerations. The principal challenge facing late 18th-century Great Britain was realizing – in the sense of attaining – the greater economic complexity and wealth that was synonymous with the steam engine. Likewise, the principal challenge facing the early 20th-century United States was realizing the greater economic complexity and wealth that was synonymous with electric unit drive (process and product technologies).

Failure to tailor the ICS to the corresponding technology can be costly, as evidenced by Britain's failure in the late 19th century to exploit what was a home-grown technology, namely electro-magnetic power. The basic research on electro-magnetism-and hence, the electro-magnetic motor-was carried out in 19th-century Great Britain by such notables as Michael Faraday, Charles Wheatstone, Lord Kelvin, Joseph Swan and others. However, the British failed to implement this new technology, something that would be carried out by Thomas A. Edison and George Westinghouse in the United States. *The UK Coal Conservation Sub-Committee*, set up by Viscount Haldane in 1916, made numerous references to this "puzzle." What had gone wrong? Why had the British failed to capitalize, to exploit on what was a home-grown technology. In the same year, *The Board of Trade* struck an *Electrical Trades Committee*, whose given purpose was to investigate the position of the electrical trades after the war. Sir Henry Self and Elizabeth Watson summarized its findings as follows:

> *Reference was made in no uncertain terms to the crippling handicaps of the local and political considerations which had prevented Great Britain from reaping the fruits of the outstanding preeminence which it had received in original constructive research and development of electricity generation at the hands of pioneers such as Faraday, Wheatstone, Kelvin, Swan, Hopkinson, and many others. The loss of that outstanding lead, the history of industry in the intervening years, and the evidence taken during their examination of the position led the Committee to the following conclusions.*
>
> *(Self and Watson 1952, 35)*

In other words, local regulation, specifically by the gas and coal industry, had thwarted the development of the electric power industry in Great Britain. Rules-based laisser-faire would have, as it did in the United States, allowed for the presence of both technologies, with the spoils going to the winner.

This result also provides a rationalization of the *deus ex machina* view of the market – that is, as a superior ICS – as the optimality of a rules-based ICS in a dynamic, complex setting, one characterized by on-going technological change (process and product). As was the case in late 19th-century Great Britain, there may exist a set of processes/products whose value/potential escapes the grasp of government officials (hierarchical ICS). In such cases, it could be argued that the optimal strategy is best be left to the "specialists" – that is, to those who have more information than the *n* agents and gatekeeper in the hierarchical ICS. A good example of this is *FedEx*, the brain-child of a Yale undergraduate economics student in the 1960s who outlined the idea of an overnight parcel-delivery service in a term-paper. His professor, legend has it, didn't see much merit in the idea, and gave him a C+. The rest is "history," so to speak.

These results also bring into focus many of the issues raised in the recent institutions-growth literature. This literature examines the relationship between institutions and economic growth. For example, some have argued that causality runs from limited government to economic growth, while others show it running in the opposite direction. Unfortunately, the microfoundations of this literature – that is, the underlying mechanics – are not well understood. Just how institutions affect growth is not well understood.

Core Principle II: Summary and Conclusion

Core Principle II focuses on the question of information and coordination in complex economic environments. It was shown that information and coordination costs act as a constraint on societies as a whole, hampering in some cases, preventing in others, increases in economic complexity made possible by technology shocks. We maintain that this problem was at the heart of Adam Smith's magnum opus, *An Inquiry into the Nature and Causes of the Wealth of Nations*, published over two centuries ago. Getting in the way of increased specialization at the time (economic complexity) was the extent of the market. What ensued was an often-acrimonious debate over laisser-faire – that is, over free markets. As we have attempted to show in this section, both ICSs (discretion-based and rules-based) have their merits and their costs. Discretion-based ICSs, however, have performed rather poorly in the presence of new technologies.

While discretionary ICSs (distributed and hierarchical) played an integral role in the emergence and early evolution of economic complexity, their usefulness had waned considerably by the 19th century. Attempts at designing discretionary ICS-based industrial societies have, not surprisingly, met with little success. Examples of such societies include early 19th-century France, the 20th-century Soviet Union, and Communist China. Based largely on the writings of Claude Rouvroy, Comte de St-Simon, early 19th-century France, led by Napoleon, embarked on an ambitious program of industrialization organized around a hierarchical ICS. The resulting *technocracy* would, in St-Simon's eyes, close the gap with Great Britain, and in the process increase economic complexity. The Soviet Union and China held similar ambitions. The results are there for all to see. Hierarchical ICSs have underperformed, relative to comparable rules-based ICSs, owing to, among others factors, high information and coordination costs.

As we have attempted to show here technology and technological change are not sufficient conditions for heightened economic complexity and greater material wealth. As with all other forms of complexity, organization is of equal importance. Heightened specialization and trade require cost-efficient, highly effective ICSs. The latter range from discretionary ICSs to rules-based ICSs, to combination discretionary-rules-based ICSs. When it comes to ICS's, no one ICS dominates all others. Early innovations in economic complexity were the result of discretionary, hierarchical ICSs. In time, these proved to be too costly and ineffective, prompting a shift to rules-based ICS's in the form of free markets. The shortcomings (efficiency-wise) of markets, in turn, prompted the emergence of a hybrid ICS in the form of localized hierarchies-rules-based ICSs, with large vertically integrated firms operating in what are free-markets.

These results are interesting for a number of reasons. First and foremost is their synthetic nature. The view of economic complexity presented here synthesizes over 200 years of political economy and 8,000 years of economic complexity. In doing so, it refocuses the debate surrounding "economic systems" around dynamic considerations, notably the ability to coordinate potential economic complexity. An interesting by-product is a theory of the origins of large-scale specialization and exchange (LSSE) as an equilibrium to a Schelling-type coordination game. More often than not, LSSE required discretionary ICSs, a fact history bears witness to.

Core Principle II: Applications

The Markets versus Hierarchies Debate

The science of wealth has, over the course of the past two centuries, defined and been defined by what is, in essence, an institutional question, namely do markets outperform government hierarchies? From the early Physiocrats to the current Neo-Conservatives, the debate has centered and continues to center on whether rules-based, decentralized, non-hierarchical ICSs dominate the hierarchical-based ICSs that have been the dominant ICS in the history of Western civilization from the early Sumerians?

The debate has been and continues to be multidimensional. However, one dimension stands out, namely the relationship between ICS and the level and rate of growth. More specifically, are rules-based markets more conducive to economic growth? Or is it the reverse? As we shall see in this book, this debate has implications for virtually every field in modern-day economics, from economic growth, to macroeconomics, to income distribution, to price theory.

Core Principle III: The Industrial Exchange Sequence

In each of the first two core principles, time plays an important role in the analysis. In the case of value chains/bushes, value added and ultimately value (goods) are created in real time. Finished goods are not produced instantaneously (i.e. at a point in time), but rather, are produced over time, ranging from weeks, to months to years. In the case of value chains, entrepreneurs/managers are, however, called upon to coordinate the various links in vertically integrated value chains in real time.

This has important implications for the study of economic aggregates (macroeconomic variables). The first is what we refer to as the absence of instantaneity (or the presence of hysteresis).[13] Decisions taken in the past will invariably have a bearing on the present and future; those taken in the present will have an effect on the future etc. It therefore follows that agents' expectations, especially those of the decision makers (i.e. entrepreneurs), will have an important bearing on the present and the future. Consequently, problems can arise at any time and at any stage of production (both at the individual firm level and at the aggregate level). To better understand and appreciate the role of time – and expectations – in production, we turn to Core Principle III, the Industrial Exchange Sequence (IES). The IES, shown in Table 2.5, is a temporal representation of firm-level and aggregate economic activity. It consists of six sequential activities, namely *Vision/Planning*, *Financing*, *Production*, *Variable-Factor Income Distribution*, *Sales* and *Fixed-Factor Distribution*.

The IES mimics the actual behavior of individual firms in real time as they go about their activities. A good way to think about the IES is as a representation of an entrepreneur who enters an industry. To begin with, he conceives of a product and the corresponding value chain/bush.[14] He then arranges for the financing of his endeavor. This consists of securing credit lines from the bank (to finance the day-to-day transactions and operations) and finding willing investors (to finance the capital equipment). Once in place, he then goes about making the necessary arrangements to purchase various intermediate inputs, energy and labor so that production can take place. As payments to capital are a residual form of income, it stands to reason that transactions on the labor and energy markets will simultaneously determine the level of output (value added) as well as variable-factor income distribution. Put differently, the decision to hire a certain number of workers at a fixed wage determines both output and distribution. Lastly, the entrepreneur sells

TABLE 2.5 The Industrial Exchange Sequence

Firm Level	*Vision/Planning Stage*	*Financing Stage*	*Production Stage*	*Variable Income Stage*	*Sales Stage*	*Fixed Factor Income Stage*
Aggregate	*Macroeconomic Expectations Stage*	*Monetizing Stage*	*GDP Stage*	*Aggregate Labor Income Stage*	*Gross Domestic Expenditure Stage*	*Aggregate Dividend Stage*

his product(s) in the output market, thus completing the cycle. At this juncture, he will reimburse outstanding debts (i.e. the outstanding balance on his credit line). What is left is then distributed among the managers and shareholders. In this sense, factor payments to capital are a residual, paid out from the proceeds of its net-of-variable-cost sales. Typically, these payments (dividends) are made on a quarterly or annual basis.

Industrial Exchange Sequence

The Vision Stage

All economic activity begins with an idea, with a plan. This is represented in the IES as the vision stage, where the idea of a product/process takes shape. It should, however, be noted that these visions are abstractions.

Despite this fact, the conception stage is extremely important as it harbors the very origins of economic activity. The more abstractions or visions there are in an economy, the greater will be wealth and the overall level of economic activity.

Affecting the overall number or level of abstractions are a number of factors, including the general, economy-wide level of creativity/imagination, as well as the level of overall confidence. The more entrepreneurs/managers are confident in the future, the greater will be the number of abstractions, and consequently, the greater will be the level of output. For example, if entrepreneurs/managers believe that GDP and consequently, aggregate consumption will increase by 4 percent in the coming year, then they will be more likely to increase hiring, investment and output.

This highlights the integral role played by expectations in macroeconomic phenomena. The more optimistic are entrepreneurs/managers as a group, the greater will aggregate output be. This is sometimes referred to as a self-fulfilling prophecy. The more people believe in something, the greater are the chances it will occur. This explains in part why government officials are typically – in fact, universally – optimistic. That it was otherwise would be anathema to growth and prosperity.[15]

The Financing Stage

Armed with a vision, entrepreneurs/managers must then find the necessary financing in order to realize their project. Typically, financing will consist of bank credit. Firms obtain a credit line that is used to finance the purchase of intermediate inputs, as well as the variable inputs used in the value-added process. These include energy, typically in the form of electricity, and labor.

Notice that capital is absent from this list. This is not an omission but rather owes to the fact that as Frank Knight pointed out in 1921, the owners of capital are residual claimants. That is, their earnings accrue once the firm has financed, produced and sold its output on the relevant market. This reflects a fundamental difference between factor payments made to labor and those made to capital. The former are made prior to the sale of the output (value added) while the latter are made afterward. This is reflected in the fact that a firm's earnings are made either at the end of the fiscal year or on a quarterly basis. Put differently, the owners of capital are not paid a wage or salary the way the owners of labor are.

Clearly, the ability to secure the necessary credit is a key condition to the successful execution of an entrepreneurial/managerial vision. This highlights the important role of money and monetary institutions in economic growth. Failure to provide the necessary bank credit to entrepreneurs/managers can result in an important contraction/failure to increase in economic activity.

The Production Stage

The production stage is by far the most important of all stages as it is there that wealth per se is created in the form of material transformation. Energy and organization combine to transform raw materials and intermediate inputs into useful goods and services. Labor and capital typically provide the framework in which energy/force does the relevant work. All inputs are essential; however, not all are physically productive. Following classical mechanics, only energy/force is physically productive.

The Variable Factor Income Stage

The variable factor income stage is contemporaneous with the Production Stage in that it occurs simultaneously. When entrepreneurs/managers decide on output levels, they implicitly decide on the level of variable costs, and hence, on variable factor income, given the equivalence between costs and income.

The Expenditure Stage

This is the penultimate stage, and the ultimate raison d'être of economic activity, namely consumption or expenditure. Firms will typically send their goods to merchants who will put them up for sale. Consumers will then purchase them using the income obtained in factor markets. The receipts are then used to defray the cost of intermediation (by merchants) and the cost of the goods themselves. The latter consist of payments made to manufacturers.

The expenditure stage highlights the important role of merchants in the economic process. Like entrepreneurs/managers, their decisions are based on visions or abstractions, in this case of what the state of markets will be. More specifically, they place orders with manufacturers based on their expectations of where the market will be. If merchants as a whole become pessimistic, then orders will fall, setting in motion a downward spiral. Similarly, like entrepreneurs/managers, they finance their activities using bank credit.

It is important to understand that merchants provide valuable services. This is evidenced by the fact that retail mark-ups are oftentimes in the 40–60 percent range.

In other words, for every dollar spent at a retailer, half of the value is provided by the merchant, on average.

The Fixed Factor Income Stage

This corresponds to the ultimate stage and consists of factor payments made to fixed factors, mainly equity capital, once the goods and services have been sold on product markets. In actual fact, it corresponds to firms' quarterly, bi-annual, or annual earnings. What is important to understand is the residual nature of firm profits/earnings. Unlike variable factor input payments made at the time of production, fixed-factor income payments are made after the good/service in question has been delivered to the market.

CAPSULE: MONETIZING OUTPUT IN A WICKSELLIAN PURE CREDIT ECONOMY

The distinctive feature of a monetary economy, according to UCLA economics professor Robert Clower, is not the existence of money or a medium of exchange, but rather that goods exchange for money and money for goods, but not goods against goods. This raises the question, how is output or wealth monetized – that is, for exchange to take place? In short, a firm's output has to be monetized so that in aggregate, output is monetized.

The first step, in the IES, is for firms to purchase their variable inputs using trade credit – or simply, bank credit. In most cases, this amounts to roughly 65 percent of aggregate output (i.e. GDP). However, 35 percent remains unmonetized as profits are a residual. Unlike wages that are paid out ex-ante (i.e. before output reaches the market), profits are paid out ex-post – that is, once output is sold, taking on the form of quarterly or annual dividends.

The second step consists of firms borrowing money to finance investment – a form of bridge finance obtained in anticipation of dividends owning. When dividends are paid out, the outstanding debt is reimbursed.

If we assume that all wage income is consumed, then consumption will constitute 65 percent of GDP and investment 35 percent.

Trade credit is the resulting medium of exchange, changing hands to begin with from firms to workers and then from workers to firms in the spirit of Clower's tautology.

Core Principle III: Applications

The IES presents numerous advantages especially as a diagnostic tool. For example, in macroeconomics, it provides a framework in which to define and diagnose disequilibria. Overall macroeconomic equilibria can, within the IES, be defined as a situation in which all stages are equal. That is, GDP according to the aggregate visions stage is equal to that of the finance stage, which is equal to that of the expenditure stage. Accordingly, disequilibria can occur at any one of the stages. For example, it could occur at the financial stage owing to a lack of sufficient credit. That is, there is insufficient credit (bills of exchange) to support the desired or planned level of output. Or it could occur at the income stage, where there is insufficient overall income (variable factor input and fixed factor input payments) to purchase the output. Or, at the expenditure level, where the level of expenditure is less than the level of output.

Core Principle III: Summary and Conclusion

The IES sequence of economic activity is a refinement of the typical circular flow diagram. Its advantage lies in the fact that it highlights the temporal nature of production and the role of time in decision making both at the firm level as well as at the aggregate, economy-wide level. This will be especially useful in Chapter 5 which examines the history of macroeconomic thought.

Who Makes the Market?

The IES provides a convenient framework to address one of the key questions in macroeconomics, namely who makes the market? In other words, who is ultimately, responsible for creating demand, both at the individual firm level and at the aggregate level? The answer, ultimately, is firms, collectively. Firms make the market via their behavior in the variable-factor input market as well as in the fixed-factor input market. The more variable factors they employ, the greater is variable factor income (energy and labor), and likewise for the fixed factors.

CAPSULE: WHY THE US GOVERNMENT BAILED THE BIG BANKS OUT IN 2008?

The IES highlights a number of fundamental, yet overlooked (by mainstream economics) aspects of the current exchange technology in market-based economies. These include the role played by banks and financial institutions in trade and exchange, the role of expectations in macroeconomic equilibria, the important role of firms in the "market making" process, and the residual nature of profits. As it turns out, private banks, via their ability to create and extend credit to firms, provide the de facto medium of exchange in Western industrialized economies-oftentimes referred to as the money supply. As such, private banks are the source of the nation's money supply. Consequently, central banks are called upon to regulate, but are not ultimately responsible for the nation's money supply. Specifically, using a series of instruments, they attempt to control the level of outstanding credit in the economy.

With this in mind, one easily understands why the US government, via the Federal Reserve, came to the rescue of large Wall Street banks in the aftermath of the 2008 Financial Meltdown. Not doing so would have compromised the integrity of the US economy as a whole. Put differently, it was a matter of life and death, that is, economic life and death.

Summary and Conclusion

This chapter has presented the three core principles that underline our critical history of economic thought. Developments in the various fields will be examined accordingly. By far, the most critical of the three is the first, namely the physical or scientific view of material processes. As pointed out, wealth consists of goods and services and goods and services are produced by material processes, which are governed by the laws of applied physics and engineering. These laws are immutable and universal. The other two are more descriptive, intended to highlight various debates and situations that have arisen over the last 200 years.

The upshot is that because economic thought was and continues to be largely the work of moral philosophers (including latter-day scholars), the bulk of what is considered to be modern economic thought is unscientific either because it violates the laws of the physical world, because it either cannot or has not been tested, or both. We realize that this is a harsh judgment and one that will undoubtedly be challenged. However, we believe in calling a spade, a spade.

Questions for Discussion

1 In your opinion, should the known laws of the universe apply to economic phenomena, or should the study of economics be exempt from them? Explain.
2 What is the most fundamental difference between broadly defined energy and broadly defined organization factor inputs?
3 Explain how the market mechanism solves the coordination problem. What role do prices play?
4 How and why do hierarchical organizations dominate more distributed, collegial organizations.
5 In your opinion, do innovation and technological change more likely in hierarchical or market environments? Explain.
6 Explain the role of financial intermediaries (banks) in macroeconomic equilibria.
7 Are payments to labor and capital analogous? How are they similar and how are they different?
8 Macroeconomists oftentimes refer to self-fulfilling equilibria. Explain, using the IES, how such equilibria occur, and how governments can minimize any possible effects.

9 To your knowledge, has the superiority of markets over hierarchy ever been proved scientifically? That is, by isolating all other factors and focusing on the CCS?

Notes

1 Energy cannot be physically consumed, but rather simply transformed. However, for our purposes, we will refer to its use as consumption.
2 The key Neolithic innovations included the development of large-scale agriculture and metallurgy, both of which involve tapping into the earth's abundant supply of energy (solar radiation and heat).
3 Second law efficiency is defined as the ratio of the useful exergy output to the total exergy input for a given process or device.
4 Simple tools provide mechanical advantage by multiplying the force we exert on a tool at the cost of increasing the distance we need to sustain the force. This trade-off occurs because simple tools (ideally) do not alter the amount of work done. Work is the product of distance and force, so by increasing the distance via a tool one can decrease the force required. The ratio between the force exerted by the tool and the force applied to the tool defines the mechanical advantage.
5 For more on this, see Beaudreau (2017).
6 Physiocracy, Greek for government (cracy) by nature (physio). Or, put differently the laws of nature (science) govern wealth and growth.
7 Accordingly, the Physiocrats viewed agriculture as the only productive sector as it powered (via the calories it generated) itself as well as all other sectors of the economy. The latter were, as such, seen as "sterile" in the sense that they simply transformed food calories into output – in short, they did not add to the energy constraint.
8 This is typically referred to as the value of the marginal product.
9 Conventionally defined labor had been rendered redundant by the force, the power of the steam that was driving industrial material processes.
10 The market informs and coordinates via the price mechanism. If demand exceeds supply, prices rise, informing both sides of the market and coordinating the behavior of both consumers and producers.
11 It could be argued that the hand metaphor has its origins in moral philosophy, the hand being a reference to the biblical hand of God. In Calvinism, God works through each individual, not organized, hierarchical structures like the Vatican. It bears reminding that Adam Smith and Jean-Baptiste Say were both Calvinists.
12 A good example is the American 13 colonies, where each was established as a chartered company. Examples include the Massachusetts Company, the Virginia Company and the Carolina Company.
13 In other words, decisions and choices made in the past are not affected by current conditions (e.g. price variations).
14 In this regard, it is a horizontal representation of the vertical value chain.
15 For example, if a government were to announce that GDP would fall by 50 percent, there is good reason to believe that it would as decision-makers would, anticipating a 50 percent decrease in sales, cut employment and output by 50 percent.

References

Beaudreau, B.C. (1998) *Energy and Organization, Growth and Distribution Reconsidered*, Westport, CT: Greenwood Press.

Beaudreau, B.C. (1999) *Energy and the Rise and Fall of Political Economy*, Westport, CT: Greenwood Press.

Beaudreau, Bernard C. (2017) The Economies of Speed, KE=1/2mv2, and the Productivity Slowdown, *Energy*, 124, pp. 100–113.
Beiser, A. (1983) *Modern Technical Physics*, Menlo Park, CA: The Benjamin/Cummings Publishing Company.
Berg, M. (1980) *The Machine Question and the Making of Political Economy*, Cambridge: Cambridge University Press.
Berndt, E. and Wood D. (1975) Technology, Prices and the Derived Demand for Energy, *The Review of Economics and Statistics*, pp. 259–268.
Betts, J. (1989) *Essentials of Applied Physics*, Englewood Cliffs, NJ: Prentice-Hall.
Chandler, A.D. (1977) *The Visible Hand: The Managerial Revolution in American Business*, Cambridge, MA: Harvard University Press.
Coase, R. (1937) The Nature of the Firm, *Economica*, 4(16), pp. 386–405.
Durlauf, S.N. (1997) A Formal Model of Theory Choice in Science, *Economic Theory*, 14(1) pp. 113–130.
General Electric Company (1937) The General Electric Machine Tool Speed Show, https://www.youtube.com/watch?v=CUYajEF7X-U&t=26s
Glaeser, E.L., F. Lopez-De-Silianes, Andrei Scheilfer (2004) Do Institutions Cause Growth, *Journal of Economic Growth*, 9, pp. 271–303.
La Porta, R. et al. (1998) Law and Finance, *Journal of Political Economy,* 106(6), pp. 1113–1155.
Leibenstein, H. (1968) Entrepreneurship and Development, *American Economic Review,* 58, pp. 72–83.
Marshall, A. (1890) *Principles of Economics*, London: Macmilllan.
Newcomb, S. (1886) *Principles of Economics*, New York: Augustus M. Kelley.
Nye, D.E. (1990) *Electrifying America: Social Meanings of a New Technology*, Cambridge, MA: MIT Press.
Smith, A. (1776) *An Inquiry into the Nature and Causes of the Wealth of Nations*, New York: Modern Library.
Sobel, R.M. (1972) *The Age of Giant Corporations: A Microeconomic History of American Business 1914–1970*, Westport, CT: Greenwood Press.
Soddy, Frederick. (1924) *Cartesian Economics, The Bearing of Physical Sciences upon State Stewardship* London: Henderson.
Solow, R (1974) The Economics of Resources or the Resources of Economics, *American Economic Review* 64(2), pp.1–14.
Tryon, F.G. (1927) An Index of Consumption of Fuels and Water Power, *Journal of the American Statistical Association* 22, pp. 271–282.
Tylecote, M. (1957) *The Mechanics Institute of Lancashire and Yorkshire Before 1851*, Manchester: Manchester University Press.
Williamson, O. (1985) *The Economic Institutions of Capitalism*, New York: NY: Free Press.
Wilson, E.O. (2012) *Consilience: The Unity of Knowledge*, Cambridge, MA: Harvard University Press.

3

GROWTH THEORY

Introduction

Simply put, economics is the science of wealth. As such, while it is concerned with the myriad issues related to wealth, it is first and foremost about the creation of wealth as well as its growth over time. Adam Smith's magnum opus*, An Inquiry into the Nature and Causes of the Wealth of Nations*, set the agenda for the emerging discipline. Economics would be about the nature of wealth (material processes) and its causes (growth). Two hundred and fifty years later, the nature and causes of the wealth of nations continue to dominate the economics agenda. The Productivity Slowdown of the 1970s combined with the inability of Western industrialized nations, via a multitude of measures and policies, to restore growth levels to post-WWII levels have resulted in a renaissance of sorts for growth theory. Ignored for most of the 20th century, it now occupies "the" central place in economics.

In this chapter, we examine growth theory critically. We will be particularly interested in the reasons why, despite over two centuries of study, the "causes" of growth remain elusive? For example, growth in the post-WWII era averaged roughly 3.5 percent annually, half of which is attributed to labor and capital growth, and the other half is of unknown origin, referred to by Stanford University economics professor Moses Abramovitz as "our measure of ignorance" and more recently, by MIT economics professor Robert Solow as a "residual."

This chapter, like all subsequent ones, will be organized as follows. First, it will be structured temporally around the two centuries of political economy, namely the 19th and 20th centuries. Then, within each century, it will be organized around two themes, namely the relevant history (e.g. in this chapter, of economic growth) and the corresponding thought, or history of thought. In the former, a historical narrative of, in this case, economic growth, using the core principles of Chapter 2 will be presented.

DOI: 10.4324/9781003527060-3

This corresponding "thought" will then be set against this narrative, thus allowing for an in-depth critical evaluation. Guiding us through this critical examination will be the building blocks of the scientific method, namely hypotheses and test results. As in all chapters, we will be particularly interested in identifying the issues and debates, which prompted scholars and writers in general to inquire into the growth process.

Definition

By growth theory, it should be understood the set of theoretical abstractions that describe wealth creation (the level and rate of growth). Put differently, what are the factors that determine the level and rate of growth of material wealth? The level of material wealth is typically measured in monetary units (e.g. dollars, euros and yen) while its rate of growth is measured in percentage terms.

The Problem of Economic Growth

As pointed out in the introduction, science has been, is, and will continue to be reactionary in nature, responding to the challenges and problems of any given era. This raises the question: What were/are the challenges and problems that underlie growth theory? As we shall show in this chapter, the challenges and problems have varied over time, ranging from the early 19th-century desire on the part of Western industrial societies to industrialize, to the late 20th-century Productivity Slowdown, which witnessed a marked decrease in the rate of per capita GDP growth.

What You Will Learn in This Chapter

In this chapter, you will:

- Learn about economic growth throughout the ages, with the emphasis on the past two centuries (industrialization).
- Learn about the various technological innovations that contributed in a non-negligible way to increasing material wealth and consequently, the standard of living in the West.
- Learn about how throughout the past two centuries, Western industrialized economies have rarely operated at full capacity.
- Learn about those who attempted to understand these changes.
- Learn about how the debate over the causes of wealth degenerated into a debate over distribution. That is, distribution of the overall level of wealth to the various factor inputs.
- Learn why the failure of production theory to move beyond the obvious (i.e. the physics of growth) resulted in chaos and confusion, and a series of mysteries and paradoxes. Among these are the Productivity Slowdown and the information paradox.

By the End of This Chapter, You Should Understand

- How and why a poor understanding of the underlying physics of material processes plagued the economic growth literature from its very inception and continues to plague it.
- The reasons for the failure of the economics profession to understand what is its "bread and butter issue" namely the equations of motion of wealth.
- Why, barring a paradigm change in fundamentals, mainstream growth theory will continue to fall short of its ultimate objective, namely explaining and predicting economic growth.

The 19th Century

History of Growth in the 19th Century

The shift from the domestic system of production to the factory system, based on new sources of power (water, steam), had a profound impact on the industrial and economic landscape of the UK. For example, the ownership of factor inputs (energy and organization) was no longer concentrated (i.e. within the family unit), but rather, was diffuse. Workers which had up until then been a source of motive power were reduced to supervisory inputs (i.e. machine operatives), overseeing the workings of steam-powered machinery. Producers no longer coordinated production activity in house, but rather did so in a market environment. So great were these changes that moral philosophers and political economists would devote the next hundred years to understanding them, with, as shall be shown, mixed results.

Missing from the resulting literature (economic thought), whether classical, Marxian and neoclassical, however, is any mention of energy in general, and hydraulic and steam power in particular. Production continued to be modeled in terms of capital and labor. Energy is notable for its absence. This, we argue, was not inconsequential. Energy-related innovations were changing the industrial landscape; yet, in political economy, they were nowhere to be found. This is not to say that political economy was impervious to the changing industrial landscape; rather, it was impervious to the root cause. To most political economists of the time, the introduction of new machinery was the relevant technological shock.

In this chapter, using the model of production, exchange and distribution developed in Chapter 2, we re-examine the origins and evolution of 19th-century political economy. As pointed out in the introduction, the approach taken is altogether different from conventional history of economic thought. First, we abstract from the writings of classical, radical and neoclassical moral philosophers and examine, using the analytical framework presented in Chapter 2, the transition from the domestic to the factory system. This allows us to identify the major problems and issues related to the introduction of the revolutionary form of inanimate energy that was "fire power." This is then followed by an in-depth re-examination of classical, radical and neoclassical political economy, its motives, its influences, its contributions and its shortcomings.

Steam Power and the Industrial Revolution

This section is devoted to evaluating the effects of "fire power" on production, distribution and exchange in Great Britain in the late 18th and early 19th centuries. Particular attention will be paid to the various problems "fire power" raised. Among these are the problems of exchange and distribution.

The Domestic System

To better understand and appreciate the impact of "fire power" on industry in the UK, we begin by describing production, distribution and exchange activity in the years leading up to the industrial revolution. Prior to the introduction of the Watt-Boulton reciprocating steam engine, work (i.e. output) in Great Britain was, for the most part, the result of the application of muscular (human and animal) force. Draft animals, supervised by farmers, provided the necessary force to till the soil. Human, muscular force, however, was required to harvest crops. Clearly, the stronger the draft animals, the more work could be done per unit of animal feed. The heightened interest in animal breeding in the pre-industrial period can, as such, be viewed as a means of increasing the relevant η, the level of thermodynamic efficiency. The same is true of the tool industry, where the emphasis was on high-grade, durable metals, capable of doing more work per unit force—in this case, muscular.

In 17th-century Great Britain, most forms of production activity were carried out on a small scale, often times by the household unit. Food was grown, wool was produced, thread was spun, cloth was woven and tools/furniture were fashioned. Among the specialized activities were steel making, and, to a lesser degree, grain milling and, of course, religion—salvation. Autarky was, in general, the rule. Exceptions, however, involved the production of goods, most often textiles, by households for the market. Merchants from cities would contract work out to households in the surrounding countryside, supplying the raw material and purchasing the finished products. This is known as the "domestic system," "putting out system" and the "cottage industry." Peter Stearns describes this period as follows:

> *With all these developments, however, Western technology and production methods remained firmly anchored in the basic traditions of agricultural societies, particularly in terms of reliance on human and animal power. Agriculture had scarcely changed in method since the fourteenth century. Manufacturing, despite some important new techniques, continued to entail combining skill with hand tools and was carried out in very small shops. The most important Western response to new manufacturing opportunities involved a great expansion*

> *of rural (domestic) production, particularly in textiles but also in small metal goods. Domestic manufacturing workers used simple equipment, which they usually bought themselves, and relied on labor from the household. Many combined their efforts with farming, and in general their skill levels were modest. The system worked well because it required little capital; rural households invested a bit in a spinning wheel or a hand loom, while an urban-based capitalist purchased the necessary raw materials and, usually, arranged for the sale of the product. Output expanded because of the sheer growth of worker numbers, not because of technical advancement; indeed, the low wages paid generated little incentive for technical change.*
>
> *(Stearns 1993, 18)*

What is particularly interesting, as far as we are concerned, is the nature of production, exchange and distribution. The household unit (producer) provided the necessary energy, tools and supervision to transform say raw wool into thread, thread into finished cloth, or, for that matter, finished cloth into clothing. The energy was, in general, muscular in nature; the tools were primitive by today's standard, and the supervision was provided by the workers themselves. Given that the energy and organization in question were owned by the household (i.e. the household unit), there was no distribution problem – as described earlier (i.e. outside of the household). The income received from the merchants (payments for services rendered) went to the household (producer), not to the individual factors, per se.

The resulting exchange technology did not pose any problems. The overall demand for trade credit was, but for the merchant's profit, equal to the value of total output. Trade credit was provided by local and regional banks. The relevant credit instruments included bills of exchange, promissory notes, etc. Merchants demanded trade credit in the amount of the cost of their raw materials (cotton, wool, linen), and the cost of transformation (adding value).

Not surprisingly, the domestic system went largely unnoticed, not being the subject of any natural or moral philosophical treatise in the pre-industrial period. The supply of human, animate and muscular energy put an upper limit on the per-capita amount of output/work, and, hence, of the growth of output and work. One could argue that in the absence of energy-related innovations (e.g. steam engine), growth would have been limited to growth of animate, muscular energy, which, at the time, tracked population growth.

Enter the Steam Engine

Two events in 18th-century Great Britain changed the industrial landscape forever. The first was Richard Arkwright's water-wheel-driven spinning jenny, while the second was the development and widespread application of the Watts-Boulton reciprocating steam engine. Analytically speaking, Arkwright's water-powered spinning jenny was of monumental importance, as it altered fundamentally the nature of work. The force required to spin cotton and wool would, from this point on, no longer be animate, but inanimate. Spinning wheels (spindles) would be powered by hydraulic power, transmitted by way of belting, gearing and shafting. This de facto lifted the energy constraint that had limited the level of per capita wealth since the beginning of time. Never again would human muscular power limit the amount of work done. According to Peter Stearns:

> *More impressive developments occurred in the preparatory phases in cotton, James Hargreaves invented a spinning jenny device about 1764, which mechanically drew out and twisted fibers into threads—though this advance too initially was applied to handwork, not a new power source. Carding and combing machines, to ready the fiber prior to spinning, were developed at about the same time. Then in 1769, Richard Arkwright developed the first water-powered spinning machine; it twisted and wound threads by means of flyers and bobbins operating continuously. These first machines were relevant only for the cheapest kind of thread, but other inventions by 1780 began to make possible the spinning of finer cotton yarns. These new devices also could be powered by steam engines as well as waterwheels. The basic principles of mechanized thread production have not changed to this day, though machines were to grow progressively larger, and a given worker could tend to a number of spindles.*
>
> *(Stearns 1993, 23)*

However, by moving production out of cottages (putting-out) into factories (gathering-in), it raised the problem of exchange and distribution. How would resulting total value added be apportioned among the owners of capital (i.e. the mill), the owners of lower-level supervisory skills (i.e. men, women and children) and the owners of the hydraulic resource? Moreover, given that the producer (manager) was, in most cases, also the owner of the capital (equity capital), a non-negligible fraction of factor payments would be residual in nature, paid out after the finished output was sold to merchants (i.e. the fixed factor input payment).

It is important to point out that these epoch-defining changes predate the introduction of the steam engine in industry. A good example of this is Matthew Boulton's Soho Manufactory in Bolton where the Hockley Brook (water wheel) powered the machines used to manufacture buttons, watch chains, plated wares et cetera (collectively referred to as toys). Earlier in 1765, he had left Birmingham to avoid operating an expensive horse mill.

Hockley Brook, however, was not without problems of its own. For example, in the summer, water levels were, often times, insufficient to power the wheels, bringing the manufactory to a halt. To overcome this problem, Boulton turned to steam power, ordering a Savary engine to pump water and, in the process, turn the water wheels. According to Richard Hills:

> *In light of subsequent history, one of the most important people to consider using a Savary engine was Matthew Boulton when he wished to supplement the*

water resources of the Hockley Brook which powered his new Soho Manufactory. He had purposely moved out of Birmingham in 1765 to avoid operating an expensive horse mill, but the growth of the Manufactory presented him, with a similar dilemma once more. So his mind turned to employing a steam engine to lift water from the tail race of the waterwheel back to the mill dam.

(Hills 1989, 40)

Realizing that steam could drive machinery directly—as opposed to via waterwheels—Boulton began work with James Watt in 1768 on what was to become the defining energy innovation of the 18th century, namely the Boulton-Watt rotary-drive steam engine. These developments are essential to understanding Adam Smith's *An Inquiry into the Nature and Causes of the Wealth of Nations*. According to the record, Smith knew Boulton and Watt, and had personally visited the Soho Manufactory prior to 1776. Hence, there is every reason to believe that he was aware of both the atmospheric (with condenser) and reciprocating dual-acting steam engines and the potential both represented for England.

The mid-to-late 18th century/early 19th century, it therefore follows, was a transitional period, with animate, muscular energy being replaced by inanimate, hydraulic-based energy, which, in turn, was replaced by inanimate, fossil-fuel-based energy in the form of steam power. According to Katrina Honeyman:

During the period 1780–1825, cotton factories varied not only in scale but also in type. S. D. Chapman has identified what he sees as three main types. The Type A mill was a small-scale operation, often employing hand-operated Jennies or mules and possibly horse capstans for driving card machines. The cost of establishing and equipping this type of mill was about £1,000–£2,000. The Type B factory was more often purpose-built and comprised three or four storeys. It came in two sizes: one designed to hold approximately 1,000 spindles and requiring up to 13,000 investment; and one at least twice as large with up to 3,000 spindles, costing from £5,000. These are often referred to as Arkwright-type mills. Type C was larger, generally steam-powered, and cost about £10,000. This category of mill was not usual until the early 19th century.

(Honeyman 1982, 57)

The substitution of inanimate power for animate, muscular power occurred over a period of roughly 100 years (1760–1860). According to data on laborers in the UK from 1806 to 1862, there were as many factory workers as handweavers, and that by 1862, the latter had, for all intents and purposes, disappeared from the land. Inanimate energy had completely displaced animate energy. Industrialization being born of inanimate energy—in this case, the consumption of coal—it follows that the rate of growth of output would be an increasing function of the rate of growth of coal consumption, ceteris paribus. Table 3.1 reports both the level and rate of growth of coal production in the UK at five-year intervals from 1755 to 1900. From a level of 4.230 million tons in 1755, it had increased 12,049 percent to 50.968 million tons

TABLE 3.1 Total Coal Consumption, Great Britain, 1755–1900

Year	*Coal Consumption*	*Rate of Growth*
1760	4,520	–
1765	4,950	0.095
1770	5,520	0.115
1775	6,120	0.108
1780	6,750	0.102
1785	7,550	0.116
1790	8,570	0.145
1795	9,570	0.116
1800	10,960	0.145
1805	12,960	0.182
1810	14,790	0.141
1815	16,590	0.121
1820	18,900	0.139
1825	20,900	0.105
1830	24,800	0.186
1835	29,560	0.191
1840	35,270	0.193
1845	41,706	0.182
1850	50,968	0.222
1855	64,500	0.265
1860	80,000	0.240
1865	98,200	0.227
1870	110,400	0.124
1875	133,300	0.207
1880	147,000	0.102
1885	159,400	0.084
1890	181,600	0.139
1895	189,700	0.044
1900	225,200	0.187

Source: Mitchell (1988).

Note: Five-Year Growth Rate

in 1850. By 1870, it had more than doubled to 110.4 million tons. At the end of the century, it had more than doubled again to 225.2 million tons.

Referring to Column 3, we see that five-year growth rates ranged from a low of 6.8 percent in 1755–1760, to a high of 24.0 percent in 1855–1860. Given their broad nature, these data must be interpreted with caution. Ideally, data on industrial consumption of coal in the UK, not the overall total output of coal, would be required. Such data, unfortunately, do not exist. What do exist, however, are data collected by the Factory Inspectors, in accordance with the Factory Act of 1833 on the use of steam and water power in various UK industries from 1835 onward. These data, in combination with employment data also contained in, provide useful information on the extent of inanimate energy deepening in the UK industry, especially in the textiles sector.

Table 3.2 presents data on power employed, measured in horsepower, in the cotton, wool and flax/jute/hemp/Chinagrass factories from 1835 to 1870, as well as the corresponding employment data. The sources of both series are the various returns filed by the Factory Inspectors and published in the Sessional Papers of the House of Lords. Before turning to these data, it bears reminding that workers in factories no longer exerted themselves physically as was the case in the domestic system, but, instead, supervised the spinning machines and looms (power looms). Some, however, were assigned the task(s) of managing feedstocks (inputs and

TABLE 3.2 Total Power Consumption, Textiles, Great Britain, 1835–1903

Cotton					
Year	*Steam HP*	*Water HP*	*Total HP*	*Workers*	*Total HP/Worker*
1835	na	na	na	219	na
1838	46	12	58	259	0.2239
1850	71	11	82	331	0.2477
1856	87	9	96	379	0.2532
1861	281	12	293	452	0.6482
1867	190	12	202	401	0.5037
1870	299	8	307	450	0.6822
Wool					
Year	*Steam HP*	*Water HP*	*Total HP*	*Workers*	*Total HP/Workers*
1835	na	na	na	55	na
1838	17	10	27	87	0.3103
1850	23	10	33	154	0.2142
1856	31	9	40	167	0.2395
1861	53	11	64	173	0.3699
1867	85	12	97	262	0.3702
1870	103	12	115	239	0.4811
Miscellaneous					
Year	*Steam HP*	*Water HP*	*Total HP*	*Workers*	*Total HP/Workers*
1835	na	na	na	33	na
1838	7	4	11	42	0.2619
1850	11	3	14	68	0.2058
1856	14	4	18	80	0.2250
1861	32	4	36	94	0.3829
1867	42	5	47	135	0.3489
1870	52	5	57	146	0.3904

Source: Mitchell (1988).

outputs). As such, by dividing total horsepower say in the cotton industry by the total employment, one arrives at a crude measure of inanimate energy per worker/supervisor. That is, the amount of energy—and hence, work—workers supervised. The evolution of this ratio over time provides a measure of energy deepening.

Take, for example, the cotton industry, which in 1838, had 46,000 horsepower of steam power, and 12,000 horsepower of water power, for a total of 58,000 horsepower of inanimate energy. Given the presence of 259,000 workers, it stands to reason that the relevant $E_c(t)/S_c(t)$ ratio stood at 0.223938. This is to say that each worker supervised the equivalent of 0.223938 of a horsepower of inanimate energy. Referring to Column 4, we see that this ratio increased monotonically in time, from 0.223938 in 1838 to 0.682222 in 1870.[3] In practical terms, this implies that supervisors (workers) in the cotton industry were overseeing three times as more inanimate power in 1870 than in 1838, a span of only 32 years. As power is synonymous with work, it follows that they were supervising three times more work in 1870 than in 1838.

This jump in inanimate power consumption per worker can be attributed to two factors, the first of which being the declining use of handlooms, referred to earlier. Animate energy as a power source declined steadily from 1838 and, by 1870, had virtually disappeared. The second factor is the various technological improvements in the generation of steam power. Foremost among these is the development by Richard Trevithick and Arthur Woolf of the high-pressure, non-condensing steam engine. The latter increased the "indicated" horsepower of existing and new engines far beyond their rated "nominal" horsepower.

Despite the dearth of data on output growth in various British industries for the period under consideration (1800–1900), what is clear is that work as defined in the EO sense increased at unprecedented rates in the UK. Never before had a country, nation or people increased, in so little time, the amount of work performed. All of this, of course, was achieved by tapping into a store of energy 450 million years old, in the form of coal (*Carboniferous Era*). Not only did the consumption of coal increase in this period, but the efficiency with which it was used also increased, increasing manifold the ability of the UK to do work.

The Importance of Speed

The manifold increase in UK manufacturing output in the 19th century resulted from a process of energy deepening which characterized much of this period. The energy deepening, in question, was achieved in two distinct ways, namely intensively and extensively. Starting with the latter, extensive energy deepening refers to the increase in the number and capacity of spindles and looms in the cotton industry. With Arkwright's spinning jenny, the number of spindles in the UK cotton spinning industry increased manifold. Similarly, with the advent of power looms, the weaving capacity, as measured by the size and number of looms, increased manifold.

A second source of energy deepening was the many speed-ups that characterized the UK textiles industry in the 19th century. Existing machines, be they carding, spinning or weaving, were accelerated, making for greater output per period of time. Characteristic of such "speed-ups" was an increase in power consumption per period in time, in keeping with the basic premises of EO production analysis (Chapter 2). Improvements in steam engines throughout the 19th century, along with improvements in spinning and weaving *per se*, paved the way for increases in the throughput rates per unit of capital (i.e. spindle or loom). Among these was the development and commercial use of the high-pressure steam engine by Richard Trevithick and Arthur Woolf, which increased markedly the speed of execution, and consequently, the rate of output (throughput).

References to speed-ups in the early 19th century are few and far-between. However, the few that do exist convey the essence of the power revolution that was playing itself out in Great Britain. Take, for example, William Longston's testimony on working conditions in the textiles industry before the Committee on the Factories Bill.

9397. Is the intensity of application and of labour altered, either against or in favour of the operative and of the children employed in mills and factories?—I was a great number of years out of any factory, but those who were my acquaintances during my boyhood have often conversed with me, and they very frequently say that it cannot be less than double in intensity and exertion of physical application.

9398. State why you believe that the labour of those employed has doubled since the first introduction and use of cotton machinery, or at least since you first knew it?—The reason why I believe so is from some calculations which I have been obliged to make, and by my own observation during the time I was manager of a mill in 1830 and 1831, when I had some of the same operations under my own observation.

9399. Have you any objection to put in those calculations—Certainly not.

[The following document was then put in and read.]

9400. It appears by this document that the work done is very greatly increased between the years 1810 and 1832; has the machinery been so altered as to produce that amazing difference, or does it result from accelerating the speed of the machinery?—It is from accelerating the speed generally; and another cause is, that more and more exertion is required from the individual working at the machine; these are the two causes.

9401. Those two causes, then, prove what you have been asserting, namely that double the labour and attendance is now requisite that was formerly required?—I think so.

9403. In spite of the improvements of machinery?—Yes; I believe those that are now working in the same employment as I did when I was a boy, do double the work.

9403. So that there may be a great improvement in machinery, and at the same time a great increase in actual labour to each operative?—Yes.

9404. Has that been, as far as your experience has extended, the consonant result of improvements of machinery in those mills, namely, that the labour of the hands has increased with every improvement in the machinery; rather than diminished?—Yes; the improvements in the machinery have been great, and the same physical exertion, and the same physical exertion, and the same attention as was formerly applied, would certainly produce, in proportion to the altered state of machinery, a much greater quantity and better articles; but, added to that, the increased exertions make the quantities to be such as just now surprised you.

(Committee on Factories Bill 1832, 430)

As is clear from his testimony, machinery speed-ups increased considerably the amount of "work" demanded of the corresponding supervisors–that is, workers. This was the direct result of the fact that not all processes were automated. Faster turning spindles and faster operating looms required more exertion on the part of the "operatives"—that is, those who supervise the machinery (machine operatives). As the data presented show, output per lower-level supervisor (stretcher) increased by 200 percent from 1810 to 1833. In the case of mule yarn-spinning, the number of hanks spun, for 480 spindles ceteris paribus, increased by 50 percent between 1806 and 1833.

The Role of Capital and Labor

The shift from the domestic system to the factory system altered the nature of both capital and labor. Labor, a source of energy (animate, muscular) and thus of motive drive in the domestic system, was reduced to a supervisory input, overseeing the workings of continuous-flow machinery – machinery that could theoretically operate 24 hours, seven days a week. The men, women and children who, in the domestic system, had spun and woven cotton, wool, linen etcetera would, from now on, supervise the workings of steam power-driven spinning and weaving machines, and managing the various feedstocks (inputs and outputs) in factories. Alfred Marshall would describe this far-reaching change in 1890 in the following terms:

We may now pass to the effects which machinery has in relieving that excessive muscular strain which a few generations ago was the common lot of more than half the working men even in such a country as England ... in other trades, machinery has lightened man's labours. The house carpenters, for instance, make things of the same kind as those used by our forefathers, with much less toil for themselves ... . Nothing could be more narrow or monotonous than the occupation of a weaver of plain stuffs in the old time. But now, one woman will manage four or more looms, each of which does many times as much work in the course of a day as the old hand loom did; and her work is much less monotonous and calls for much more judgment than his did.

(Marshall 1890, 218)

The key word here is "manage." The woman he refers to now "manages," and, hence, no longer weaves. Moreover, as he points out, each power loom "does many times as much work in the course of a day as the old hand loom did." Conventionally defined labor productivity, it follows, increased manifold. E. Baines, in the *History of the Cotton Manufacture* published in 1835, refers to a tenfold increase in productivity for weavers.

A very good hand weaver, 25 or 30 years of age, will weave two pieces of 9-8ths shirting per week, each 24 yards long, containing 100 shoots of weft in an inch; the reed of the cloth being a 44 Bolton count, and the warp and weft hanks to 40 hanks to the lb.

In 1823, a steam-loom weaver, about 15 years of age, attending two looms, could weave seven similar pieces in a week.

In 1826, a steam-loom weaver, about 15 years of age, attending to two looms, could weave twelve similar pieces in a week; some could weave fifteen pieces.

In 1833, a steam-loom weaver, from 15-20 years of age, assisted by a girl about 12 years of age, attending to four looms, can weave eighteen similar pieces in a week; some can weave twenty pieces.

(Baines 1835, 240)

However, at this point in time, an important distinction is in order, namely, that between energy-based measures of productivity and organization-based measures of productivity. In the domestic system, workers physically exerted themselves, carding, spinning and/or weaving, in addition to supervising the workings of their animate energy (i.e. their muscles) and the tools (rudimentary spinning wheels and hand looms). In the factory system, their job task (job definition) was reduced considerably. Specifically, it would consist, almost uniquely of supervision. As such, it follows that the relevant productivity measure as found in the factory system is organization-based (see Table 3.1 on page).

Capital also underwent a major transformation. Specifically, the simple tools of the domestic system (spinning wheels and hand looms) were fitted with a power source (rotary power). Machinery, as a result, consisted of rudimentary tools driven by an inanimate power source. Complex shafting, belting and gearing systems were used to transmit the torque generated by steam engines to the spindles and the looms. Capital costs per spindle or per square yard of weaving capacity increased substantially, owing to power-related costs, and to the need for more reliable spindles and looms. Under the domestic system, spinning wheels and hand looms were fashioned out of wood (hardwood and softwood), harvested, in most cases, in local forests. The demands of high-throughput, continuous-flow production, however, were such that metal spindles and looms were needed, increasing, as such, the cost of capital. This, as it turns out, was true of all steam power-driven industries.

As shall be argued later, these costs figured prominently in the works of classical political economists. The new drive technology required massive investments, both in steam engines and in the accompanying tools. Saving and investment would, over the next half century, occupy center stage in political economy.

History of Economic Thought: 19th-Century Growth Theory

The steam engine ushered in a new era in Western civilization, an era of unlimited wealth, an era based on a new source of energy in the form of coal and fossil fuels in general. In this section, we examine contributions to what today is known as economic growth theory. That is, the study of "nature" and the "causes" of "the wealth of nations." As is the case in most, if not all, intellectual endeavors, interest in wealth and it causes in the 19th century was the result of the many challenges – and problems – that resulted from the introduction and application of the new power-drive technology. Perhaps the most important is what we refer to as the existence of a structural output gap (between potential and actual output). Whether it be theoretical or practical, the steam engine increased potential wealth markedly. Factories could be operated around the clock, 7 days a week, 52 weeks a year. The potential for wealth had never been so great. Getting there, however, would prove to be a challenge.

Adam Smith and the Nature and Causes of the Wealth of Nations

The Nature and Causes of the Wealth of Nations published in 1776 is somewhat of an oddity, for a number of reasons. First, it has no precedent. That is, it is not part of a larger literature on the "nature" and "causes" of the wealth of nations. Second, it is by no means clear why he took pen to paper to write what many regard today as the bible of modern economics. After all, he wasn't a professional political economist per se as evidenced by the fact that, like David Ricardo a half-century later, there were no follow-up works.

Most agree that it was an attempt on his part to influence the public debate over the larger question of freedom or liberty. After all, he advocated in favor of the loosening government controls/oversight.

In this section, we present a different argument, one based on our interpretation of what we feel is the most telling insight in the book, namely that the "degree of specialization or simply "specialization" is determined by the extent of the market." Put differently, we maintain that the *Wealth of Nations* was first and foremost a critique, a critique of what Smith saw as the inability of the UK economy to move in the short run to the new higher level of wealth defined by the power-drive technology that was the steam engine.

From Chapter 2, it follows that the introduction of a new energy source, or power-drive technology, will potentially increase machine/process speeds, thus increasing potential output. In such cases, a gap will be opened between potential output and actual output.

This gap, we argue, is germane to understanding the *Wealth of Nations*. In short, the *Wealth of Nations* should be understood as a critique, namely of the inability of a market economy to close the gap between potential GDP in England with the widespread adoption of the steam engine, and actual GDP, a gap that owed to the "extent of the market." Not wanting to simply identify the problem, Smith proposed a solution, namely free trade. The latter would extend the market and in so doing, incite firms to specialize, by which it should be understood, adopt the new power-drive technology that was the steam engine.

His approach can be summarized as follows. First, show how the steam engine can increase output and labor productivity. Second, show how the extent of the market *de facto* affects the decision to specialize (adopt the new technology) and third, show why and how free trade increases the extent of the market.

Another way of seeing the question at hand is as a coordination failure. Without the intervention of a third party, a market economy cannot make a spontaneous and instantaneous transition to the new growth path defined by the steam engine – what Smith referred to as "fire power." It is important to keep in mind that he was a personal friend of both Watt and Boulton and had visited the Soho Factory on many an occasion. In other words, the potential for higher productivity or the existence of a new technology does not necessarily guarantee higher income and expenditure. The latter has to come from elsewhere.

In the following excerpt from Chapter 1 of *The Wealth of Nations*, Smith outlines what became classical output and growth theory. That is, wealth is an increasing function of employment.

> *Of the Causes of Improvement in the productive Powers of Labour, and of the Order according to which its Produce is naturally distributed among the different Ranks of the People*
> *Book I, Chapter I*
> *Of the Division of Labor*
>
> *This great increase of the quantity of work which, in consequence of the division of labour, the same number of people are capable of performing, is owing to three different circumstances; first to the increase of dexterity in every particular workman; secondly, to the saving of the time which is commonly lost in passing from one species of work to another; and lastly, to the invention of a great number of machines which facilitate and abridge labour, and enable one man to do the work of many.*
>
> *First, the improvement of the dexterity of the workman necessarily increases the quantity of the work he can perform; and the division of labour, by reducing every man's business to some one simple operation, and by making this operation*

*the sole employment of his life, necessarily increases very much the dexterity of the workman. A common smith, who, though accustomed to handle the hammer, has never been used to make nails, if upon some particular occasion he is obliged to attempt it, will scarce, I am assured, be able to make above two or three hundred nails in a day, and those too very bad ones.*28 A smith who has been accustomed to make nails, but whose sole or principal business has not been that of a nailer, can seldom with his utmost diligence make more than eight hundred or a thousand nails in a day. I have seen several boys under twenty years of age who had never exercised any other trade but that of making nails, and who, when they exerted themselves, could make, each of them, upwards of two thousand three hundred nails in a day.*29 The making of a nail, however, is by no means one of the simplest operations. The same person blows the bellows, stirs or mends the fire as there is occasion, heats the iron, and forges every part of the nail: In forging the head too he is obliged to change his tools. The different operations into which the making of a pin, or of a metal button,*30 is subdivided, are all of them much more simple, and the dexterity of the person, of whose life it has been the sole business to perform them, is usually much greater. The rapidity with which some of the operations of those manufactures are performed, exceeds what the human hand could, by those who had never seen them, be supposed capable of acquiring.*

*Secondly, the advantage which is gained by saving the time commonly lost in passing from one sort of work to another, is much greater than we should at first view be apt to imagine it. It is impossible to pass very quickly from one kind of work to another; that is carried on in a different place, and with quite different tools. A country weaver,*31 who cultivates a small farm, must lose a good deal of time in passing from his loom to the field, and from the field to his loom. When the two trades can be carried on in the same workhouse, the loss of time is no doubt much less. It is even in this case, however, very considerable. A man commonly saunters a little in turning his hand from one sort of employment to another. When he first begins the new work he is seldom very keen and hearty; his mind, as they say, does not go to it, and for some time he rather trifles than applies to good purpose. The habit of sauntering and of indolent careless application, which is naturally, or rather necessarily acquired by every country workman who is obliged to change his work and his tools every half hour, and to apply his hand in twenty different ways almost every day of his life; renders him almost always slothful and lazy, and incapable of any vigorous application even on the most pressing occasions. Independent, therefore, of his deficiency in point of dexterity, this cause alone must always reduce considerably the quantity of work which he is capable of performing.*

*Thirdly, and lastly, every body must be sensible how much labour is facilitated and abridged by the application of proper machinery. It is unnecessary to give any example.*32 I shall only observe, therefore,*33 that the invention of all those machines by which labour is so much facilitated and abridged, seems to have been originally owing to the division of labour. Men are much more likely* *to discover easier and readier methods of attaining any object, when the whole attention of their minds is directed towards that single object, than when it is dissipated among a great variety of things. But in consequence of the division of labour, the whole of every man's attention comes naturally to be directed towards some one very simple object. It is naturally to be expected, therefore, that some one or other of those who are employed in each particular branch of labour should soon find out easier and readier methods of performing their own particular work, wherever the nature of it admits of such improvement. A great part of the machines made use of*34 in those manufactures in which labour is most subdivided, were originally the inventions of common workmen, who, being each of them employed in some very simple operation, naturally turned their thoughts towards finding out easier and readier methods of performing it. Whoever has been much accustomed to visit such manufactures, must frequently have been shewn very pretty machines, which were the inventions of such workmen,*35 in order to facilitate and quicken their own particular part of the work. In the first fire-engines,*36 a boy was constantly employed to open and shut alternately the communication between the boiler and the cylinder, according as the piston either ascended or descended. One of those boys, who loved to play with his companions, observed that, by tying a string from the handle of the valve which opened this communication, to another part of the machine, the valve would open and shut without his assistance, and leave him at liberty to divert himself with his play-fellows. One of the greatest improvements that has been made upon this machine, since it was first invented, was in this manner the discovery of a boy who wanted to save his own labour.*

(Smith 1776, 12)

To summarize, according to Smith, labor productivity is increasing in three factors, namely (i) increased productivity due to specialization, (ii) less down time from having to constantly change tasks and (iii) the introduction of machinery.

Labor-Centric View of Mechanization/Steam Engine

This raises a number of questions, notably why did Smith choose to describe the new technology from a labor-centric point of view? Instead of modeling wealth as an increasing function of work/energy (in keeping with classical mechanics), he chose to focus on labor. Energy and capital equipment were subordinated to labor. Both served to increase labor productivity.

Clearly, this made little sense from a physical point of view. After all, the steam engine, by replacing muscle-based force/energy with inanimate force/energy, had de facto trivialized labor as a factor input, rendering it a supervisory input, overseeing the workings of machines. From the physical point of view, labor was no longer productive as it no longer powered the material processes in question.

How then are we to understand Smith's reasoning? Why focus on labor when steam was the crux of the issue? Why marginalize what most observers, then as now, consider to be the single most important innovation of modern times? Here, we maintain that his decision owed to two factors, namely ignorance and propaganda. While an engineering marvel, the steam engine was a scientific enigma. Little was known of heat engines. That is, as sources of work. In fact, thermodynamics, the science of heat, was a century away. Hence, it should come as no surprise that Smith, the moral philosopher, was unable to integrate in a meaningful way, the steam engine in his analysis.

This is not to say that Smith was oblivious to the role of the steam engine. At various places in the Wealth of Nations, he refers to the Watts-Boulton steam engine as "fire power," which indicates a certain familiarity with the new technology. However, the lack of a "general" theory of production, one that included energy as well as broadly defined organization (capital, supervision), precluded a more in-depth – and accurate – analysis of the effects of the steam engine on wealth.

The second factor was propaganda by which it should be understood the politics of the steam engine. Smith was fully aware that inanimate energy-powered machinery was looked upon as suspect by the various worker guilds throughout England. The reason was straightforward, namely the steam engine threatened the livelihood of skilled labor (guilds). To allay their fears, Smith purposely "subordinated" steam to labor. The steam engine and associated machinery, he argued, would increase labor productivity, not destroy jobs. Workers would as such be better off. In many regards, his task was not unlike that of the current denizens of information technology, namely convincing workers that computers and computer technology would not cost them their jobs, but rather would increase their productivity.

Second on Smith's list of to-dos was realizing the UK's new potential. The steam engine would increase potential UK output by a factor of between 40 and 100. The problem, of course, was getting there. To this end, massive investments in steam engines and associated machinery would be needed, not to mention the corresponding infrastructure (i.e. of supplying coal) needed to move inputs and outputs.

Getting in the way, Smith reasoned, were the institutions of the 18th century, namely mercantilism, controlled largely by the state in conjunction with royal merchants (i.e. those having a government charter). Resources that had been allocated by the state, he argued, would need to be reallocated to the emerging manufacturing sector.

> *All systems of political preference and State restraint cause scarce resources to be employed less economically than would otherwise have been the case. Allocative inefficiency, unattractive in itself to a puritan who valued productivity and looked down on waste, thus had the further disadvantage that it acted as a brake on the growth of nations: "Every system which endeavours, either, by*

> *extraordinary encouragements, to draw towards a particular species of industry a greater share of the capital of the society than what would naturally go to it; or, by extraordinary restraints, to force from a particular species of industry some share of the capital which would otherwise be employed in it; is in reality subversive of the great purpose which it means to promote. It retards, instead of accelerating, the progress of the society towards real wealth and greatness; and diminishes, instead of increasing, the real value of the annual produce of its land and labour."*
>
> *(Smith 1776, 208])*

The solution: free and open financial markets. Savings would as such be directed toward high-yielding investments.

Smith's third concern was the problem posed by the high throughput, continuous flow production techniques made possible by the steam engine. As noted, the latter increased factory output by a factor of between 40 and 100, an outcome he referred to as specialization. The problem, however, was with the market, specifically with demand/buyers. Put differently, could the market somehow "absorb" the resulting output? Smith referred to the underlying conundrum as "specialization being determined by the extent of the market." The extent of the market, or the size of the market, was a key factor affecting the entrepreneur's decision to adopt the new technology.

What was Smith's solution? Free trade. Free trade would, by eliminating tariffs and other impediments, extend the market, making specialization, by which it should be understood, the adoption of the steam engine, viable. As shall be argued later, the case in favor of free trade throughout the late 18th and early 19th century was based in large measure, on growth concerns, as opposed to the traditional gains from trade argument found in the trade literature.

Adam Smith's the Wealth of Nations: Ideology or Science?

Considered to be the cornerstone of modern economics, Smith's contribution to political economy cannot be overstated. However, the question remains: Is his work ideological, a form of propaganda, or scientific? The absence of any reference to classical mechanics (i.e. Newtonian physics) as well as the absence of any data/evidence, or for that matter, any testable hypotheses forces us to conclude that the "Wealth of Nations" is, in large measure, ideology/ propaganda. In what is considered to be the "bible" of modern-day market-based economics, there is no attempt on the part of the author to provide systematic proof of the various hypotheses presented.

His account of the underlying laws of production (i.e. Chapter 1) is little more than an account of Paleolithic era (i.e. pre-industrial) material processes based on human force/energy and learning curves enhanced by machinery. Moreover, it is completely orthogonal to the scientific laws (Newtonian physics) of the day that describe work (i.e. material processes) in what was the beginning of the age of mechanized power, an age that began with the steam engine. More telling, in the presence of the steam engine or "fire power" as he described it, labor was no longer productive physically, being called upon to supervise or oversee steam-powered machinery. As it turned out, never again would labor be physically productive. As for his defense of free trade, it too is devoid of any scientific rigor, being more impressionistic than scientific. Moreover, it violates a key feature of international trade, namely as a zero-sum game, market-wise. For equilibrium to hold, any increase in exports must be matched by an equivalent increase in imports. In short, free trade cannot increase the "extent of the market" without decreasing it at the same time – unless of course the exports in question consist of manufactures (i.e. goods that benefit from specialization) and the imports, of raw materials.

CAPSULE: THE WEALTH OF NATIONS AS CRITIQUE

Celebrated as the bible of modern economics, questions remain as to Adam Smith's motive(s) for penning this much-celebrated monograph. Was it to showcase the steam engine? Was it to highlight the merits of free markets over a command economy? Was it to make a case for free trade?

There is, however, a case to be made for the Wealth of Nations as a critique, a critique of free markets, of how a new technology is adopted, of how a technology shock is not a sufficient condition to move the economy onto the corresponding higher growth path. The key concept in Chapter 1 is the notion that "specialization is determined by the extent of the market." By specialization, it should be understood the adoption of the steam engine (fire power). No mention is made of how specialization affects the extent of the market. Rather causality goes from the market to specialization. Thus, the existence of a coordination failure. Specialization does not affect the extent of the market. In other words, it does not affect wages.

To resolve this failure, Smith proposed free trade, or a widening of the market, the foreign market. This, in his view, will be growth enhancing as it increases the extent of the market.

What Caused the Industrial Revolution?

The development of the atmospheric steam engine (circa 1769) as well as the Boulton-Watt reciprocating steam engine (circa 1799) is largely seen as having launched the industrial revolution, an event that changed the course of human history, allowing mankind to tap into and exploit the earth's abundant supply of energy, ushering a period of seemingly unbound wealth. But what led to this momentous event? What factors were at play? And why in England and not continental Europe or Asia?

These questions have dogged political economy and economics from the late 18th century. As Adam Smith pointed out, specialization or the introduction of the steam engine (fire power) was determined by the extent of the market. Hence, it would stand to reason that the industrial revolution was more than just the steam engine, that a whole host of factors were at play.

The literature on the origins of the industrial revolution is twofold in nature, consisting of material explanations and non-material explanations. The former consist of technological developments or market-based developments that resulted in the manifold increase in productivity (machine speed) in the 19th century. Non-material explanations, as their very name implies, point to social/cultural factors that led ultimately to a fundamental change in behavior, leading eventually to a revolution in the creation of wealth.

Table 3.3 presents the many theories, broken down by category. Material theories point to such things as the development of the steam engine, increasing wages in the late 18th century, expanded foreign trade, an increase in per-capita income etc. Non-material theories point to changes in governance (i.e. the Glorious Revolution of 1688), changes in values (e.g. McCloskey's Bourgeois Dignity) and changes in science (e.g. Mokyr's Republic of Letters). According to Northwestern University economics professor Joel Mokyr, the enlightenment spawned an era of useful scientific innovation in England, the cumulative effect of which led in time to the industrial revolution.

While this literature is rich in details and narratives, it suffers from an important shortcoming, namely the lack of any conclusive test or proof. In other words, it is virtually impossible to test these theories for the simple reason that the event in question is unique. Put differently, the sample consists of one observation. The authors have, as such, resorted to writing what are exhaustive descriptive accounts

TABLE 3.3 Theories of the Industrial Revolution

Non-material	
Republic of letters	Moykr (2010)
Bourgeois dignity	McCloskey (2010)
Property rights	North and Weingast (1989)
Material	
Energy-related developments	Wrigley (2010)
High wages	Broadberry and Gupta (2009)
Cheap coal, costly labor	Allen (2009)
Overseas trade	Deane and Cole (1964), Davis (1979)
Slavery	Williams (1944)
Contact with the Atlantic Economy	Acemoglu et al.'s (2005)
Higher per-capita income	de Vries (1994)
High food prices	Cole (1973)
Demand and supply factors	Gilboy (1932)

of the events of the late 18th/early 19th centuries. Not surprisingly, the debate remains fractious with little hope of uncovering a definite cause.

Other Potential Causes of the Output Gap

Perhaps the key element in the *Wealth of Nations* is Smith's argument to the effect that "specialization is determined by the extent of the market." By this, it should be understood that the transition to mechanization or industrialization is characterized by an indeterminacy, namely that demand determines supply, but that supply ultimately determines income and consequently, demand, making for what is a coordination failure of sorts. Entrepreneurs will refrain from adopting the new technology for lack of demand, thus pre-empting mechanization, higher productivity and worker income, and consequently, higher demand. Another way of seeing this is in terms of an output gap, one between potential GDP and constrained (i.e. by the extent of the market) actual GDP. While Adam Smith was one of the first to raise the problem of the structural output gap, he was by no means alone. Throughout much of the 19th century, the problem of making the transition to the new, steam engine-based growth path garnered the attention of virtually every political economist, from David Ricardo, to Robert Owen, to Swiss economist Jean-Charles-Léonard Simonde de Sismondi, to German economist Karl Marx. Running throughout this body of work is the view that the transition to new higher growth paths in response to technological change was not instantaneous, was not automatic but rather was plagued by inertia, and in many cases, by an unforeseen downturn in economic activity. Companies that "specialized" by which it should be understood, adopted the new technology, decreased their demand for labor (supervisors), thus decreasing worker income and overall demand. Paradoxically, the introduction of a new productivity-increasing technology was transformed paradoxically into an employment and wealth decreasing enterprise.

What is important to understand in so far as 19th century growth theory is concerned is the fact that the problem of the output gap described here, while not a growth issue *per se*, was by far the single most important factor contributing to understanding the creation of wealth and thus of growth theory. The reason is simple, namely that 19th-century writers needed to define/describe potential output and hence the underlying technology (i.e. that it was 40 or 100 times greater) in order to define the corresponding output gap, before identifying the suspected causes. As such, they found themselves having to describe both the old and new technologies and the extent of the resulting gap. Given that growth theory was in its infancy, we find considerable variation in the writings of these "pioneers."

David Ricardo

Other than Adam Smith, David Ricardo is perhaps the best-known classical political economist. Chief among his concerns was moving the British economy on to the new, higher growth path as defined by the steam engine. Among the impediments he identified were higher agricultural prices and the resulting higher wages, as well as the "extent of the market." Lesser issues included the taxation of the owners of capital.

In the 1810s, the price of wheat and other cereals (known collectively as corn) had increased markedly, owing to Napoleon's continental blockade, as well as the presence of the Corn Laws, which consisted of tariffs on cereal imports into Britain. Continued growth in the UK had pushed the price of cereals (viz. Corn) up, increasing wages and lowering profits. Benefitting from the higher prices were the landowners, or the Lords. As such, land rents and profits in manufactures moved in opposite directions.

Ricardo argued that higher cereal prices, by raising wages, impeded growth. His reasoning was simple, namely that the resulting higher wages, by reducing profits, reduced savings and investment, thus lowering capital formation and growth in the manufacturing sector. Insufficient investment, by preventing or limiting the application of the steam engine to all sectors and industries of the UK economy, impeded the transition to the new, higher equilibrium growth path.

This brings us to the question at hand, namely Ricardo's understanding of growth and of production processes in general. As it turns out, his understanding of production processes both before and after the steam engine was highly rudimentary. Like Smith, he emphasized the role of labor in production. And like Smith, his knowledge of the mechanics underlying the steam engine was virtually non-existent. Throughout *The Principles of Political Economy and Taxation*, he referred to the steam engine under the generic heading of "machinery." Just what machinery did, and how it did it, were questions that were not broached.

Robert Owen

Like David Ricardo, Robert Owen was not a moral philosopher, but rather a businessman. More specifically, he was the owner/manager of New Lanark Mills in New Lanark, Scotland. Like Smith and Ricardo, he argued that the UK economy had failed to make the transition to the new, higher growth path defined by the steam engine. The reason: money income had failed to increase commensurately with potential output, making for a fundamental disequilibrium. More specifically, wage income had not kept pace with productivity growth, resulting in stagnation and unemployment.

Owen attributed the very existence of the output gap to what he refers to as "a rapid advancement in scientific improvements and arrangements, introduced, more or less, into all the departments of productive industry throughout the empire."

> *It is well known that, during the last half century in particular, Great Britain, beyond any other nation, has progressively increased its powers of production, by a rapid advancement in scientific improvements and arrangements,*

introduced, more or less, into all the departments of productive industry throughout the empire.

The amount of this new productive power cannot, for want of proper data, be very accurately estimated; but your Reporter has ascertained from facts which none will dispute, that its increase has been enormous; – that, compared with the manual labour of the whole population of Great Britain and Ireland, it is, at least, as forty to one, and may be easily made as 100 to one; and that this increase may be extended to other countries; that it is already sufficient to saturate the world with wealth, and that the power of creating wealth may be made to advance perpetually in an accelerating ratio.

(Owen 1820, 2)

Like many of his contemporaries, Owen was unable to describe in any detail, the effects of the steam engine on Britain's capacity to create wealth, invoking such terms as "scientific improvements and arrangements" in lieu of a detailed discussion of the underlying physics of the new energy source that was steam. Put in terms of machine operating speed, an increase in output in the order of 40 times would imply that the output rate of a single worker (supervisor) would have increased 40-fold with the introduction of machinery. To put that in perspective, in Adam Smith's pin factory, a pin-making machine would have produced 40 times the output of a manual pin worker. If the latter could produce a pin in 10 minutes, the machine could produce 40.

Jean-Charles-Léonard Simonde de Sismondi

The problem of insufficient income and the resulting insufficient demand was front and center in the writings of Swiss political economist Jean-Charles-Léonard Simonde de Sismondi who today is considered by most to be father of (dynamic) macroeconomic modeling. Like Owen, he maintained that output growth, the result of the wholesale application of the steam engine, had outstripped income growth. More specifically, he pointed to a lag between the former and the latter, resulting in a "growth-based" disequilibrium. This, he argued, had its roots in the underlying wage-game played by firms in general. Specifically, no single firm had an incentive to increase wages in response to an increase in productivity. As such, the resulting Nash equilibrium had zero wage increases in response to technological change, which at the aggregate level resulting in underincome. As the following passage taken from *Nouveaux principes d'économie politique*, published in 1819 shows, firms have no private interest in increasing overall money income in response to the introduction of a "procédé nouveau," a new process technology.

Le vendeur n'a pas par lui-même aucun moyen d'étendre son débit, qui ne réagisse sur ses confrères; il leur dispute une quantité donnée de revenu qui doit remplacer son capital; et plus, il réussit à en garder pour lui même; moins il en laisse pour les autres. Il ne dépend nullement du producteur d'augmenter les revenus de la société ou du marché qu'il sert de manière qu'ils puissent s'échanger contre une augmentation de produits...Entre commerçants, on regarde comme une mauvaise action de se séduire réciproquement ses pratiques; mais, la concurrence que chacun exerce contre tous ne présente point une idée aussi précise; et un commerçant n'a pas moins d'empressement à étendre son débit aux dépens de ses confrères qu'à le proportionner à l'accroissement des richesses, lorsque celles-ci lui offrent l'échange d'un nouveau revenu. Jusqu'ici, dans l'un ou l'autre cas, la découverte d'un procédé nouveau a causé une grande perte nationale, une grande diminution de revenu, et par conséquent, la consommation.

(Simonde de Sismondi 1819, 269)[1]

Again, like his contemporaries, Simonde was unable to describe in any scientific detail, the effects of the steam engine on Britain's capacity to create wealth, beyond a reference to a "procédé nouveau," a new process technology.

Charles Babbage

As it turned out, the first scholar to provide a truly scientific account of the effects of steam on output was polymath Charles Babbage, who in *On the Economy of Machinery and Manufactures* published in 1835, examined the effects of the introduction of the steam engine through the prism of classical mechanics, or more explicitly, force. According to him, the steam engine had increased the overall level of force or energy consumed, thus contributing to a manifold increase in output.

What is important to point out is the fact that Babbage's work is the first-ever scientific study of the steam engine. Until then, machinery (viz. the steam engine) had been described in general terms, without any reference to the underlying physics. Babbage, a polymath, was able to go beyond generalities to describe

TABLE 3.4 Charles Babbage's Sources of Advantages Arising from Machinery and Manufactures

1	There exists, perhaps, no single circumstance, which distinguishes our country more remarkably from all others, than the vast extent and perfection to which we have carried the contrivance of tools and machines for forming those conveniences of which so large a quantity is consumed by almost every class of the community.
2	The accumulation of skill and science, which has been directed to diminish the difficulty of producing manufactured goods, has not been beneficial to that country alone in which it is concentrated; distant kingdoms have participated in its advantages.
3	The large proportion of the population of this country, who are engaged in manufactures.

(Continued)

TABLE 3.4 (Continued)

4	
5	Of additions to human power. With respect to the first of these causes, the forces derived from wind, from water, and from steam, present themselves to the mind of every one; these are, in fact, additions to human power, and will be considered in a future page.
6	The economy of human time is the next advantage of machinery in manufactures.
7	The simple contrivance of tin tubes for speaking through, communicating between different apartments, by which the directions of the superintendent are instantly conveyed to the remotest parts of an establishment, produces a considerable economy of time.
8	The art of using the diamond for cutting glass has undergone, within a few years, a very important improvement.
9	Employment of materials of little value.
10	Of tools.
11	To arrange 20,000 needles thrown promiscuously into a box, mixed and entangled in every possible direction, in such a form that they shall be all parallel to each other, would, at first sight, appear a most tedious occupation; in fact, if each needle were to be separated individually, many hours must be consumed in the process.
12	Another process in the art of making needles furnishes an example of one of the simplest contrivances which can come under the denomination of a tool.
13	Various operations occur in the arts in which the assistance of an additional hand would be a great convenience to the workman, and in these cases tools or machines of the simplest structure come to our aid: vices of different forms, in which the material to be wrought is firmly grasped by screws, are of this kind, and are used in almost every workshop; but a more striking example may be found in the trade of the nail-maker.
14	Another, though fortunately a less general substitution of tools for human hands, is used to assist the labour of those who are deprived by nature, or by accident, of some of their limbs.
15	Division of the objects of machinery.
16	Of those machines by which we produce power, it may be observed that although they are to us immense acquisitions, yet in regard to two of the sources of this power – the force of wind and of water – we merely make use of bodies in a state of motion by nature; we change the directions of their movement in order to render them subservient to our purposes, but we neither add to nor diminish the quantity of motion in existence.
17	The force of vapour is another fertile source of moving power; but even in this case, it cannot be maintained that power is created.
18	In stating the broad principle that all combinations of mechanical art can only augment the force communicated to the machine at the expense of the time employed in producing the effect, it might, perhaps, be imagined that the assistance derived from such contrivances is small.
19	When a mass of matter is to be removed a certain force must be expended; and upon the proper economy of this force the price of transport will depend.

Source: Babbage (1835), 230.

the specifics, namely to the underlying physics. Babbage clearly anticipated the energy-organization approach to modeling material processes described in Chapter 2 by emphasizing the role of force or power in "manufactures."

Unfortunately, his work was all but ignored by mainstream classical political economists who contented themselves with generalities (i.e. machinery). The focus of their analysis continued to be the worker whose "productive powers" and hence, physical productivity are enhanced by the introduction of machinery. This raises the question why? Why was political economy impervious to scientific analysis? Why was force/energy ignored in favor of labor which, by then, had become a minor factor input, providing supervisory services? The answer can be found in the writings of Karl Marx.

Karl Marx

Like Jean-Charles-Léonard Simonde de Sismondi, German moral philosopher Karl Marx was drawn to England by the industrial revolution. And like Simonde, he was particularly interested in its shortcomings, notably by its apparent inability to move to the new growth path defined by the new power-drive technology that was the steam engine. Like Owen and Simonde, he attributed this to the failure of wages (wage income) to increase in response to higher productivity, resulting in stagnation and unemployment. Like Owen, he advocated social change and the replacement of private property and the market by a hierarchical, top-down government that would coordinate economic activity (socialism and eventually, communism). The problem, however, was its very labor-centricity. Industrialists (or capitalists) attributed higher output to the introduction of machinery, not to anything labor had done. As Babbage had pointed out, labor's physical contribution to wealth creation had actually diminished.

This raised an important ethical problem. How could higher wages be justified when labor's contribution had *de facto* been diminished? If anything, wages should fall, not rise. There is every reason to believe that Marx was aware of this dilemma. In fact, it could be argued that his was one of the first political economists (other than Charles Babbage) to understand and appreciate the physics of the steam engine. Consider, for example, the following passage taken from Chapter 15 of *Das Kapital.*

> *Mathematicians and mechanicians, and in this they are followed by a few English economists, call a tool a simple machine, and a machine a complex tool. They see no essential difference between them, and even give the name of machine to the simple mechanical powers, the lever, the inclined plane, the screw, the wedge, etc. As a matter of fact, every machine is a combination of those simple powers, no matter how they may be disguised. From the economic standpoint, this explanation is worth nothing, because the historical element is wanting. Another explanation of the difference between tool and machine is that, in the*

case of the tool, man is the motive power, while the motive power of a machine is something different from man, is, for instance, an animal, water, wind. and so on. According to this, a plough drawn by oxen, which is a contrivance common to the most different epochs, would be a machine, while Claussen's circular loom, which, worked by a single labourer, weaves 96,000 picks per minute, would be a mere tool. Nay, this very loom. though a tool when worked by hand, would, if worked by steam, be a machine. And, since the application of animal power is one of man's earliest inventions, production by machinery would have preceded production by handicrafts. When in 1735, John Wyalt brought out his spinning machine and began the industrial revolution of the eighteenth century, not a word did he say about an ass driving it instead of a man. and yet this part fell to the ass. He described it as a machine "to spin without fingers."

All fully developed machinery consists of three essentially different parts, the motor mechanism, the transmitting mechanism, and finally the tool of working machine. The motor mechanism is that which puts the whole in motion. It either generates its own motive power, like the steam engine, the caloric engine, the electro-magnetic machine, etc., or it receives its impulse from some already existing natural force, like the water-wheel from a head of water, the windmill from wind, etc. The transmitting mechanism, composed of flywheels, shafting, cogwheels, pulleys, straps, ropes, bands, pinions, and gearing of the most varied kinds, regulates the motion, changes its form where necessary, as, for instance, from linear to circular, and divides and distributes it among the working machines. These two parts of the whole mechanism are there solely for putting the working machines in motion, by means of which motion the subject of labour is seized upon and modified as desired. The tool or working machine is that part of machinery with which the industrial revolution of the eighteenth century started. And, to this day it constantly serves as such a starting point whenever a handicraft, or a manufacture, is turned into industry carried on by machinery.

(Marx 1867 181)

Clearly, these passages indicate that Marx was well aware of (i) the role of motive power and (ii) the diminished role of human force (brawn) in material processes. Yet, in spite of this, he couched most of his analysis (e.g. Chapters 1–7 of *Das Kapital*) in the classical labor theory of value, according to which labor and labor alone determines value. In essence, Marx was drawing on the early writings of Adam Smith and David Ricardo, both of whom modeled wealth as an increasing function of labor. Which raises the question, why? Why adopt what was essentially an outdated, theoretically irrelevant view of production?

The answer lies in the problem of income distribution in general and underincome and underconsumption in particular. Like Owen and Simonde, Marx was of the view that wages and wage income should rise. And to justify such an increase, he would need a reason which, in this case, came via the labor theory of value. In other words, he was clearly aware of the fact that labor had become a minor factor input, yet chose to strategically couch most of his analysis in the labor theory of value. That is, in order to justify (i) his call for higher wages and (ii) to rationalize his form of worker-based governance. In other words, by putting the worker at the center of the production process, he was strategically giving it more bargaining power, not to mention more clout when in actual fact, labor (read: former manual workers and artisans) was becoming irrelevant – that is, a minor, non-physically productive factor input.

The fallout was instantaneous. Its implications were damning. Not only was labor the only productive factor input, but also capital was physically unproductive and as such, profits and profit income amounted to a form of theft – that is, from labor, the true proprietors of wealth. It is important to keep in mind that these conclusions are not specific to Marx, but rather follow from classical production theory in general where the only physically productive factor input is labor.

Understandably, this had devastating effects on classical political economy. If capital was not physically productive, then how could profits – roughly 30 percent of national income – be justified morally, physically and of course legally?

As a result, classical political economy had an enormous problem on its hands: how to justify profit income in the absence of physical productivity. In other words, how can payments to the owners of capital be justified when capital itself is not productive? As shown in *Core Principle I* in Chapter 2, capital or tools are not physically productive as they are not a source of force/energy. As such, from a scientific point of view, the classical political economists were scientifically correct in their view of capital as not being physical productive.

The problem, scientifically speaking, was with labor. Prior to the introduction of the steam engine, labor was, for all intents and purposes, physically productive, human brawn powering virtually all pre-industrial manufacturing material processes – the exception being milling. The industrial revolution, however, changed all of that. Once a source of force/energy, labor had metamorphosized into a supervisory input, a management input, operating and overseeing machinery. This explains, among other things, why women and children became commonplace in UK manufacturing. In short, what is conventionally referred to as work had become child's play. Moreover, classical production theory, being based on labor as the sole productive factor input, was mis-specified from the get-go as the steam engine had rendered human force/energy redundant.

Nassau Senior

While classical thought focused on labor, the record shows that many writers or political economists at the time were increasingly aware of the role of power in general and steam in particular in wealth creation. This was the case of British lawyer-turned political economist Nassau Senior, who like other 19th-century writers, broached all aspects of the subject matter in his classic, Political Economy published in 1854. Under the rubric "Statement of Advantages derived from the Use of Capital," he opined:

> *The principal advantages derived from Abstinence, or, to express the same idea in more familiar language, from the Use of Capital, are two: first, the Use of Implements; and second, the division of Labour.*
>
> *Implements, or tools, or machines (words which express things perhaps slightly different in some respects, but precisely similar so far as they are the subjects of Political Economy) have been divided into those which produce power, and those which transmit power. Under the first head are comprehended those which produce motion independently of human labour. Such are, for instance, those machines which are worked by the force of wind, of water, or of steam,*
>
> *The second head comprises what are usually termed tools, such as the spade, the hammer, or the knife which assist the force, or save the time of the workman, but receive their impulse from his hand.*
>
> (Senior 1854, 67)

To Senior, tools (capital) are not physically productive as they receive their impulse (read: force-energy) from the workman's hand. Clearly, he understood classical mechanics, specifically the role of force (or impulse) as the sole physically productive factor. However, the heading under which he elaborated these concepts connotes the notion that capital increases labor productivity. In short, labor is still front and center.

The Classical Response

Various choices were available to classical political economists in the wake of the radical writers' somewhat compromising conclusions and allegations. They could reject all of classical production theory and start from scratch using Babbage's *On the Economy of Machinery and Manufactures* and/or Marx's Chapter 15 as guides, or conversely, simply decree, *ex cathedra*, capital to be physically productive and thus deflect any and all criticism. Put otherwise, nip the problem of profits in the bud. As it turned out, this is what it opted for.

The Birth of Neoclassical Production Theory

Thus far, we have shown that the obstacles for the British economy to make a successful transition to the new higher equilibrium growth path defined by the new steam engine-based technology prompted much interest and work on the question of growth, or what we have defined here as growth theory. As it turned out, these developments spawned one of the most important, one of the most enduring, and one of the most acrimonious debates in all of political economy, namely the role/contribution of capital in modern industrial production processes.

In the wake of Engels and Marx's critique, classical political economy was faced with a conundrum, namely how to justify profits? After all, capital was absent from their analysis, entering parametrically in labor productivity. Their answer: simply decree capital to be physically productive in direct violation of classical mechanics. Starting with William Stanley Jevons and ending with Alfred Marshall, classical production theory metamorphosized into neoclassical (or new classic) production analysis where both labor and capital are assumed to be physically productive.

William Stanley Jevons

William Stanley Jevons is an interesting and intriguing figure, in so far as the question of production is concerned. In "The Coal Question, An Inquiry into the Probable Exhaustion of Our Coal Mines" published in 1865, he declared:

> *Day by day it becomes more evident that the Coal we happily possess in excellent quality and abundance is the mainspring of modern material civilization. As the source of fire, it is the source at once of mechanical motion and of chemical change. Accordingly it is the chief agent in almost every improvement or discovery in the arts which the present age brings forth. It is to us indispensable for domestic purposes, and it has of late years been found to yield a series of organic substances, which puzzle us by their complexity, please us by their beautiful colours, and serve us by their various utility. And as the source especially of steam and iron, coal is all powerful. This age has been called the Iron Age, and it is true that iron is the material of most great novelties. By its strength, endurance, and wide range of qualities, this metal is fitted to be the fulcrum and lever of great works, while steam is the motive power. But coal alone can command in sufficient abundance either the iron or the steam; and coal, therefore, commands this age---the Age of Coal. Coal in truth stands not beside but entirely above all other commodities. It is the material energy of the country---the universal aid---the factor in everything we do. With coal almost any feat is possible or easy; without it we are thrown back into the laborious poverty of early times.*
>
> *(Jevons 1865, 14)*

In other words, coal was the basis of modern civilization, of the industrial revolution and of Britain's overwhelming success. Consequently, in Jevons' eyes, it was imperative for society to concern itself with its future.

In 1871, a mere six years later, he published his magnum opus, *The Theory of Political Economy*, outlining what was to become neoclassical production theory Jevons (1871). In a nutshell, wealth was an increasing function of labor and capital. In short, capital had simply been decreed to be physically productive, increasing output, but at a decreasing rate, *ceteris paribus*. However, the most startling thing was the total absence of coal, of energy, of force. Thus, it had gone from hero in 1865 to zero in 1871, in a span of six years.

Unlike his classical forebearers, he couched the analysis in the language of thermodynamics, namely differential calculus. The total product curves (labor and capital) presented mimicked second-law efficiency schedules, being monotonically increasing and concave. Ironically, what was absent was the very raison d'être of thermodynamics and hence, differential calculus, namely energy.

Alfred Marshall

Along with Stanley William Jevons and Léon Walras, Alfred Marshall is considered one of the founding fathers of the neoclassical school. However, unlike Jevons, Marshall's understanding of material processes in general and the role of the steam engine and thus of coal in the industrial revolution, was primitive to say the least. In fact, one could argue that his account of production differed little from that of Adam Smith a century earlier. His analysis is couched in terms of labor and labor productivity. His account of the role of machinery is comparable to that of Smith, and light years from that of Charles Babbage and Karl Marx.

This is altogether surprising, given that by 1890, thermodynamics and its fundamental laws had revolutionized classical physics, providing the set of laws that governed the material processes that collectively defined the industrial revolution. While that are numerous references to energy, none refer to coal, hydraulics or wind. There are no references to the steam engine, to the Watt-Boulton reciprocating steam engine, nor to power.

However, his *Principles of Economics* did contain a number of interesting insights, especially with regard to the nature of the labor input. As pointed out earlier, the steam engine had altered the nature of labor from a source of force/energy to a supervisory input, a fact that Marshall acknowledged in the following quotations.

> *Nothing could be more narrow or monotonous than the occupation of a weaver of plain stuffs in the old time. But now one woman will manage four or more looms, each of which does many times as much work in the course of the day as the old hand-loom did; and her work is much less monotonous and calls for much more judgment than his did. So that for every hundred yards of cloth that are woven, the purely monotonous work done by human beings is probably not a twentieth part of what it was.*
>
> (*Marshall 1890, 218*)

> *New machinery, when just invented, generally requires a great deal of care and attention. But the work of its attendant is always being sifted; that which is uniform and monotonous is gradually taken over by the machine, which thus becomes steadily more and more automatic and self-acting; till at last there is nothing for the hand to do, but to supply the material at certain intervals and to take away the work when finished. There still remains the responsibility for*

> *seeing that the machinery is in good order and working smoothly; but even this task is often made light by the introduction of an automatic movement, which brings the machine to a stop the instant anything goes wrong.*
>
> (Marshall 1890, 218)

There can be little doubt that despite its encyclopedic nature, *Principles of Economics* came up glaringly short in so far as production theory was concerned.

Philip Wicksteed

In 1894, Philip Wicksteed published *An Essay on the Co-ordination of the Laws of Distribution* where he sought to prove mathematically that a distributive system which rewarded factory owners according to marginal productivity would exhaust the total product produced. But it was his 1910 *The Common Sense of Political Economy* which most comprehensively presents Wicksteed's economic system. The 1932 work by Lionel Robbins, *An Essay on the Nature and Significance of Economic Science*, picked up and developed his ideas.

In *An Essay on the Coordination of the Laws of Distribution*, he restates the neoclassical theory of production in functional form.

> *This would perhaps not be a convenient form in which to express the law, of exchange value for general purposes; but it is useful to us at present because it suggests a formula of Distribution. In fact we may regard the total satisfaction enjoyed by the community as a "product" and the several services and commodities as the factors of production. Each factor then receives a share of the product regulated by its marginal efficiency as a producer. Here is a general law of distribution put into our hand. Is it applicable to the internal or " domestic " distribution of the whole share that falls to each service or commodity, regarded in its turn as a product to be shared amongst the several factors that produced it? Let the special product to be distributed (P) be regarded as a function (F) of the various factors of production (A, B, C,...). Then the (marginal) significance of each factor is determined by the effect upon the product of a small increment of that factor, all the others remaining [p.9] constant. It is suggested that the ratio of participation in the product on which any factor, K, can insist (by threat of withdrawal), will be dK/ dP per unit, and its total share will be K dK /dP.*
>
> (Wicksteed 1894, 307)

Thus, by the end of the 19th century, not only had neoclassical production theory become the norm, but also it cast had been cast in functional form, making it amenable to analysis using differential and integral calculus. Unknown, however, was the exact numerical contribution of labor and capital to the overall product, something that would come in 1928 when Americans Charles Cobb and Paul Douglas would provide the first numerical estimates of the relevant output elasticities.

Carl Menger and the Birth of the Austrian School

Nowhere was the criticism of Karl Marx and *Das Kapital* greater than in Austria where a number of former classical economists would outline an alternative, more palatable – in their eyes – view of productivity, exchange and prices, collectively known as the Austrian School. Austria at the time was a very conservative, hierarchical society, a society that had not industrialized and a society that was best characterized by inertia. The upshot of Marx's *Das Kapital* was an outright condemnation of market economies and a vote for a social or communal organization of society in which decisions would be taken by a hierarchical third party.

Not surprising, this was not well received by the more progressive elements in Austrian society that advocated for a British-like form of industrialization.

A number of economists in Vienna launched a counter-attack, a counter-attack that would revolve around methodological individualism, marginalism and the virtues of private markets. They included Carl Menger and Eugene Bohn-Bawerk, both of whom provided were staunch critics of Marx.

In time, the resulting body of literature would come to be known as the Austrian School, a school that focused on the virtues of free markets, individualism and, most of all, anti-government sentiment. One of its sons, Friedrich Van Hayek would go on to earn a Nobel Prize, largely for his defense of markets and freedom and his condemnation of Keynesian-style government intervention.

19th-Century Growth Theory: Summary and Conclusion

The 19th century marked the beginning of the systematic study of wealth. Unfortunately, instead of marking the beginning of the scientific study of wealth, drawing from the tributary fields of classical mechanics and thermodynamics (in short, from natural philosophy), it marked the beginning of a unique form of growth ideology, one propagated by moral philosophers. As shown, the steam engine had altered labor's traditional role in material processes as a source of force/energy. Fire power, as Smith referred to it, had become the only physically productive factor input, a fact pointed out by William Stanley Jevons in 1865.

For a number of reasons, ranging from naiveté (classical political economy) to ideology (Marxism) to survival (neoclassical political economy), political economy chose to ignore this fundamental, epoch-defining development. The result was a set of theories of production whose underlying principles/assumptions violated basic physics and more importantly ignored the key factor input, energy. The scientific *élan* found in Charles Babbage's pioneering work was ignored and instead gave way to the ideology and propaganda on the part of the radical economists as well as that of the classical apologists, the neoclassicals.

The result was damning as the events of the 20th century would show. While neoclassical production theory was as convenient as it was elegant, it would fail to provide the necessary theoretical tooling to understand the second industrial revolution as well as the subsequent unprecedented growth rates of the post-WWII period (i.e. the Golden Age of Capitalism).

The 20th Century

Economic Growth in the Early 20th Century

The shift from the domestic to the factory system, as pointed out earlier, lifted and pushed back the energy constraint which had, for over 200,000 years, constrained *Homo sapien*'s (*neanderthalensis and sapiens*) ability to transform the earth's abundant supply of raw materials into goods and services. It, however, had not been lifted completely, owing, in large measure, to the steam power transmission technology, namely belting, gearing and shafting. Further, not all production processes lent themselves to mechanization (i.e. driven by steam power). Part of this owed to the size of economically viable steam engines (especially high-pressure engines and steam turbines), limiting potential applications to large concerns.

Enter a new power transmission technology, namely, electro-magnetic motors (hereafter, electric motors) and electricity. Unlike steam engines, electric motors came in different sizes and more importantly, different—read, faster—speeds. As they began appearing in factories (in replacement of steam engines), the energy constraint was, once again, lifted and pushed back, in this case, further than ever before. Production processes that had, *hitherto*, not been mechanized were. Henry Ford's electric motor-driven assembly line is a case in point. Static material-handling processes of which the final assembly of the automobile is a case in point (i.e. the craft system) were replaced with continuous-flow materials handling processes, driven by direct-current (DC) electric motors. Secondly, production processes, which had been mechanized (i.e. powered by steam), were converted to electric power, resulting in even greater speeds (throughput rates), and consequently, higher throughput and productivity. The result: the second industrial revolution. Electric power transformed industry, increasing throughput rates, and mechanizing processes, which had, until then, resisted inanimate power. Handheld electric power tools are a case in point. Electric drills, saws and planners replaced hand-powered drills, saws and planners.

A parallel development was the development of the petro-chemical industry/sector, based largely on electrolysis, resulting in the world's new-found ability to synthesize various elements and materials. Electrolysis is based on electricity, which, with the advent of large public utilities, was abundant and inexpensive. Unlike the first industrial revolution where few new products or materials were introduced, electricity widened significantly the product mix. A telling example is the introduction of electric-powered home appliances.

This section proceeds in the same way as the last. To begin with, we examine the impact of electric power on growth, paying particular attention to the manufacturing sector. This is then followed by a look at its impact on growth theory. How did the economics profession view this shock if at all? More versatile than belting, gearing and shafting, electric unit drive (EUD) de facto removed the energy constraint, setting the stage for 75 years of energy deepening and the resulting record levels of economic growth.

Getting to the proverbial Garden of Eden, however, was not without obstacles and setbacks. As was the case with the steam engine, greater process speeds are not a sufficient condition for growth in actual output. Money income has to growth commensurately. Otherwise, the problem of underincome arises.[2] As we shall show in this section, the shift from the steam engine to electric drive and the ensuing rise in rated productive capacity, productivity *etcetera* resulted in an acute case of underincome. Specifically, rated productive capacity in US manufacturing increased faster than money income in the 1910s, 1920s and 1930s.

We begin by examining the impact of electric drive on output, distribution and exchange using the analytical framework developed in Chapter 2. This will then be followed by a look at how these changes affected growth theory in general. Whereas steam power revolutionized production processes by moving production out of "cottages" and into factories, electric power revolutionized production processes in three fundamental ways. First, by replacing steam engines with electric motors, throughput rates (i.e. machine speeds) were increased. To the naive observer, nothing will have changed, yet, output may increase by 100 percent as cases where speed is doubled. Second, by making power available on a smaller scale, production processes which had, up until then, resisted the shift to steam power were mechanized. Third, the required capital in the case of EUD actually decreased as cumbersome belting, gearing and shafting was replaced by individual electric motors (i.e. EUD).

It will be argued that for these and other reasons, the introduction of electric drive went largely unnoticed in early 20th-century political economy, where, for the most part, technological change was associated with new, often times, more costly machinery. The effects of electric power on productivity, output, employment and expenditure, however, could not be ignored.

Electricity Production in the Early 20th Century

As pointed out earlier, electric power is a misnomer, electricity not being a source of energy, but rather a transmission technology. Early developments in electromagnetics bear this out. When Michael Faraday discovered that an electric force exposed to a magnet repelled the latter, the force in question had been generated by the thermal energy in his body. Throughout the ensuing period, electric power continued to be generated from non-electric (i.e. non-atomic) sources. Only recently have we learned how to exploit the energy contained in the atom. Atomic power, however, represents but a fraction of current world total power consumption, the bulk coming from fossil-fuel and hydraulic-based energy sources, both of which are both based on solar radiation, and ultimately, the nuclear fusion of the sun's abundant supply of hydrogen into helium.

Table 3.4 provides data on the installed generating capacity in US electric utilities and industrial electricity-generating plants from 1902 to 1951, by type (i.e. hydro, steam and internal combustion). In 1902, total installed generating capacity stood at 2,987,000 kilowatts. By 1930, it had reached 41,828,000 kilowatts, a 1,277 percent increase, which corresponds to an annual average annual increase of 42 percent. As the numbers in Table 3.4 indicate, most of the growth in electricity-generating capacity in the United States in the 20th century in general and the early 20th century in particular, was coal and fossil fuel based. This was also true of other industrialized nations such as the UK, Germany and France. The point is that the second industrial revolution did not witness the emergence of a new power source, but rather, the emergence of a new power-drive technology, namely electricity.

Electric Unit Drive and Its Effects on the US Economy

Few were the sectors of the US economy not affected by the new power transmission technology. Production processes that hitherto had been driven by belting, gearing

TABLE 3.5 Installed Generating Capacity, Federal and Industrial (000 kwhs), United States, 1902–1951

Year	*Total*	*PUE*	*Federal*	*Industrial*	*PUE/ Total*	*Federal/ Utilities*
1925	84,666	61,451	103	23,215	0.72	0.001
1926	94,222	69,363	518	24,869	0.73	0.007
1927	10,1390	75,418	668	25,972	0.74	0.008
1928	108,069	82,794	356	25,275	0.76	0.004
1929	116,747	92,180	300	24,567	0.78	0.003
1930	114,637	91,112	465	23,525	0.79	0.005
1931	109,373	87,350	497	22,023	0.79	0.005
1932	99,359	79,393	445	19,966	0.79	0.005
1933	102,655	81,740	458	20915	0.79	0.005
1934	110,404	87,258	357	23,146	0.79	0.004
1935	118,935	95,289	555	23,648	0.80	0.005
1936	136,006	109,316	1,072	26,690	0.80	0.009
1937	146,476	118,213	1,843	27,563	0.80	0.015
1938	141,955	113,812	3,029	28,143	0.80	0.026
1939	161,308	127,642	5,476	33,666	0.79	0.042
1940	179,907	141,837	8,584	38,070	0.82	0.060
1941	208,306	164,788	10,793	43,518	0.78	0.065
1942	233,146	185,979	16,893	47,167	0.79	0.090
1943	267,540	217,759	24,485	49,781	0.79	0.112
1944	279,525	228,189	28,867	51,336	0.81	0.126
1945	271,255	222,486	28,000	48,769	0.81	0.125

Source: U.S. Department of Commerce (1975), Series S44, S45, S53, S74–S77.

and shafting (i.e. transmitting steam and hydraulic power) were converted to EUD, resulting in substantially higher throughput rates. Production processes and sectors that had previously resisted "mechanization" were mechanized. Among these one finds the mining sector, the petrochemical sector, and the material handling sector in general. Electric motor-powered conveyor belts and pumps increased throughput rates in all of these sectors, resulting in vastly greater productivity. Analytically speaking, the introduction of EUD should be viewed as an extension of the first industrial revolution where, as argued earlier, inanimate power replaced animate, muscular power. Now, however, the chemical energy contained in fossil fuels would drive electro-magnetic generators (aka dynamos), the output of which would, in turn, power production processes.

This section examines the effects of this far-reaching change on production, distribution and exchange using the Core Principles developed in Chapter 2. As we shall show, the shift from cumbersome belting, shafting and gearing-based drive to electric drive, while a watershed in the history of power-drive technology (Nye 1990; Rosenberg 1972; Devine 1983), went largely unnoticed in political economy. Unlike the shift from muscular to steam power which, to most, defined the industrial revolution, it failed to generate much interest among political economists. Working with models in which capital and labor were the only factors of production, the shift to a new power-drive technology was, for the most part, ignored. In fact, the effect would be seen as negative given that electric-power drive was less capital intensive, thus lowering the measured capital input (Devine 1990).

By paving the way for increased levels of energy consumption, the shift to EUD increased output considerably. Few were the sectors which were not affected. Productivity per lower-level supervisor (machine operatives) increased, in some cases doubling. Once again, this raised the problem of distribution. Who would appropriate the new set of energy rents? Also, it raised the problem of exchange, specifically, the problem of money income growth. More productive firms have no private incentives to increase wage income. Merchants, in turn, have no private incentives to increase orders from consumer and capital goods firms. Since profits are a residual income form (see IES in Chapter 2), it follows that both wage and profit income fail to rise.

Electric Drive, Energy Consumption and Productivity

According to Warren D. Devine Jr, the shift from shafting, belting and gearing drive to EUD stands as one of the most rapid and complete transitions in "energy use" in history.

> *Perhaps the most rapid and complete transition in energy use was the shift from steam power to electric power for driving machinery. Steam power prevailed at the turn of the century, with steam engines providing around 80 percent of the*

total capacity for driving machinery. By 1920, electricity had replaced steam as the major source of motive power, and by 1929—just forty-five years after their first use in a factory—electric motors provided 78 percent of all mechanical drive.

(Devine 1990, 21)

While ignored by the economics profession, this new technology galvanized the attention of the engineering profession, broadly defined. Process and power engineers could hardly contain their enthusiasm. Consider, for example, the following quote taken from a speech by Matthew S. Sloan, president of the New York Edison Company, to the annual dinner of trust companies in Chicago in February 1929:

Mr. Sloan compared this age which he termed the "new industrial revolution" with "the industrial revolution" in the eighteenth century, when the steamboat and locomotive came into use. As steam brought in the machine era, electricity, he said, has brought in the era of mass production which has so greatly affected the general economic situation and social conditions. Thus, electricity, he said, is responsible for our present production. With all its attendant circumstances of lowered unit costs, lowered prices, increased wages, intensifying merchandising, wider markets, higher standard of living. Electricity-motivating machinery has multiplied the working power of the nation many times, he said, and the generating stations of the country now have a capacity of 35,000,000 horsepower, of the ability to do the work of about 350,000,000 men. In 1900, the generating capacity was only 3,000,000 horsepower.

(New York Times, February 15, 1929, 3)

In the same year, the *President's Conference on Unemployment*, chaired by Herbert C. Hoover, identified the electrification of the US industry as the "single most important change in US industry." In its report, it described this far-reaching change as follows:

Characteristic also has been the rise in the use of power—three and three-quarters times faster than the growth of population—and the extent to which power has been made readily available not alone for driving tools of increased size and capacity, but for a convenient purposes in the smallest business enterprise and on the farm and in the home. Factories no longer need to cluster about the source of power. Widespread interconnection between power plants, arising out of an increasing appreciation of the value of flexibility in power and made possible by technical advances during recent years, has created huge reservoirs of power so that abnormal conditions in one locality need not stop the wheels of industry. The increasing flexibility with which electricity can be delivered from power has enabled manufacturers and farmers to meet high labor costs by the application of power-driven specialized machines; and, power in this

> *flexible form has penetrated into every section of the United States, including many rural areas. The survey shows that as a nation we use as much electricity as all of the rest of the world combined. Through the subdivision of power, the unskilled worker has become a skilled operator, multiplying his effectiveness with specialized automatic machinery and processes.*
>
> (*National Bureau of* Economic Research 1929, *xi)*

The shift to EUD is easily understood in terms of EO production analysis. Specifically, electric drive, by lifting the constraints imposed by belting, shafting and gearing transmission technology, allowed for greater inanimate energy consumption per period of time (i.e. $E(t)$). Higher energy consumption increased throughput rates (read: process speeds) throughout all sectors of the US economy, and for that matter, in industries the world over, increasing conventionally measured productivity. Output per lower-level supervisor (i.e. conventionally defined labor productivity) increased substantially. In sectors where water, wind or steam power had failed to penetrate, EUD provided a flexible, made-to-scale, source of power, increasing productivity. As pointed out earlier, and highlighted in these quotes, there was hardly a sector of the US economy that had not been affected in one way or another by electric drive.

Consider, for example, the mining sector, which had, throughout the 19th century, resisted "mechanization." Historian David E. Nye describes the application of electricity in the mining sector as follows:

> *Mine owners had many uses for electricity. Electric lights gave safe illumination that did not exhaust scarce oxygen supplies. Electric-alarm systems signaled danger or disaster. Electric drills were more portable than other drills: "Where electric power is used, small wires take the place of cumbersome pipes necessary for the transmission of steam or compressed air." Portable electric pumps often replaced steam engines, to keep pits free from water. An electric hoist had similar advantages over a steam-driven hoist; it was "more easily installed, and when in place takes up much less room than a steam outfit of the same hoisting capacity. It does away with the boiler, coal bins, and piping.".... The greatest single change electricity made in the mines was the elimination of the mules, which were replaced by squat, powerful electric locomotives. With such equipment one company in Pennsylvania produced 11,000 tons of coal a month in the 1890's without using a single mule. With similar equipment New York and Scranton Coal Company saved five or six cents per ton of coal extracted and the Hillside Coal and Iron Company saved almost $20,000 per year on the cost of mules and laborers.".... At Green Ridge Colliery, for example, a station engineer, a motorman, and helper could run an electric locomotive that replaced six mule drivers, four boy helpers, and seventeen mules.*
>
> (Nye 1990, *205)*

No greater testimony to/of the prominent role of EUD in the rise of the 20th-century US industry is there than the concerns of the laggard nations, the most important of which was Great Britain. As America's industrial might increase with every additional megawatt of electric power, Great Britain, mired in the glory of steam and, more importantly, a web of regulation, could only concede defeat. Beginning in 1916, a number of committees were struck to study the problem. The first was *The Coal Conservation Sub-Committee*, set up in 1916 under Viscount Haldane, which, in turn, appointed a sub-committee to investigate the question of electric power supply in the UK. Its report, issued in 1918, dealt in considerable detail with "the use of electric power in industry, and recommended reorganization of the generation and main transmission on a regional basis under the central supervision of a 'Board of Electricity Commissioners' with wide powers" (Self 1952, 35). In the same year, the Board of Trade appointed an Electrical Trades Committee to consider the position of the "electrical trades" after the war. Sir Henry Self summarized its findings in the following terms:

> *Reference was made in strong terms to the crippling handicaps of the local and political considerations which had prevented Great Britain from reaping the fruits of the outstanding preeminence which it had received in original constructive research and development of electricity generation at the hands of pioneers such as Faraday, Wheatstone, Kelvin, Swan, Hopkinson, and many others. The loss of that outstanding lead, the history of industry in the intervening years, and the evidence taken during their examination of the position, led the Committee to the following conclusions:*
>
> i *That Government should recognize the dependence of the State, both from military and industrial standpoints, upon the supply of electrical energy as a "key industry."*
> ii *That the distribution of electrical energy should be regarded no longer as parochial but as a national question of urgent importance.*
> iii *that the present system of electrical generation and distribution is behind the times and is a serious handicap in international competition.*
> iv *That the present conditions are mainly due to faulty legislation and to divided and therefore weak executive control.*
> v *That the determination of questions concerning concentration of generating plant with the resulting economy of coal and other savings. requires immediate attention.*
> vi *That only by such steps can the electrical manufacturing industry of this country be fully developed, not only for the home trade, but as a consequence of the great industry now maturing overseas; that the gain to the State from a well-planned scheme of reconstruction will be inestimable; and that the items which are capable of reasonable calculation, such*

> *as saving in fuel, reduction in factory costs, and increased output will together represent not less than 100,000,000 pounds per annum.*
>
> (Self 1952, *35)*

What is particularly noteworthy is the reference made in point (ix) of the "great industry now maturing overseas." This clearly demonstrates that the Electrical Trades Committee was well aware, as early as 1916, of the threat posed by the electrification of the US industry. Similar conclusions were reached by the Williamson Committee, struck by the Board of Trade in 1917:

> 1 *That when British industry is subjected to the test of keen international competition after the war, its success will depend upon the adoption of the most efficient methods and machinery, so as to reduce manufacturing costs as much as possible.*
>
> 2 *That a highly important element in reducing manufacturing costs will be the general extension of the use of electric power supplied at the lowest possible price, and it is by largely increasing the amount of power used in the industry that the average output per head. and, as a consequence, the wages of the worker can be raised.*
>
> 5 *That a comprehensive system for the generation of electricity, and, where necessary, reorganizing its supply should be established as soon as possible.*
>
> (Self 1952, *37)*

In 1924, David Lloyd-George, then Liberal member of Parliament, struck an informal committee, the purpose of which was to address the "inter-linked questions of coal and electricity." The results of the inquiry were published in a report entitled *Coal and Power Inquiry* which called for "compulsory powers of acquisition, coordination and regulation to enable the Electricity Commissioners to grant to approved bodies the right of supplying power within substantial defined areas" (Self 1952, 52). H.H. Ballin summarized the Inquiry's findings as follows:

> *With our various competitors going ahead swiftly in the direction of the greater utilization of power, a policy of preventing power development in industry would leave our workers in the position of having to compete on unequal terms so that the incompetence of management would have to be made up by the toil of the workers. It ushers in a vista of endless strikes, industrial trouble and internal strain. The way out is to be found in the direction of scientific production and utilisation of power.*
>
> *(Lloyd-George 1924, 99)*

How did the resulting energy deepening affect conventionally defined productivity in US manufacturing? That is, how did it affect $W(t)/S_l(t)$ (see Table 2.3)? As it turns out, this is a particularly difficult issue, given data limitations. The data for productivity in this period are sparse and incomplete. This notwithstanding, we proceeded in two distinct ways. First, we considered the case of the Ford Motor Company's Highland Park plant which, in 1913, moved from static assembly to EUD dynamic assembly, commonly known as mass production. Second, various EO productivity measures developed in Chapter 2 were estimated for this period.

The choice of the Ford Motor Company (FMC) as a case study was based on its early use of electric drive (Nye 1990; Beaudreau 1996). Its founder, Henry Ford, had been chief mechanical engineer at the Detroit Edison Illuminating Company from 1886 to 1899, a period of 14 years. In earlier work (Beaudreau 1996), it was argued that this period in Ford's life is key to understanding of the development of high-throughput continuous-flow manufacturing at the FMC and, ultimately, in the United States. From then on, Ford was, to put it mildly, a power zealot, as evidenced by his lifelong friendship with Thomas Edison, and his attempt at securing the rights to the Muscle Shoals hydroelectric project in 1919. His single most important contribution to production technology was the application of EUD to virtually all facets of automobile production and assembly material processes, resulting in record increases in productivity (Nye 1990; Beaudreau 1996).

To see this, consider Table 3.6, taken from Beaudreau (1996), which presents throughput data measured in terms of time. Prior to the introduction of electric drive-powered assembly lines, it took, on average, 20 minutes to assemble a magneto. In the initial phase of electric drive-powered assembly lines (i.e. conveyor belts), this was reduced to 13 minutes, followed by a further reduction to 7 minutes, and ultimately, to 5 minutes. Productivity, it therefore follows, had quadrupled. Even greater productivity gains were achieved in chassis assembly where the required time went from 12 hours, 28 minutes, to 6 hours, and eventually, to 1 hour 33 minutes.

From a level of 8.36 in 1912, labor productivity climbed, mercurially, to 20.89 in 1915, which corresponds to a 150 percent increase. The conversion to electric

TABLE 3.6 The Ford Motor Company, Assembly Process Productivity

Process	*Phase*	*Assembly Time*	*Index*
Magneto	Initial	20 minutes	100
	I	13 minutes, 10 seconds	66
	II	7 minutes	35
	III	5 minutes	25
Transmission Cover	Initial	18 minutes	100
	I	9 minutes	50
Chassis Assembly	Initial	12 hours, 28 minutes	100
	I	6 hours	48
		1 hour, 33 minutes	12

Source: Beaudreau (1996), 143.

TABLE 3.7 The Ford Motor Company, Production Data, 1909–1916

Year	*Model-Ts*	*Employees*	*Ratio*
1909	13,840	1,655	8.36
1910	20,727	2,773	7.47
1911	53,488	3,976	13.45
1912	82,388	6,867	11.99
1913	189,088	14,366	13.16
1914	230,788	12,880	17.91
1915	394,788	18,892	20.89
1916	585,388	32,702	17.90

Source: Beaudreau (1996), 152.

drive had more than doubled productivity. In the 1926 edition of the *Encyclopaedia Britannica*, Ford described "mass production" in the following terms:

> *Mass production is not merely quantity production, for this may be had with none of the requisites of mass production. Nor is it merely machine production, which also may exist without any resemblance to mass production. Mass production is the focusing upon a manufacturing project of the principles of power, accuracy, economy, system, continuity, and speed.*
>
> *(Ford 1926, 821)*

The operant words here are power and speed. Mass production, *à la Ford*, was about speed.[3] In little time, electric drive as developed at the Ford Motor Company spread throughout the United States, and, for that matter, the world over. According to historian David S. Hounshell:

> *The story of mass production at the Ford Motor Company was not something only historians of a later generation would delve into and try to understand. Henry Ford's contemporaries, many of whom were competitors, closely watched the doings at Highland Park, attempting to understand and emulate the revolutionary developments. Henry Ford encouraged their interest. Unlike the Singer Manufacturing Company, the Ford Company was completely open about its organizational structure, its sales, and its production methods.... As a consequence of Ford's openness, Ford production technology diffused rapidly throughout American manufacturing.*
>
> *(Hounshell 1984, 260)*

Consumption of electric power in US manufacturing increased dramatically in the ensuing years. It went from a level of 9,250 million kilowatt hours in 1912, it had more than doubled by 1917 (i.e. 20,750 million kilowatt hours), and, doubled again by 1927. Cast in per-worker terms, in 1912, each manufacturing employee supervised 1,111 kilowatt hours of electric power. This doubled by 1917, tripled by 1923, and quadrupled by 1926. Conventionally defined productivity increased in-step. Productivity indexes (i.e. $W(t)/S_l(t)$) for this period show a marked increase. For example, the NBER productivity index goes from a level of 29.2 in 1913 to a level of 46.5 in 1926, a 60 percent increase (U.S. Department of Commerce (1975), Series D130, 124, D802).

Like steam power a century and a half earlier, the shift to electric drive increased throughput rates, and, consequently, conventionally defined labor productivity. It is important to point out, however, that labor per se was not more productive; rather, it was being called upon to supervise the more and more work done, in this case, by the EUD-powered machinery. The second industrial revolution was, in many regards, a continuation of the first industrial revolution. Like the first, the key ingredient was increased power and the resulting faster machine/process speeds.

Growth Theory in the Early 20th Century

Ironically, it turns out that what is perhaps the greatest process-based innovation of all time was ignored by the economics profession. Productivity was soaring, as was potential output. Whole new sectors of the economy were being developed. These included consumer durables (household appliances, automobiles). This begs the question, why? Why was the economics profession oblivious to these changes?

The reason, we argue, owes in large part to the very nature of economic growth theory at the time. Remember, by the end of the 19th century, production theory focused exclusively on capital and labor. All other factor inputs were virtually ignored, making for a situation in which the shift to EUD (the electrification of industry) went largely unnoticed. In fact, if anything, economic theory would have predicted a decrease in output and productivity given that the capital requirements (for EUD) were substantially lower.

There were, nonetheless, some discordant voices. Among these were those of Thorstein Veblen, Paul Douglas, Rexford G. Tugwell, F.G. Tryon and, to a lesser degree, Irving Fisher. As had been the case in early 19th-century Great Britain, interest in growth theory per se was not spontaneous, but rather, the result of economic stagnation and growing unemployment. More specifically, it was a response to the apparent inability of the US economy to move to the new higher growth path.

Thorstein Veblen

Perhaps the earliest whistleblower (i.e. that the US economy had failed to make the transition to the new equilibrium growth path) was University of Chicago political economist, Thorstein Veblen. Trained as a neoclassical economist, Veblen came to believe that there was something egregiously wrong with the for-profit economy, something that de facto prevented it from making a smooth transition to new, technological change-based higher growth path. According to him, cost-minimizing businessmen, by reducing the wage bill in response to electrification, "sabotaged" the transition, resulting in stagnation and unemployment.

> *Without some salutary restraint in the way of sabotage on the productive use of the available industrial plant and workmen, it is altogether unlikely that prices could be maintained at a reasonably profitable figure for any appreciable time. A businesslike control of the rate and volume of output is indispensable for keeping up a profitable market, and a profitable market is the first and unremitting condition of prosperity in any community whose industry is owned and managed by business men. And the ways and means of this necessary control of the output of industry are always and necessarily something in the way of retardation, restriction, withdrawal, unemployment of plant and workmen-whereby production is kept short of productive capacity.*
>
> *(Veblen 1921, 8)*

Veblen felt that the profession was ill-equipped to analyze technological change, given the emphasis of neoclassical production theory on capital and labor. This led to his life-long interest in technology and in engineering. More to the point, he called for the creation of new form of social, political and economic analysis and governance, known as Technocracy. That is, governance (i.e. the relevant information and coordination strategy) by engineers.[4]

Veblen's call for a new theory of wealth was heeded by a group of engineers at Columbia University in the 1920s. The result was a new economics, namely, the "economics of abundance." Among its leading authors—and there were many—were Stuart Chase and Howard Scott. Defining the economics of abundance were (i) the role of energy in general, and electric power in particular in production processes, and consequently in early 20th-century US economic growth, (ii) the purported flawed nature of the for-profit economy, distribution system, and/or money supply process, and (iii) the call for change, whether it be in the conduct of business or government regulation. Regarding the role of energy, their publications/writings begin by extolling the virtues of the new "power age." Consider, for example, the following excerpt from Howard Scott et al's *Introduction to Technocracy*, published in 1933:

> *A century ago these United States had a population of approximately 12,000,000 whereas to-day our census figures a total of 122,000,000—a tenfold increase in the century. One hundred years ago, in these United States, we consumed less than 75 trillion British thermal units of extraneous energy per annum, whereas in 1929, we consumed approximately 27,000 trillion British thermal units—an increase of 353 fold in the century. Our energy consumption now exceeds 150,000 kilogram calories per capita per day; whereas in the year 1800 our consumption of extraneous energy was not less than 1600 or more than 2000 kilogram calories per day.... The United States of our forefathers, with*

12,000,000 inhabitants, performed the necessary work in almost entire dependence upon the human engine, which, as its chief means of energy conversion, was aided and abetted only by domestic animals and a few water wheels. The United States to-day has over one billion installed horsepower. In 1929, these engines of energy conversion, though operated only to partial capacity, nevertheless had an output that represented approximately 50 percent of the total work of the world. When one realizes that the technologist had succeeded to such an extent that he is to-day capable of building and operating engines of energy conversion that have nine million times the output capacity of the average single human being working an eight hour day, one begins to understand the acceleration, beginning with man as the chief engineer of energy conversion and culminating with these huge extensions of his original one-tenth of a horse power. Then add the fact that of this 9,000,000 fold acceleration, 8,766,000 has occurred since the year 1900.

(Scott et al 1933, 42)

CAPSULE: THE CONTINENTAL COMMITTEE ON TECHNOCRACY

To non-economists, the developments of the 1920s, especially the conversion to EUD, were astounding. The roaring twenties witnessed phenomenal productivity and output growth. Engineers marveled at the prospects for the future.

However, to economists, nothing had happened. After all, there was no spike in either capital or labor – in fact, capital expenditures fell as EUD was less capital intensive as the belting, gearing and shafting it replaced.

This was incomprehensible in the eyes of a group of engineers from Columbia University. The world was changing. Yet, those whose job it is to follow this, appeared oblivious.

They then took matters into their own hands, setting out to rewrite economics with an eye to physics and engineering. And so was born, the Technocracy movement, devoted to the task of rewriting production theory around the theme of energy, the only physically productive factor input.

Another good example is the following excerpt taken from Chapter 1 of Stuart Chase's The Economics of Abundance, entitled "Forty to One":

Suppose that the thirteen million people living in the United States in 1830 had awakened on the morning of January 1, 1831, with forty times the physical energy they had gone to bed with the night before. An active picture meets the mind's eye; a very active picture. A lumberman can fell forty times as many trees in a week, a housewife sweep forty times as many square feet of floor; forty

> *barns can be built in the time hitherto required for one—and forty chests and forty chairs. Porters can transport forty times their accustomed load in a day; weavers ply their shuttles forty times as fast—if the shuttles can brook the strain; and children raise forty times their normal rumpus.*
>
> *Assuming no increase in the invention of labor-saving devices—and where would be the point with such an exuberance of labor available—what might we logically expect in the way of economic changes in a culture essentially handicraft? From an economy of scarcity, with barely enough to go around, the young republic would almost immediately enter an economy of abundance.*
>
> (Chase 1934, 1)

In the same chapter, Chase defines "Abundance" in terms of a series of propositions.

1. *A condition where the bulk of the economic work is performed not by men, but by inanimate energy, drawn from coal, oil and water power. Such a condition was reached in the United States toward the close of the 19th century, circa 1880.*
2. *A point at which living standards per capita reach an average, which is, at least potentially, twice as high as ever obtained under scarcity conditions. Reached circa 1900.*
3. *A point at which the curve of invention, following, as it does, a geometric increase, becomes the dominant factor in economic life – precisely as the Nile was the dominating factor in the economic life of Egypt. Circa 1870.*
4. *A point at which the scientific method supersedes the use and want of the craftsman in the production of most material goods. Circa 1900.*
5. *A point where output per man hour becomes so great that total productive labor must thereafter decline, even as output grows. A point at which labor ceases to be a measure of output – as it always has been in preceding ages. Circa 1920.*
6. *A point at which overproduction carries a more serious threat to the financial system than shortage. Circa 1880.*
7. *A point at which specialization has destroyed all practicable local self-sufficiency and made economic insecurity for all classes latent, growing, and ultimately intolerable, given no change in financial methods. Circa 1900, with the closing of the American frontier.*
8. *A point at which consumption becomes a greater problem than production. Circa, 1920. "Our economy," says F.L. Ackerman, "is so set up that it produces goods at a higher rate that it produces income with which to purchase them."*
9. *A point at which the industrial plant is, substantially, constructed, requiring relatively smaller outlays for capital goods in the future, and where pecuniary savings are not only unnecessary in their old volume, but seriously embarrassing, Circa, 1925.*

10 *A point where, due to the presence of the technical arts, costs, prices, interest rates, debts, begin a descent with zero as their objective. Circa 1920. (Chase 1934,12)*

The economics of abundance should be understood for what it was, namely a rejection of neoclassical economics with its emphasis on scarcity. The main issue, in so far as the study of economics was concerned, was not scarcity, but rather abundance. And abundance carried with it, a number of problems, the most egregious being underincome and underconsumption.

Unfortunately, Technocracy and the economics of abundance had little real effect on the theory of growth, and economics in general. After all, both proposed a radical reformulation of production theory on the basis of process engineering in general, and on the energy input in particular. In many regards, they were the spiritual disciples of 19th-century political economist and mathematician, Charles Babbage, and to a lesser degree, Karl Marx.

Paul Douglas

University of Chicago political economist Paul Douglas was the author of what is unquestionably the most lasting contribution to production and growth theory in the early 20th century, namely the Cobb-Douglas production function, known to literally all students and practitioners today. Ironically, Douglas' interest in production theory stemmed not from an interest in technology per se, but rather from his interest in distribution, more specifically from his view that distribution problems were the root cause of economic stagnation in the 1920s. Accordingly, technological change in the 1910s and 1920s had increased profits, leaving wages unchanged. This, Douglas argued, led to weakness in product markets and eventually to economic stagnation and unemployment.

In a nutshell, Douglas believed that wages were too low that they had not kept pace with productivity. But the problem, as had been the case with Robert Owen and Karl Marx in the 19th century, was in justifying what he believed was needed, namely higher wages. In other words, he needed more than a hunch. To this end, he turned to what he felt was science. This entailed estimating what he felt was a fundamental law of production, namely the neoclassical production function, in search for output elasticities. These, he reasoned, would guide wage and profit policies.

He then set out to estimate the parameters of a CRS neoclassical production function. With the help of mathematician/statistician Charles Cobb, he came to the conclusion that labor's share of GDP stood at 0.75, while capital's share stood at 0.25. The technology scaler, A, was estimated at 1.01. He referred to this as a law. Any increases in productivity would need to be distributed in a 75–25 percent basis.

These were then used to calculate what he referred to as the Value Product Unit Labor, which was then compared to real wages in manufacturing. In 1922, labor productivity growth had outpaced real wage growth by 13 percent, thus confirming Douglas' initial hunch (see Table 3.8).

Summary and Conclusion

As it turned out, the early 20th century would mark the end of the macroeconomic disequilibrium-based interest in growth theory. As we have shown the early 20th century was essentially a continuation of the 19th century in the sense that technological change and the resulting stagnation were at what motivated work on growth theory. What differed, of course, was the technology shock, namely EUD-based acceleration and the localization, the United States.

TABLE 3.8 Charles Cobb and Paul Douglas' Estimates of the Difference between Labor Productivity and Wages

Year	*Value Product per unit Labor (Average 1899–1908=100)*	*Real Wages (Average 1899–1908=100)*	*Per Cent Deviation*	*Business Annals*
1899	101	99	−2	
1900	95	98	+3	Brief Recession
1901	99	101	+2	
1902	95	102	+7	
1903	93	100	+8	
1904	96	99	+3	Mild Depression
1905	106	103	−3	
1906	111	101	−9	
1907	105	99	−6	
1908	96	94	−2	Depression
1909	97	102	+5	
1910	95	104	+9	
1911	96	97	+1	Mild Depression
1912	103	99	−4	
1913	106	100	−6	
1914	98	99	+1	Depression
1915	110	99	−10	
1916	115	104	−10	
1917	104	103	−1	War
1918	98	107	+9	War
1919	102	111	+9	
1920	114	114	0	
1921	117	115	−2	Depression
1922	136	119	−13	

Source: Cobb and Douglas (1928), 164.

Post-WWII Growth Theory

The post-WWII period (1945–1975) was characterized by exceptionally high rates of growth, earning it the moniker, the golden era of capitalism in Western industrialized democracies. As it turned out, this period was particularly fertile in developments in so far as growth theory is concerned. Whereas growth had until then been seen in terms of capital and labor, it would now be seen in terms of technology. The first true growth models would be developed, launching a new sub-field, known as growth theory.

In this section, we proceed as before, namely by first providing a detailed description of growth in the post-WWII period, followed by the developments in growth theory.

Post-WWII Growth

WWII was both a military and economic watershed. In 1939, US GNP stood at $209.4 billion (constant 1958 dollars). By 1944, it had reached $361.3 billion, a 73 percent increase. In 1939, the US industry consumed 78,603 million kilowatt hours of electric power; by 1944, it was consuming 156,365 million kilowatt hours, a phenomenal 100 percent increase. Metaphorically speaking, the war had unleashed the potential which had been building throughout the early part of the century, putting the US economy on a new, higher growth path. The challenge, according to President Harry Truman, was staying on it. In his 1945 budget speech to the new Congress, he referred repeatedly to the country's "productive capacity," implicitly referring to the gap between actual and potential output:

> *The American people have learned during the war the measure of their productive capacity, and they will remember the experience in the peace to come. It is the responsibility of business enterprise to translate market opportunities into employment and production. It is the responsibility of the Government to hold open the door of opportunity and assure sustained markets. Then and only then can free enterprise provide jobs.*
>
> *(Senate Congressional Record, January 7, 1945)*

The end of the war did not, however, mark the end of energy deepening. In hindsight, what had happened during the war was but a preview of things to come. In the decade from 1945 to 1955, total industrial consumption of electric power more-than-doubled going from 146,261 million kilowatt hours in 1945 to 334 to 334,088 million kilowatt hours. From 1955 to 1965, it increased by another 60 percent. By 1965, the United States consumed more electric power than all other countries combined. Never before in the history of mankind had per-capita energy consumption increased so rapidly.

This "energy orgy" came to a sudden, unexpected end with the oil/energy crisis in the 1970s. Responding to the falling real oil prices, members of the Organization of Petroleum Exporting Countries (OPEC) orchestrated an artificial crisis in 1973, resulting in the quadrupling of oil and other energy prices. With this came the end of what had been over a century of declining real energy prices (Jorgenson 1983). Per-worker energy consumption, monotone increasing for most of this century, stopped rising, resulting in zero productivity growth.

This section examines the massive energy deepening which characterized this period. As was the case in the mid-to-late 19th century, there was no new energy form or transmission technology per se; instead, the emphasis was on energy deepening, defined as an increase in the consumption of a given type of energy—in this case, electric power—per unit time. As pointed out earlier, the 19th century witnessed a marked increase in horsepower per factory worker (see Table 3.5) the result of various improvements to steam engines (e.g. high-pressure steam engines, steam turbines). As in the previous chapter, the main focus will be on the relationship between the energy deepening of the post-WWII period and growth. It will be shown that they had important indirect effects, including the development of growth accounting and, more importantly, the current interest in the Productivity Slowdown, and economic growth in general (e.g. real business cycle theory, endogenous growth theory).

Also, it will be argued that developments in labor law, especially, the Wagner Act which legalized collective bargaining, in consumer credit, and in the financing of government expenditure had important macroeconomic implications. Specifically, they contributed in a non-negligible way to resolving the problems of exchange and distribution as defined earlier (underincome and stagnation). For example, by tying real wages to conventionally defined productivity (contemporaneously or lagged), collective bargaining removed the wage, and hence, money income inertia (underincome) that had characterized the 19th and early 20th centuries. Rising productivity, the result of the massive energy deepening of the 1950s and 1960s, resulted in higher nominal and real wages, higher money income, and consequently, higher output and expenditure. Merchants increased their demand for consumer and capital goods, contributing to an increase in firm profits. In combination with the increasing use of consumer credit, growing government expenditure, increasing exports, the institution of collective bargaining solved, if not totally, partially, the problem of underincome. For a short period in the history of material civilization, Western industrialized economies, specifically the United States, realized, almost instantaneously, the potential associated with energy deepening.

As far as data and information in general are concerned, the post-WWII period was a watershed of sorts. Prior to the Great Depression, economic data in the United States, and in most Western industrialized democracies, were scant, if not altogether inexistent. This all changed with the rise of Keynesian macroeconomics. Specifically, governments began collecting detailed economic data, providing a wealth of information about production, exchange, and distribution. In this section, these are used to study production, distribution and exchange in three Western industrialized economies, namely the United States, Germany and Japan, with particular emphasis on the manufacturing sector for the post-WWII period. At war's end, the first two were the leading consumers of electric power. The third, on the other hand, ranked far behind.

Electric Unit Drive-Based Energy Deepening and Manufacturing Productivity

By the end of WWII, electric-motors had supplanted belting, shafting and gearing as the dominant energy transmission technology (Devine 1990; Nye 1990). Fossil fuels and hydraulic resources, however, remained the ultimate power source, in the United States, Germany and Japan, as well as in most other industrialized nations. While in the early part of the century, most manufacturing firms generated their own electric power, by the end of WWII, most were purchasing it from publicly regulated electric power utilities. In 1945, electric utilities' installed generating capacity stood at 50,111,000 kilowatts, which, by 1955, had more than doubled to 114,472,000 kilowatts. By 1965, it had, once again, doubled, reaching 236,126,000 kilowatts. US industrial generating capacity in this period increased, but at a considerably slower rate, going from 12,757,000 kilowatts in 1945 to 18,973,000 kilowatts.

Industrial power consumption increased at record rates in this period. Production processes were speeded up; throughput rates increased, resulting in higher plant output per period of time. What is particularly remarkable is the fact that most of this occurred with the existing capital and labor. For example, in the pulp and paper industry, existing paper machines turned faster, increasing productivity. According to business historian Alfred D. Chandler:

> *In modern mass production, as in modern mass distribution and modern transportation and communications, economies resulted more from speed than from size. It was not the size of the manufacturing establishment in terms of number of workers and the amount and value of productive equipment, but the velocity of throughput and the resulting increase in volume that permitted economies that lowered costs and increases output per worker and per machine.*
>
> *(Chandler 1977, 244)*

In earlier work (Beaudreau 1995, 1996, 1998), Chandler's "velocity of throughput" was modeled using a modified KLEM (capital, labor, energy materials) production function, the CLEP (capital, labor and electric power) production function, and proceeded to estimate the relevant output elasticities directly using post-WWII input and output data for US, German and Japanese manufacturing. These were then used in lieu of factor shares as the relevant weights in standard growth accounting exercises. Specifically, a well-behaved, twice differentiable, monotonic and quasi-concave production function was assumed, such as (1), where Q = value added, EP = electric power, L = employment, and K = capital. Christensen and Jorgenson (1970) and Gollop and Jorgenson (1980) define the rate of growth of total factor productivity, $tfp = dTFP / dt1 / TFP$, as $tfp = q - s_{EP}ep - s_K k - s_L l$, where $q = dQ / dt1 / Q$, $ep = dEP / dt1 / EP$, $l = dL / dt1 / L$ and $k = dK / dt1 / K$ and s_i is the estimated output elasticity for $i = EP,\ L,\ and\ K$.

$$Q(t) = F\left[EP(t),\ L(t),\ K(t)\right] \tag{3.1}$$

The relevant output elasticities (s_i) were estimated directly (i.e. as opposed to indirectly using the cost function). Specifically, data on value added, electric power consumption, total employment and capital for US, German and Japanese manufacturing were used to estimate the Cobb-Douglas KLEP production function:

The estimated output elasticities for all three countries are presented in Table 3.8. What is particularly striking are the similarities across countries. In all three cases, electric power consumption is, by far, the most important factor input, as evidenced by output elasticities of 0.537244, 0.747482 and 0.605599, respectively.

Pre- and Post-Energy Crisis Growth

Table 3.10 reports the relevant growth rates for manufacturing value added (*Q*), electric power (*EP*), labor (*L*) and capital (*K*), as well as the relevant fixed-weight aggregate input index (AI) (Hisnanick and Kymm 1992; Gullickson and Harper 1987) for three time periods: 1950–1984, 1950–1973 and 1974–1984.

Unlike previous studies that found a non-negligible gap between rates of output growth and rates of aggregate input growth (in essence, the Solow residual), these results indicate that growth in US, German and Japanese manufacturing value added is fully explained by growth in the relevant fixed-weight factor input growth indexes (Beaudreau 1995, 1998). For the complete period 1950–1984, US

TABLE 3.9 KLEP Output Elasticities: US, German and Japanese Manufacturing

Independent Variables	*US*	*Germany*	*Japan*
EP	0.537244	0.747482	0.605599
	(26.551)	(3.135)	(3.017)
L	0.399727	0.121134	0.197653
	(18.231)	(3.332)	(1.847)
K	0.075049	0.131383	0.196748
	(3.768)	(0.543)	(1.608)
Constant	0.075049	0.046106	-0.019274
	(9.956)	(1.426)	(0.271)
R^2	0.98438	0.95821	0.98314
F	1008.5140	229.2853	613.1780

Source: Beaudreau (1998), 98.

TABLE 3.10 Output and Input Growth Rates: US, German and Japanese Manufacturing

US			
	1950–1984	*1950–1973*	*1974–1984*
USVA	3.684	3.469	0.121
USAI[a]	3.674	3.472	0.310
USEP	4.052	5.371	0.246
USN	0.662	0.900	−0.091
USK	3.694	3.614	3.4008
German			
	1963–1988	*1962–1973*	*1974–1984*
GERVA	3.462	6.522	1.486
GERAI[a]	3.433	5.190	1.080
GEREP	3.894	5.883	1.366
GERN	−0.785	0.592	−0.938
GERK	3.945	5.620	1.406
Japanese			
	1965–1988	*1965–1973*	*1974–1988*
JAPVA	3.826	8.844	3.099
JAPAI[a]	3.566	9.856	1.538
JAPEP	3.559	11.320	0.965
JAPN	−0.082	3.297	−0.367
JAPK	7.520	13.536	5.182

Source: Beaudreau (1998), 99.

[a] Index of aggregate input based on estimated coefficients.

manufacturing value added increased at an average annual rate of 3.684 percent, while the aggregate input increased at 3.655 percent. For the first sub-period 1950–1973, it increased at 3.469, while the aggregate input increased at 3.466 percent. In the second sub-period, 1974–1984, it increased at an average annual rate of 0.121, while the aggregate input increased at 0.310.

Chief among the causes of growth in US, German and Japanese manufacturing value added was electric power consumption. In the US case, electric power consumption increased at an average annual rate of 4.052 percent over the period 1950–1984. Per worker consumption of electric power in US manufacturing in this period went from 12,534 kilowatt hours in 1950 to 41,688 kilowatt hours in 1984, an increase of 232 percent (U.S. Department of Commerce). When multiplied by the relevant output elasticity (i.e. 0.537244), the growth in electric power consumption in US manufacturing accounts for 82 percent of overall output growth (i.e. 3.17/3.68), which corroborates the predictions of EO production analysis. Prior to the energy crisis (i.e. 1973), electric power consumption in manufacturing increased at an average annual rate of 5.371 percent. Output increased at an average annual rate of 3.466 percent. Electric power consumption growth, it then follows, accounts for 83 percent of output growth (i.e. 3.88/3.46). In the post-energy-crisis period, electric power consumption increased at an average annual rate of 0.246, while output increased at an average annual rate of 0.121.

Pre- and Post-Energy Crisis Productivity Growth

Following Gullickson and Harper (1987) and Hisnanick and Kymm (1992) who examined the sources of productivity growth in US manufacturing using $lp = q - n$ (see Equation 3.2) as the appropriate measure of labor productivity, pre- and post-energy crisis productivity rates were estimated for US, German and Japanese manufacturing. Referring to Table 3.11, we see that the rate of growth of labor productivity is, in all three cases, entirely explained by increasing electric power and capital intensities, defined here as $ep - n$, the shift away from labor to electric power, and $k - n$, the shift away from labor to capital.

$$lp = q - n = \beta_1 \left[ep - n \right] + \beta_2 \left[k - n \right] + tfp \qquad (3.2)$$

Over the entire sample period (i.e. 1950–1984), US labor productivity increased at an average annual rate of 3.022 percent. During this period, the electric power-labor ratio increased at an average annual rate of 3.39 percent, which when multiplied by the relevant elasticity (i.e. 0.537244), yields a value of 1.820 percent, which measures the effects on labor productivity of the substitution of labor for electric power referred to by Dale Jorgenson (Jorgenson 1983). Also, during this period, the capital-labor ratio increased at an average annual rate of 3.032 (Column 2), which when multiplied by the relevant output elasticity (0.075049) yields a value of 0.191, which measures the effects on labor productivity of the substitution of labor for capital. The sum of these two effects accounts for 99.5 percent of the growth in labor productivity in US manufacturing (3.011/3.022).

Prior to the energy crisis, labor productivity increased at an average annual rate of 3.569 percent, of which 3.400 percent can be attributed to labor-electric power substitution (energy deepening) and 0.170 percent can be attributed to labor-capital substitution. Together, these two effects overstate the overall increase in labor productivity by 1 percent. In the ensuing decade, labor productivity increased at an average annual rate of 0.212 percent, of which 0.180 percent can be attributed to labor-electric power substitution and 0.219 percent can be attributed to labor-capital substitution.

Similar results are reported for German and Japanese manufacturing, the upshot being that the increase in labor productivity observed in all three countries can, in large part, be attributed to increases in electric power use, consistent with the EO approach to material processes.

TABLE 3.11 Productivity Growth: US, German and Japanese Manufacturing

US			
Period	*1950–1984*	*1950–1973*	*1974–1984*
uslp	3.022	3.569	0.212
ustfp	0.010	−0.002	−0.1889
β1(usep-usn)	1.820	3.400	0.180
β3(usk-usn)	0.191	0.170	0.219
German			
Period	*1963–1988*	*1963–1973*	*1974–1988*
gerlp	3.247	5.930	3.424
gertfp	0.007	1.315	0.3942
β1(gerep-gern)	3.750	3.954	1.722
β3(gerk-gern)	0.489	0.660	0.307
Japanese			
Period	*1965–1988*	*1965–1973*	*1974–1988*
japlp	3.908	6.547	3.466
japtfp	0.208	−1.126	1.567
β1(japep-japn)	3.204	5.463	0.806
β3(japk-japn)	1.495	3.210	1.091

Source: Beaudreau (1998), 101.

Electric Unit Drive-Based Energy Deepening as Seen by Political Economists

While they ignored energy and the role of energy in the creation of wealth throughout the 18th, 19th and early 20th centuries, political economists could not ignore the phenomenal growth in output in general, and output per worker (conventionally defined labor productivity) in this period. Among the first to acknowledge the existence of a gap between conventionally used factor inputs (capital and labor) and output were Jan Tinbergen in Europe and Moses Abramovitz in the United States. Both had devised indexes of input (capital and labor) and output growth, and found, using post-WWI data, the presence of an unexplained, upward drift in output indexes. Abramovitz referred to this gap as "our measure of ignorance."

Credit for the earliest explicit calculation belongs to Tinbergen, who in a 1942 paper, published in German, generalized the Cobb-Douglas production function by adding an exponential trend to it, intended to represent various "technical developments." He computed the average value of this trend component, calling it a measure of "efficiency," for four countries: Germany, Great Britain, France, and the United States, using the formula $trend = y - 2/3n - 1/3k$, where y, n and k are the average growth rates of output, labor and capital, respectively.

Note how similar this was to Robert Solow who would let these weights change, shifting the index numbers from a fixed weight geometric to an approximate Divisia form. Nobody seems to have been aware of Tinbergen's paper in the United States until much later.

> *The developments in the U.S. originated primarily at the NBER where a program of constructing national income and "real" output series under the leadership of Simon Kuznets was expanded to include capital series for major sectors of the economy, with contributions by Creamer, Fabricant, Goldsmith, Tostlebe and others.*
>
> *(Griliches 1995, 3)*

Unfortunately, in spite of half of century of work in the field of growth accounting since, our "measure of ignorance" has not decreased (Maddison 1987; Gullickson and Harper 1987; Aghion and Howitt 1998). It has changed names (e.g. tfp-total factor productivity), been cloaked in formal and informal models, been tested against every possible datum, yet, in the end, it stands as a living testimony to what by now were over two centuries of residuals.

The Energy Crisis and Productivity as Seen by Political Economists

As pointed out earlier, the seemingly endless increase in energy consumption/use of the post-WWII period came to an unexpected and unfortunate end in the mid-1970s with the OPEC-induced energy crisis. Energy prices doubled, tripled and, eventually, quadrupled, pushing manufacturing firms up their energy demand curve. As shown in Table 3.10, energy consumption stopped growing. In hindsight, one would have thought that maybe now, at long last, energy would get the attention it deserved. "Absence makes the heart grow fonder," as the saying goes. Figuratively speaking, the hen that had laid the golden eggs (energy rents) for over two centuries was no more. As incredulous as it may appear, this was not to be, as evidenced by the continued absence of energy from production theory. Once again, the reasons are many. First, since energy had, up to then, not been defined as a factor input, the focus as far as production theory was concerned was not on energy per se, but rather, on the relationship between energy prices and the demand for capital and labor. For example, if energy and capital are complementary, then an increase in the price of the former will decrease the demand for the latter, reducing growth, and, quite possibly, in the short run, provoke a recession (Berndt and Wood 1975).

To address these questions (complementarity-substitutability), Ernst Berndt and David O. Wood developed a new, all-inclusive production function, commonly known as the KLEM production function. By eliminating the age-old distinction between factor inputs and intermediate inputs, Berndt and Wood cleared the way for the estimation of energy-labor and energy-capital, not to mention, energy-materials and energy-services, cross-elasticities.

At first blush, one's inclination is to laud what appeared to be an important breakthrough, as far as the role of energy in production is concerned. After all, it took 200 years (from Smith's Wealth of Nations in 1776–1975) for energy to break the stranglehold held by capital and labor in production theory. Finally, energy had entered the select club of factor inputs. The irony, however, is that the select club was (is) no more. The distinction between intermediate input and factor input was blurred beyond recognition. Nothing was a factor input, and nothing was an intermediate input.

Their estimates of the four output elasticities are presented in Table 3.12, where we see that the energy output elasticity to be 0.0443. This implies that a one percent increase in energy consumption results in a 0.04 percent increase in manufacturing output, leasing the authors to conclude that energy *per se* was not a key factor input in manufacturing.

This has raised questions regarding their methodology. Specifically, instead of using input and output data, they chose cost and factor share data. Implicit in the use of such data are the assumptions of constant returns to scale in production and competitive factor markets. It being the case that electric power is the dominant form of energy in manufacturing, and that the price of electric power is regulated, doing so introduces an important bias. Their results showed an energy output elasticity of 0.0442 percent. Put plainly, energy was, for all intents and purposes, insignificant.

When it was suggested that the energy crisis could lie at the root of the productivity and growth slowdown, Berndt and Wood's energy output elasticity (and

TABLE 3.12 Berndt and Wood's (1975) KLEM Output Elasticities, I3SLS Estimates of KLEM Translog Cost Function: US Manufacturing, 1947–1971

Parameter	*Estimates*	*Parameter*	*Estimates*
αK	0.0564 (36.571)	γ_{KM}	−0.0153 (−1.301)
α_L	0.2539 (112.359)	γ_{LL}	0.0739 (10.159)
α_E	0.0442 (38.078)	γ_{LE}	−0.0043 (−1.438)
α_M	0.6455 (173.348)	γ_{LM}	0.0697 (-5.942)
γ_{KK}	0.0254 (3.455)	γ_{EE}	0.0214 (2.393)
γ_{KL}	0.0001 (0.022)	γ_{EM}	−0.0068 (−0.527)
γ_{EE}	−0.0102 (−2.444)	γ_{MM}	0.0918 (3.243)

Source: Berndt and Wood (1975), 262.

TABLE 3.13 Gullickson and Harper's Estimates of Multifactor Productivity 1949–1983

Period	*Output*	*Aggregate*	*Capital*	*Labor*	*Energy*	*Material*	*Service*	*KLEMS*
1949–1983	3.1	3.0	3.8	0.8	3.3	3.2	4.6	1.1
1949–1973	4.2	3.7	3.9	1.5	5.1	3.1	5.4	1.5
1973–1983	0.6	0.3	3.6	−1.0	−0.8	0.2	3.6	0.3

Source: Gullickson and Harper (1987), 23.

others') was cited as evidence to the contrary. Something as insignificant as energy in 20th-century production processes could not possibly have halved the growth rate, and all but eliminated productivity growth, or so the story goes. In their comprehensive study of total factor productivity in US manufacturing (the results are reproduced in Table 3.13), William Gullickson and Michael J. Harper show, beyond a shadow of a doubt, that energy was not the cause.

The Energy Agnostics

Unconvinced by either the methodology or the results of growth accounting, others continued to study the role of energy in production. Among these, one finds political economists Dale Jorgenson, Zvi Griliches and Nathan Rosenberg, and production engineers Sam H. Schurr, Calvin Burwell, Warren D. Devine Jr and Sidney Sonenblum. For example, in 1983, Dale Jorgenson published the results of a study of the role of electricity in technical change (i.e. whether it was electricity using or not). Of the 35 sectors studied, 23 were found to be of the electricity-using type. Specifically, "the decline in electricity prices prior to 1973 prompted increased electrification via the substitution of electricity for other forms of energy, and through the substitution of energy for other inputs—especially labor" (Jorgenson 1983, 21). Electrification and energy deepening in the form of higher levels of electricity consumption, he went on to conclude, played a fundamental role in productivity growth.

In similar work, Sidney Sonenblum shows that technological progress in manufacturing in this period has been "related to the adoption and spread of production processes and modes of organization that are dependent on the use of electricity" (Sonenblum 1990, 277). The downside, however, in Sonenblum and Jorgenson's work is the absence of a theory of production that is sufficiently general to incorporate energy. Oddly enough, energy, in this case, electricity, affects output indirectly through "technology." Habits die hard. The spirit of the neoclassical production function with its emphasis on capital and labor, and, to a lesser degree, on technology, is very much present in Jorgenson's work, and, indeed, in all post-energy crisis work on energy.

This, in brief, is where the economics profession stands today on the role of energy in production. Despite two epoch-defining energy innovations, two centuries of energy deepening, and a cataclysmic "energy crisis," energy, the building block of material processes in general remains very much the outsider, having no place at the table.

Post-WWII Growth Theory

This period is by far the most productive in so far as growth theory is concerned. The contributions were many and varied, ranging from the Harrod-Domar Growth Model, to the Solow-Swan Growth Model, to Edward Denison's exhaustive, encyclopedic study of the causes of economic growth. Motivating work in this period were (i) the Keynesian Revolution and its dynamic ramifications, (ii) the many empirical irregularities, and (iii) the Productivity Slowdown of 1975. The Keynesian Revolution, while providing temporary relief to the millions of unemployed workers, raised a number of fundamental issues, including the long-run stability of capitalistic economies. Were free market, capitalist economies prone to large-scale crises? Did they contain, as Karl Marx pointed out, the seeds of their own demise?

To address these questions, Evsey Domar and Roy Harrod went on to show that under certain circumstances, growth rates could in fact be unstable, resulting in recurrent economic crises. This is known formally as Harrod-Domar instability.

Harrod-Domar instability lies at the very root of what is today known as the standard growth model in economics, namely the Solow-Swan Model. Robert Solow and Trevor Swan showed that with anything other than Leontief, fixed-proportions technology (i.e. with Cobb-Douglas production technology), Harrod-Domar instability was a non-issue, and that growth would be stable.

The second cause was spontaneous in nature and consisted of the various empirical irregularities found in the post-Great Depression macroeconomic time series. Specifically, when output, capital and labor time series were plotted, it became obvious that combined capital and labor growth alone could not explain output growth. In other words, there was something else at work, driving post-WWII growth rates. That something became known as the Solow Residual.

The third and by far, most important factor was the Productivity Slowdown of the 1970s. The post-WWII period was exceptional in that growth was not only high but also sustained over a 30-year period. Never before in the history of modern capitalist economies had there been a period or epoch characterized by so much prosperity. However, with the good came the bad, and the economics profession had been lulled into complacency. After all, "if it ain't broken, then don't fix it," as the saying goes. So, when growth virtually stopped in the mid-1970s, the profession, not to mention, the world, was caught off-guard.

As a testimony to its ability to change directions, the growth question soon become front and center in economics. Many of the great minds, including macroeconomists Robert Lucas and Peter Howitt, turned their attention to the question of growth. In little time, it become the most dominant issue of the late 20th and early 21st centuries. New journals were launched. Governments chimed in. With the result that today, the growth question literally defines the profession. In this section, we present the major contributions.

The "Is Capitalism Stable?" Debate

The Great Depression (1929–1939) raised a number of fundamental questions regarding capitalism, not the least of which was, "Is the capitalist, free-market system of production stable in the long run?" Or, is it prone to periodically collapse? Was this cataclysmic event a harbinger of what lie ahead? Had capitalism run out of steam, and was stagnation and decline the new normal?

It turns out that the simple Keynesian macroeconomic model provided few answers to these and related questions, owing in large measure to the fact that it was static in nature. According to Ray Harrod, only a dynamic model could provide answers to these questions. It was with this in mind that he presented one of the first "growth models" notably that which was to become known as the Harrod-Domar model, which provided the set of conditions for stable and unstable economic growth. In short, the model consists of three parameters, namely n, the rate of growth of labor; s, the savings rate; and k, the capital-output ratio. Harrod reasoned that if the rate of growth of labor was exactly equal to the ratio of the savings rate to the capital-output ratio ($n = s/k$), then stability would result. If, on the other hand, the former was less than the latter, then excess savings would be the order of the day, resulting in Harrod instability. The economy, Harrod argued, would stagnate as too few investment opportunities would exist.

The Harrod-Domar model, especially, Harrod-Domar instability, was not particularly well received by mainstream economists. After all, it predicted the eventual decline/instability of capitalism and its replacement by a hierarchical ICS-based form of economic organization (i.e. socialism or communism). Many dismissed its predictions on the grounds that new investment opportunities existed and would forever exist. Put differently, excess savings could no more exist in the long run as a man could have a baby. Leading the attack on Harrod-Domar instability were Robert Solow and Trevor Swan, who reworked Harrod and Domar's findings within the context of a standard neoclassical, Cobb-Douglas production function. In short, the Leontief, fixed-proportions technology used by Harrod and Domar was replaced with a standard neoclassical production function that allows for substitutability – in short, capital deepening. The latter *de facto* ruled out Harrod-Domar instability.

The Missing Factor: Post-WWII Input and Output Time Series

One of the more positive developments of the Great Depression was the beginning of what we refer to as the *Data Era* or the era of data collection in political economy. Prior to the 1930s, governments collected few macroeconomic and microeconomic data. At best, data were collected on foreign trade and government expenditure. This all changed in the late 1930s as the result of the Keynesian revolution, specifically to the exigencies of macroeconomic stabilization policy. Governments intent on stabilizing GDP and employment required estimates of the marginal propensity to consume and to import, in addition to detailed data on the Keynesian macroeconomic aggregates, namely GDP, consumption expenditure, investment expenditure exports and imports. Virtually every country established a data collection agency with the express purpose of providing the necessary information to conduct macroeconomic stabilization policy.

By the end of WWII, the first times series data on GDP, employment, and investment were published, ushering in a new era in the study of growth, known as growth accounting. Among the pioneers were Jan Tinbergen, Moses Abramovitz and Milton Friedman. Working within the confines of neoclassical production theory, they delved into the "causes of growth," with the firm belief that capital and labor growth would be shown to be responsible for the lion's share of GDP growth. After all, according to neoclassical production theory, industrial output was an increasing function of capital and labor. Translated into the relevant differential equation, the rate of output growth would be equal to the weighted average of the rate of growth of capital and the rate of growth of labor.

What they found, however, was disturbing, not to say earth shattering in so far as traditional production and growth theory was concerned. Specifically, their results showed that capital and labor, the cornerstones of neoclassical production theory, explained only half of GDP growth, leaving the other half unexplained. Abramovitz referred to the latter as "our measure of ignorance." In time, it became known as the Solow residual and more recently as *tfp*, total factor productivity.

The Solow residual became synonymous with the shortcomings of mainstream production theory. Clearly, neoclassical production theory had come up short. Something was missing. But what? Questions abounded. Was the Solow residual a vindication of Veblen and the Technocrats' criticisms of neoclassical production theory? Was the latter mis-specified?

Despite what was an indictment of its basic principles, neoclassical growth theory continued unchanged and unabashed. The Solow residual was formalized in terms of a technology parameter that, like capital and labor, was assumed to growth over time. And grow it did, until the mid-1970s when it stopped. A staple of post-WWII growth, the robust Solow residual of the post-WWII period disappeared in the late 1970s, never to reappear.

Not surprisingly, this Kafkian turn of events was cataclysmic. Suddenly, the Solow residual that had sustained prosperity throughout the post-WWII period was no more. Growth slowed, government deficits mounted, labor unrest increased and hope was no more. The economics profession responded by corralling resources and virtually declaring war on ignorance, in short, by declaring war on the Solow residual.

CAPSULE: DOES NEOCLASSICAL GROWTH THEORY EXPLAIN ANYTHING?

In a nutshell, post-WWII neoclassical growth theory maintains that labor and capital explain roughly half of GDP growth with the Solow residual explaining the other half. However, given that both labor and capital are not physically productive and the residual is just that, a residual, it could be argued that neoclassical growth theory in its myriad incarnations explains essentially nothing. Since capital and labor are organizational factor inputs which are not physically productive, they are necessary, but not sufficient for growth. Metaphorically, it's as if total mileage driven increased by ten percent, but the number of vehicles and drivers only increased by five percent. Can it be concluded that the number of vehicles (capital) and the number of drivers (labor) are responsible for five percent of the growth? The answer is an unqualified no, as it's the fuel (gasoline, diesel, hydrogen or electricity) that is powering the car and ultimately responsible for the ten percent increase in mileage. Neoclassical analysis would attribute the latter to labor (driver) and capital (vehicles) and a non-descript residual.

The Productivity Slowdown of 1975

The events of the mid-1970s ushered in the second "tectonic shift" of the 20th century, the Great Depression (1929–1939) being the first. From 1975 onward, the profession reacted, focusing on economic growth and its determinants. It mobilized microeconomics as well as macroeconomics, not to mention international trade. Notable economists including Nobel Prize laureates left their respective fields to focus on the question of growth. Perhaps the most notable was University of Chicago economics professor and Nobel laureate Robert Lucas who abandoned the field of macroeconomics to focus on growth theory.

This is understandable, as the goose that had laid three decades of golden eggs was no more. Or at the very least, her eggs were no longer golden. Surprisingly, however, this cataclysmic shock failed to usher in a period of paradigm change (as had been the case with the Great Depression). What we find, in large measure, are extensions of the standard neoclassical model. Particular emphasis is put on the A scaler in the Cobb-Douglas production framework, which as its name implies, was until then exogenous.

The result was endogenous growth theory, which as its name implies, endogenized or attempted to endogenize the technology scaler. Until then, economists ignored the underpinnings of technology and all matters technological. Now, all of that would change as the profession set out to understand the mechanics of technological change.

Among the more salient contributions are those of Paul Romer, Robert Lucas and Philippe Aghion and Peter Howitt. Paul Romer's contribution consisted of endogenizing technology in terms of the *Ak* framework, where *A* was modeled explicitly. Lucas, on the other hand, focused on the institutions of economic growth (science, technology, education etc.), while Aghion and Howitt revived Joseph Schumpeter's concept of creative destruction in their attempt at understanding the behavioral and technical aspects of innovation.

While promising, this literature has failed to live up to expectations. Technological change in general, and the *A* technology scaler in particular, remain unexplained with dire consequences. As we have been unable to explain past growth, the profession find itself in the unfortunate position of not being able to design science-based policy measures that are growth increasing. This constitutes one of, if not, the greatest scientific failures of the current era.

CAPSULE: INFORMATION AND COMMUNICATION TECHNOLOGY AND PROUCTIVITY GROWTH

AND PROUCTIVITY GROWTH As shown here, the industrial era was characterized, to the point of being defined, by paradigm technological shock/innovations, the steam engine and the electric motor being the two most cited and studied. Just how these two, power-based technologies affected productivity and output, however, was an open-ended question.

What transpired, however, was an interest in what Timothy Bresnahan and Manuel Trajtenberg referred to as general purpose technologies (GPTs). The latter are technologies that are adopted in many interests, raising productivity. In the 1980s, it was believed that the emerging digital revolution (computers and fiber-optics) was one such GPT, destined to increase productivity throughout the economy.

The 1980s and 1990s witnessed massive investment in information and communication technology. New industries popped up. Existing ones invested massively,

However, in 1987, Nobel laureate Robert Solow pointed out that "we see computers everywhere but in the productivity statistics," thus raising what became known as the information paradox. Compared to the steam engine and the electric motor which increased productivity and growth, ICT was alleged to be toothless.

The profession responded with a lot of arm-waving, pointing to the presence of lags and protracted adoption, the gist of which was that it was too early to pass judgment. Today, some 40 years later, it still hasn't delivered on its promises.

While growth theorists are at a loss to explain it, the EO approach presented in Chapter 2 provides a scientific justification, namely that information is not a form/type of energy. Since only energy is productive, there was and is not reason to believe that ICT, which increased information, would affect productivity – at least the way the steam engine and its many refinements did in the 19th century and the electric motor and its many refinements did in the 20th century.

Thus, if one invokes basic science, the information paradox isn't a paradox for the simple reason that it could not, did not and would not/never increase output the way innovations in power-delivery technology did from the dawn of the industrial age.[5]

Growth Theory: Ideology or Science?

In short, the question in so far as we are concerned comes down to a simple one: is growth theory, in its entirety, ideological, a form of propaganda, or scientific? Remember that by scientific, it should be understood a series of hypotheses that (i) are consistent with the fundamental laws of the universe and (ii) have been confirmed by the data (and the findings replicated), resulting in a set of "laws."

On that basis, it follows that it is not scientific. This follows from two facts, namely that (i) most of what is considered to be growth theory (production theory and the theory of growth) violates classical mechanics and thermodynamics, and (ii) the existing models have failed to explain most of post-WWII growth, not to mention, the growth slowdown, also known as the productivity slowdown.

As has been shown in this chapter, attempts at bridging the gap between physics and economics, while numerous, were and continue to be ignored. Growth theory continues to be the sole purview of moral philosophy with no input from natural philosophy.

Growth Theory: Timeline Summary

TABLE 3.14 Growth Theory: Timeline Summary

Year	*Historical Development*	*Theoretical Development*
1769	James Watt's External Condenser Steam Engine Matthew Boulton's Hockley Brook Factory	
1776		Adam Smith's Wealth of Nations
1804	Boulton-Watt Reciprocating Steam Engine	
1817		David Ricardo's
1840	Trevithick's High-Pressure Steam Engine	
1848		Karl Marx and Friedrich Engel's Communist Manifesto
1867		Karl Marx's Das Kapital

(*Continued*)

TABLE 3.14 (Continued)

Year	*Historical Development*	*Theoretical Development*
1871		William Stanley Jevons' The Theory of Political Economy
1890		Alfred Marshall's Principles of Economics
1928		Charles Cobb and Paul Douglas Estimates of Output Elasticities
1930	Great Depression	
1951		Roy Harrod and Evsey Domar's Growth Theory
1954		Solow-Swan Growth Theory
1973		OPEC-induced Energy Crisis
1975		
1975	Productivity Slowdown	
1986		Paul Romer's Ak Growth Model
1990		New Growth Theory

Growth Theory: Ideology or Science?

As Table 3.15 indicates, the bulk of growth theory is non-scientific, largely as a result of the fact that most theories/models are based on assumptions that violate the laws of the physical world (VLPW), notably the fact that labor and capital are assumed to be physically productive. Unfortunately, faulty first principles are the grounds which lead us to invalidate this field altogether. This holds true of classical, Marxian and neoclassical approaches. Not helping matters is the fact that most of the post-productivity slowdown work, including the contributions of Nobel laureates, are not testable in their original form.

This is an extremely unfortunate situation as production theory and its dynamic equivalent, growth theory, lie at the very base of each of the four other fields examined in this volume. Nothing can be right in economics until the profession gets wealth, its creation and its growth right. While this is a sobering though after some 250 years of analysis, it needs to be mentioned.

This failure can be attributed to, among other factors, the total disregard for applied physics and process engineering over the past two centuries. As we were able to show, standard production theory operates in a parallel universe with laws of its own (law of diminishing marginal productivity of labor and capital), laws that violate the known laws of the physical world. Growth theory has been reduced to labor, capital and a residual. As the first two are not physically productive, and the third is a residual, it stands to reason that growth theory explains virtually nothing. Put differently, the core theory of growth consists of two non-productive factor inputs and a residual.

TABLE 3.15 Growth Theory: Ideology or Science?

Principle/Hypothesis/Theory	*Ideology or Science*	*Justification*
Classical production theory	Ideology	VLPW, NT
Neoclassical production theory	Ideology	VLPW, NEMPCON
KLEMS production model	Ideology	VLPW
Harrod-Domar	Ideology	VLPW
Solow-Swan	Ideology	VLPW,NT
Neoclassical growth model	Ideology	VLPW,NT
Romer *Ak* model	Ideology	VLPW,NT
Schumpeterian growth	Ideology	VLPW,NT
Bourgeois dignity as a cause of the industrial revolution	Ideology	NT
Republic of letters as a cause of the industrial revolution	Ideology	NT

Summary and Conclusion

It is often said that to build a house on shaky foundations is pure folly, not to mention an outright waste of time. Unfortunately, this problem behooves all of economics. Without a solid, tested, tried and true theory of wealth and growth, the applied fields of economics cannot hope to provide light on the pressing issues of the day, and indeed of all of times. Income distribution, labor economics, international trade, macroeconomics and microeconomics all require solid fundamentals, without which nothing can be right. A theory of comparative advantage that abstracts from technology and productivity is sure to fail. Ibid for work in all other sub-fields.

This raises the question why? Why has economics been unsuccessful in its attempt at formalizing what are rather simple material processes? Why is it that thermodynamics, the science of heat, born of the same proverbial mother (i.e. the steam engine), has been wildly successful, while economics continues to struggle with the basics? These questions have not, at the time of writing, been answered.

Review Questions

1. In your view, why was the systematic study of economic growth (i.e. growth theory) non-existent prior to the beginning of the 19th century?
2. It has been argued that classical production theory is more suited to describing material processes in the Paleolithic era. That is, before industrialization. Do you agree? Why?
3. Today, growth theory is an important field in economics, rivaling macroeconomics in so far as research and interest is concerned. Was this the case in the 19th century? Explain.
4. The Neoclassical economists decreed *ex-cathedra* that capital was physically productive. In your view, was this a wise thing to do? Why? Explain.

5 *The Continental Committee on Technocracy* rejected mainstream economics on the grounds that it was divorced from the laws of physics. What were the laws of physics in question (i.e. that were being violated?). Explain
6 The Keynesian Revolution was a veritable watershed for growth theory and growth theorists? Provide at least one example of a by-product for growth theory.
7 The Productivity Slowdown was both a curse and a blessing for growth theory. It was a curse as it marked the end of the Solow Residual. On the other hand, it was a blessing as it changed the face of the science, away from macroeconomics over to growth theory. Has the latter change been successful in uncovering the laws that govern economic growth? Explain.
8 In your view, has growth theory been successful? Explain.
9 Is the notion of the marginal product of capital found in the process engineering literature? Provide an example.
10 While it has been a scientific failure of epic proportion, does the growth literature provide any value added to the policy maker?

Directions for Future Research

1 A scientifically and empirically-consistent account of economic growth in the industrial era.
2 A scientifically and empirically-consistent account of cross-country differences in growth rates (follows from 1).
3 A microeconomic model of the role of information technologies (and artificial intelligence) in growth.
4 A microeconomic model of the role of second-law efficiency in growth.
5 Studying the role of information and communication technology (ICT) and artificial intelligence (AI) in second-law efficiency.
6 The role of growth theory (and its failures) in the field of economic development.
7 The role of speed and acceleration in material processes in general.
8 Why applied physics and engineering has been and continues to be ignored by growth theorists.

Notes

1 The seller has no means of extending his trade by himself, which does not react on his colleagues; he disputes with them a given quantity of income which must replace his capital; and the more he succeeds in keeping for himself, the less he leaves for others. It is not at all up to the producer to increase the income of the society or the market which he serves in such a way that they can be exchanged for an increase in products... Among merchants, it is considered a bad action to seduce each other by their practices; but the competition which each exercises against all does not present such a precise idea; and a merchant is no less eager to extend his trade at the expense of his colleagues than to proportion it to the increase in wealth, when the latter offer him the exchange of a new income. Up to now, in one or the other case, the discovery of a new process has caused a great national loss, a great decrease in income, and consequently, consumption.

2 Underincome is defined as situations in which the level of nominal money income is less than that necessary to sustain potential aggregate wealth.
3 It was not about sequential production and/assembly as it already existed.
4 Veblen felt that markets, specifically the behavior of producers, were sub-optimal and should, as such, be replaced by professional engineers, something that would come to be known as the Technate or the Technocrats.
5 At the very best, it could increase output by increasing second-law efficiency. However, such increases would be one-shot deals and, as such, not affect growth in the long-run.

References

Acemoglu, D., S. Johnson and J.A. Robinson. (2005) The Rise of Europe: Atlantic Trade Institutional Change and Economic Growth, *American Economic Review*, 95, pp. 546–579.

Aghion, P. and P. Howitt. (1998) *Endogenous Growth Theory*, Cambridge, MA: MIT Press.

Allen, R.C. (2009) *The British Industrial Revolution in Global Perspective*, Cambridge: Cambridge University Press.

Babbage, C. (1835) *On the Economy of Machinery and Manufactures*, London: Charles Knight.

Baines, E. (1835) *History of the Cotton Manufacture in Great Britain*, London: H. Fisher, R. Fisher, and P. Jackson.

Beaudreau, B.C. (1995) The Impact of Electric Power on Productivity: A Study of U.S. Manufacturing 1950-1984. *Energy Economics*, 17(1), 231–236.

Beaudreau, B.C. (1996) *Mass Production, the Stock Market Crash, and the Great Depression: The Macroeconomics of Electrification*, Westport, CT: Greenwood Press.

Beaudreau, B.C. (1998) *Energy and Organization, Growth and Distribution Reconsidered*, Westport, CT: Greenwood Press.

Berndt, Ernst and David Wood. (1975) Technology, Prices and the Derived Demand for Energy, *Review of Economics and Statistics*, 57(3), pp. 259–268.

Broadberry, S. and B. Gupta. (2009) Lancashire, India, and the Shifting Competitive Advantage in Cotton Textiles, *Economic History Review*, 62(2), pp. 279–305.

Chandler, A.D. (1977) *The Visible Hand: The Managerial Revolution in American Business*, Cambridge, MA: Harvard University Press.

Chase, S. (1934) *The Economy of Abundance*, New York: The John Day Company.

Cobb, C. and P. Douglas. (1928) A Theory of Production, *American Economic Review*, 18, pp.139–165.

Cole, W.A. (1973) Eighteenth-Century Economic Growth Revisited, *Explorations in Economic History*, 10, pp. 327–348.

Committee on Factories Bill. (1832) Parliamentary Papers, 1831–1832, vol. XV. pp. 44, 95–97, 115, 195, 197, 339, 341–342, 430.

Committee on Recent Economic Changes. (1929) Recent Economic Changes in the United States, Volumes 1 and 2, NBER Books, *National Bureau of Economic Research*, Inc, number 29–1.

Christensen, L.R. and D.W. Jorgenson (1970), U.S. Real Product and Real Factor Input 1929-1967. *Review of Economics and Wealth* 16(1), pp. 19–50.

Davis, R. (1979), The Industrial Revolution and Overseas Trade, Leicester University Press.

Deane, W.A. and P. Cole (1964) *British Economic Growth 1688–1959; Trends and Structure*, Cambridge: Cambridge at the University Press.

Devine, W.D. Jr. (1983) From Shafts to Wires: Historical Perspective on Electrification, *Journal of Economic History* 43(2), pp. 347–372.

Devine, W.D., Jr. (1990) Electrified Mechanical Drive: The Historical Power Distribution Revolution. In Sam H. Schurr, Calin C. Burwell, Warren D. Devine, Jr., and Sidney Sonenblum, eds. *Electricity in the American Economy: Agent of Technological Progress*. Westport, CT: Greenwood Press, pp. 21–42.

de Vries, J. (1994) The Industrial Revolution and the Industrious Revolution, *Journal of Economic History*, 54, pp. 249–270.

Ford, H. (1926) Mass Production, *Encyclopaedia Britannica*, 13, pp. 821–823.

Gilboy, E.W. (1932) Demand as a Factor in the Industrial Revolution. In A.H. Cole, ed. *Facts and Factors in Economic History* (1932); rpt. in R.M. Hartwell, ed. *The Causes of the Industrial Revolution in England*. London, 1967, pp. 121–138.

Griliches, Z. (1995) *The Discovery of the Residual: A Historic Note*, Harvard Institute of Economic Research Working Paper 1743.

Gullickson, W. and M.J. Harper (1987) Multifactor Productivity in U.S. Manufacturing 1949–1983, *Monthly Labor Review*, October pp. 18–28.

Gollop, F. and D. Jorgenson (1980), US Productivity Growth by Industry, 1947–73, in Kendreich, J.W. and B.N. *Vaccara, New Developments in Productivity Measurement an Analysis*, Chicago, IL: University of Chicago Press, pp. 323–341.

Hills, R.L. (1989) *Power from Steam: A History of the Stationary Steam Engine*, Cambridge: Cambridge University Press.

Hisnanick, J. and K. Kymm (1992) The Impact of Disaggregated Energy on Productivity, *Energy Economics*, pp. 274–278.

Honeyman, K. (1982) *Origins of Enterprises: Business Leadership in the Industrial Revolution*, Manchester: Manchester University Press.

Hounshell, D.A. (1984) *From the American System to Mass Production 1800–1932*, Baltimore, MD: The Johns Hopkins University Press.

Jevons, W.S. (1865) *The Coal Question*, London: MacMillan and Co.

Jevons, W.S. (1871) *The Theory of Political Economy*, London: Macmillan and Co.

Jorgenson, D. (1982) Energy Prices and Productivity Growth, *Scandinavian Journal of Economics*, pp. 25–39.

Lloyd-George, David. (1924) *Coal and Power*, London: Hodder and Stoughton.

Maddison, A. (1987) Growth and Slowdown in Advanced Capitalist Countries: Techniques of Quantitative Assessment, *Journal of Economic Literature*, 25, pp. 649–698.

Marshall, Alfred. (1890) *Principles of Economics*, London: Macmilllan.

Marx, K. (1867) *Das Kapital*, Hamburg: Verlag von Otto Meisner.

McCloskey, D.N. (2010) *The Economic History of Britain, 1700-Present*, 1, 87–103, Cambridge: Cambridge University Press.

Mitchell, B.E. (1988) *British Historical Statistics*, Cambridge: Cambridge University Press.

Moykr, J. (2010) *The Enlightened Economy: An Economic History of Britain, 1700–1850*, New Haven, CT: Yale University Press.

New York Times, February 15, 1929.

North, D.C. and B.R. Weingast. (1989) Constitutions and Commitment: The Evolution of Institutional Governing Public Choice in Seventeenth-Century England, *The Journal of Economic History*, 49(4), pp. 803–833.

Nye, D.E. (1990) *Electrifying America: Social Meanings of a New Technology*, Cambridge, MA: MIT Press.

Owen, Robert. (1820) *Report to the County of Lanark*. May 1, 1820.

Robbins, L. (1932) *An Essay on the Nature and Significance of Economic Science*, London: Macmillan.

Rosenberg, N. (1972) *Technology and American Economic Growth*, Armonk: M.E. Sharpe.
Scott, H. et al. (1933) *Introduction to Technocracy*, New York: The John Day Company.
Self, H. and E.M. Watson. (1952) *Electricity Supply in Great Britain*, London: Allen and Unwin.
Senate Congressional Record. (1945) *Senate Congressional Record*, Washington, DC: GPO.
Senior, N. (1854) *Political Economy*, London: Griffins.
Simonde de Sismondi, J.C.L. (1819) *Nouveaux Principes d'Économie Politique*, Paris: Calmann-Lévy.
Smith, Adam. (1990[1776]) *An Inquiry into the Nature and Causes of the Wealth of Nations*, Chicago, IL: Encyclopaedia Britannica.
Sonenblum, S. (1990) Electrification and Productivity Growth in Manufacturing. In Schurr, S.H. et al. (Eds.), *Electricity in the American Economy: Agent of Technological Progress*, Westport, CT: Greenwood Press.
Stearns, P. (1993) *The Industrial Revolution in World History*, Boulder, CO: Westview Press.
U.S. Department of Commerce. (1975) *Historical Statistics of the United States*, Washington, DC: Government Printing Office.
Veblen, Thorstein. (1921) *The Engineers and the Price System*, New York: B.W. Huebsch.
Wicksteed, P. (1894) An Essay: The Coordination of the Laws of Distribution, *The Economic Journal*, 4(14), June, pp. 303–313.
Williams, E. (1944) *Capitalism and Slavery*, London: A. Deutsch.
Wrigley, E.A. (2010) *Energy and the English Industrial Revolution*, Cambridge: Cambridge University Press.

4

INCOME DISTRIBUTION

Introduction

By income distribution, it should be understood the divvying up of income, or alternatively, wealth. It sounds simple, to the point of being trivial. After all, the real problem ought to be creating income and wealth, not divvying it up. As shown in the last chapter, income and wealth creation is far from an exact science. And not surprising, income distribution, being based on income and wealth creation, is also far from an exact science. In fact, as shall be shown, income distribution ranked, ranks and will continue to rank as the most contentious, not to mention rancorous issues in all of political economy, bar none. It has been at the root of a whole counter-culture in 19th-century classical and neoclassical economics known as radical economics. Furthermore, it continues to this day to rank as one of the leading questions of the era. As we shall see, not all is settled – in fact, far from it. To better understand the stakes, we begin this chapter by defining the "problem of income distribution."

What You Will Learn in This Chapter

In this chapter, you will:

- Learn about the fundamental problem of income distribution in an industrial society.
- Learn about the role technology plays in income distribution.
- Learn about the early attempts to formalize income distribution in an industrial setting.

DOI: 10.4324/9781003527060-4

- Learn about the rise of the radical school of thought.
- Learn about the classical response to radical thought
- Learn why the neoclassical approach to income distribution violates the laws of physics.

By the End of this Chapter, You Should Understand

- How and why a poor understanding of the underlying physics of material processes has plagued the literature on income distribution from its very inception and continues to plague it.
- The reasons for the failure of the economics profession to understand what is increasingly a contentious issue.
- Why, barring a paradigm change in fundamentals, mainstream distribution theory will continue to fall short of its ultimate objective, namely explaining and predicting the distribution of income/wealth.

The Problem of Income Distribution

The problem of distribution can be formalized in terms of the following four axioms, which are based, in large part, on the energy-organization approach to modeling material processes presented in Chapter 2.

- Axiom 1: Material processes involve two inputs, broadly defined energy and broadly defined organization.
- Axiom 2: Broadly defined energy is physically productive, while broadly defined organization is organizationally productive (not physically productive).
- Axiom 3: Ownership of broadly defined energy and broadly defined organization can be either (i) concentrated or (ii) distributed.
- Axiom 4: Human labor is not a source of energy per se, but rather, is the product of nutrition-based energy (carbohydrates, proteins transformed into work).

Axioms 1–3, together, frame the problem of distribution. If Axioms 1–2 hold, and ownership is concentrated (unique) (Axiom 3), then the problem of distribution is non-existent to speak of as in this case, the unique owner (of both energy and organization) in question appropriates all of the output. If, on the other hand, ownership is distributed (diffuse), then the contemporary problem of distribution arises. By diffuse, it should be understood that the owners of the inputs are not one in the same (i.e. workers, investors, entrepreneurs, owners of energy). When ownership of the means of production is diffuse, the question then becomes how will the resulting output (wealth) be apportioned among the various owners (energy, tools, supervision)? This constitutes the fundamental problem of income distribution.

It therefore stands to reason that the "problem of distribution" is a distinctly "industrial" problem, owing to the distributed (diffuse) nature of the ownership of the means of production (factor inputs). And, not surprisingly, the problem of distribution appeared early on in the history of industrialization.

As shown in the previous chapter, it lay at the core of the "radical" or unorthodox thought. Robert Owen, Jean-Charles-Léonard Simonde de Sismondi, Thomas Malthus and Karl Marx all held that low wages in times of technological change and record productivity growth was the leading cause of economic stagnation and unemployment, preventing Great Britain from making the transition to the new, higher level of wealth. The problem, however, consisted of defining the "just" or "appropriate" wage. Just what part (viz. fraction) of the product was labor entitled to? What part was capital entitled to? What were the owners of coal, the sin quo non of the industrial revolution, entitled to? Surprisingly, no one had hard answers to these questions!

This chapter chronicles the debates over income distribution from Adam Smith to the present. It will be argued that the debate over income distribution was mis-specified from the very start. More specifically, as was shown in the previous chapter, classical production theory should, at best, be seen as a form of propaganda, used to sway both guilds and governments to the advantages of the new technology that was the steam engine (specialization). Its implications for income distribution had not been worked out formally, and in fact, it could be argued that it, per se, had never crossed the minds of its framers. We begin with a short description of the problem of income distribution in the pre-industrial era.

Historical Record

As it turns out, the historical record, while extensive, provides very little variation in terms of wealth distribution, owing in large measure, to the preponderance of communal ownership. From the Paleolithic era to the industrial era, ownership of the means of production (energy and organization) was largely communal (e.g. family, extended family, clan, tribe). Only with the advent of private property (land and tools/equipment) did the problem of distribution as we know it today arise.

Paleolithic Era

The Paleolithic era extends from 200,000 BCE to 10,000 BCE, and is characterized by animate energy-based, stone tool-using material processes. Animate energy in the form of human muscular force was used in combination with stone tools and animate supervision (the sources of energy and organization were one in the same) to add/create value (material wealth). Wealth was, as such, limited, and consisted of prepared foodstuffs, woven blankets and baskets, primitive housing, and stone tools/weapons. Muscular energy was provided by nutrition (calories), which derived from a combination of meat, fruits and vegetables. As such, food and food availability constituted the relevant energy constraint. Years of abundance were material wealth increasing, and vice versa – not unlike in the animal world.

The problem of distribution as such was inexistent, as the energy and organization in question were held in common (concentrated ownership), as was the resulting material wealth. On another level, the energy input (solar radiation) was free. However, the ability to capture this form of energy was determined by control over land – mostly by tribes and clans. The resulting wealth was then apportioned among members of the various tribes according to cultural traditions and customs (hierarchical). Examples of this include North American indigenous peoples, as well as most indigenous peoples throughout the world.

Neolithic Era

The Neolithic era witnessed the first energy shock in the form of (i) the development of large-scale agriculture, and (ii) the introduction of metallurgy. Energy consumption increased manifold (solar radiation and fossil fuel-based fire), resulting in a manifold increase in output and thus, wealth. More to the point, second-law efficiency increased in the sense that solar radiation, up until then largely wasted (i.e. was unexploited), now powered large-scale, organized photosynthesis. The result was a manifold increase in carbohydrates, proteins, and other foodstuffs. Nutrition improved markedly as did life expectancy. No longer subject to the vagaries of nature, human health and welfare improved as a result. Population increased. Whereas previous agglomerations (tribes) rarely exceeded 200 people, now population in the city-states of Mesopotamia numbered in the tens of thousands.

The increase in animate (read: muscular) energy, in combination with better tools (higher η), led to a manifold increase in the level of material wealth, as evidenced by the explosion in private consumption, public goods and culture. Underlying this was Neolithic ability to harness a greater amount of solar energy. The Roman Empire (circa 50 CE) stands as the ultimate tribute to the material wealth potential that this new Neolithic energy source afforded.

The problem of distribution, as had been the case in the Paleolithic era, was non-existent in the Neolithic, owing in large measure to the fact that ownership of broadly defined energy (i.e. land) and broadly defined organization was highly concentrated. Take, for example, the Roman landowner (senator), whose wealth derived from the solar radiation captured by the physical expanse (shield) that was his land area. As slaves are not a source of energy, but rather, a material process in and of themselves (transforming food energy into work), and landowner owned the tools, it stands to reason that the problem of distribution did not arise.

It is important to note that throughout history, slaves were not a source of energy, but rather, like all other higher-order primates, an "organic machine," transforming carbohydrates into heat, motion, and work (force).[1] Slaves were paid a subsistence wage, one that, as the word implies, allowed them to subsist, and continue transforming carbohydrates into the muscular energy/force required to perform the assigned tasks.

Modern Era

The modern era, which begins in the late 18th century and extends to the present, is characterized by two important energy shocks namely steam power (19th century) and electric power (20th century). In both cases, the energy constraint was lifted and pushed back considerably. As the data in the previous chapter show, per capita energy consumption increased over the past two centuries, as did per capita wealth. With the advent of high-throughput, continuous-flow mass production (19th and 20th centuries) came a new institution in so far as the ownership of the means of production were concerned, namely private property, specifically, of private energy (coal, hydraulics, wood, oil) and capital (tools/equipment).

Never before in the history of mankind had a new energy technology required as important an initial investment in related equipment (tools). Efficient steam engines (Watts steam engines) came in large sizes, which prompted the development of (i) the manufacturing joint-stock company and (ii) the emergence of large-scale factories, literally built around the source of power, the steam engine, itself powered by hydrocarbons (coal/charcoal/coke/wood). Labor, until then a source of motive power and organization, was reduced to an organizational factor input in the form of machine operatives (i.e. lower-level supervisors). For example, in the textile industry, hand weavers became machine operatives, overseeing the workings of steam-powered high-throughput textile looms.

In this period, the ultimate source of motive power was hydrocarbons, the calories of which provided, via the process of pyrolysis, the heat that powered the various simple and complex tools that constituted the machinery and equipment of the industrial age. Workers, investors and entrepreneurs provided the necessary organization, the result of which was an unprecedented level of material wealth. For example, according to 19th-century industrialist and social reformer Robert Owen, Great Britain's productive powers had been increased 100-fold.

> *It is well known that, during the last half century in particular, Great Britain, beyond any other nation, has progressively increased its powers of production, by a rapid advancement in scientific improvements and arrangements, introduced, more or less, into all the departments of productive industry throughout the empire. The amount of this new productive power cannot, for want of proper data, be accurately estimated; but your Reporter has ascertained from facts which none will dispute, that its increase has been enormous; that, compared with the manual labour of the whole population of Great Britain and Ireland, it is, at least, as forty to one, and may be easily made as 100 to one; and that this increase may be extended to other countries; that it is already sufficient to saturate the world with wealth and that the power of creating wealth may be made to advance perpetually in an accelerating ratio.*
>
> (*Owen 1820, 34*)

David Ricardo shared Owen's enthusiasm, as evidenced by the following passage from *The Principles of Political Economy and Taxation,* extolling the virtues of machinery.

> *Value, then, essentially differs from riches, for value depends not on abundance, but on the difficulty or facility of production. The labour of a million of men in manufactures will always produce the same value, but will not always produce the same riches, By the invention of machinery, by improvements in skill, by a better division of labour, or by the discovery of new markets, where more advantageous exchanges may be made, a million of men may produce double, or treble the amount of riches, of necessities, conveniences and amusements, in one state of society that they could produce in another, but they will not, on that account, add anything to value.*
>
> *(Ricardo 1817, 182)*

19th-Century Economic Thought: The Case of Income Distribution

To begin with, it is important to understand the context in which 19th-century political economists found themselves. Like manna from heaven, the steam engine contributed to massive increases (via greater material process speeds) in actual and potential wealth. Never before in human history had man's capacity to generate wealth been so great. Never before had he been confronted with what was a practical and an ethical problem, namely how to divvy up the spoils. How would this new-found wealth be apportioned among the owners of broadly defined energy and broadly defined organization? Who would benefit from the new technology, and by how much? Would the owners of organization (tools and supervision) be entitled to the spoils from the energy locked up in England's abundant coal?

The answers to these questions were far from obvious. Not helping matters was the absence of a well-developed understanding/theory of production. As shown in the previous chapter, classical production theory was woefully inadequate, being little more than a poor attempt at describing and illustrating material processes. As Smith and Ricardo argued, output was assumed to be an increasing function of labor input. According to the classical thought, capital affected output via its effect on labor productivity. Steam power, or "fire power" as Smith referred to it, was altogether absent from the discussion. According to the classical labor theory of value, goods and services traded at prices that reflect their relative labor content.

The Wage Fund Theory

It is important to remember that in the early stages of industrialization (1776–1848) the problem of income distribution was, for all intents and purposes, not an issue, at least in so far as the classical political economists were concerned. They did, however, provide a stylized account of income distribution in the form of the Wage

Fund. The idea of the Wage Fund is based on two things, namely an agricultural model of production (temporal) and on a primitive transactions technology. By definition, the Wage Fund is the amount of money that the firm has on hand to remunerate its variable factor, which in this case is labor. It consists largely of its sales revenue from the previous period. It is usually regarded as being fixed, for obvious reasons.

Underlying the Wage Fund is a primitive form of exchange, one based on metallic or paper money. Pure bank credit (i.e. bills of exchange) is altogether absent from the discussion. As such, firms are assumed to be constrained by existing cash balances. This, of course, is no longer the case today as, theoretically, there are no limits to a firm's variable costs as firms have access to bank credit. In other words, previous earnings have little to no bearing on the current or future level of the firm's variable costs – on what the firm can pay out in wages.

It stands to reason that because it is fixed, any increase in wages will result in a decrease in the demand for labor, and vice-versa. Ergo, an increase in the cost-of-living which forces nominal wages up, will decrease the level of employment. In the words of J. R. McCulloch:

> *Wages depend at any particular moment on the magnitude of the Fund or Capital appropriated to the payment of wages compared with the number of laborers... Laborers are everywhere the divisor, capital the dividend.*

One could argue that the Wage Fund is evidence of the theoretical shortcomings and/or archaic understanding of the workings of the emerging new industrial economy. Most firms in early 19th-century Great Britain financed (see the Finance Stage in the Macroeconomic Exchange Sequence–see Chapter 2) their variable costs using trade credit (bills of exchange) issued by the newly formed banks (commercial, industrial, merchant). Only a minority financed variable costs from profits. In short, the Wage Fund theory was little more than a stylized projection of consumption, saving and investment in an agrarian world, to that of industry.

As has been shown, classical political economy is devoid of a "theory" of income distribution per se. The Wage Fund is, at best, a description of the financing of production and exchange and the consequences for labor demand. This raises the question of why? Why was there little mention of the factors affecting the distribution of income? Why did the likes of Adam Smith and David Ricardo not elaborate a comprehensive theory of income distribution? The reason, we contend, has to do with objectives. Classical political economy was about moving the public discourse away from trade-based, government-coordinated mercantilism, over to industrial, market-based capitalism. In many ways, it was a form of propaganda, intended to focus on the sub-optimal role of government in wealth creation. Other than references to the fact that machinery would increase wages, it contained little by way of a well-articulated, scientific theory of income distribution.

As it turns out, this lack of rigor, or put differently, this lack of completeness would come back to haunt classical political economy, threatening the very foundations of British and indeed Western society, namely private property. More specifically, in the mid-19th century, the rise of radical political economy, based largely on classical production theory, threatened the very foundation of Europe. The events of the 1830s and 1840s would change the discourse forever, not to mention, come close to bringing nascent capitalism to an end.

Utopian and Radical Income Distribution Theory

By the mid-1800s, the UK economy had experienced numerous downturns, some more severe than others, and with each downturn nominal and real wages decreased, bringing with them the standard of living. The optimism that had characterized the early 19th century soon turned to pessimism.[2] Something had gone terribly wrong. The industrial revolution had failed the workers of England. Similarly, the steam engine, the purported source of unbounded wealth in the eyes of many, had failed to generate the promised wealth.

The result was growing unrest, especially in large industrial centers, where living conditions had deteriorated markedly. With the unrest came new ideas, new theories. What had gone wrong? Why was England unable to take full advantage of its new technology? Paradise promised, paradise lost.

It was against this background (growing poverty amidst unbounded potential wealth) that a number of new political, intellectual and social movements were born. Among these were the Utopian movement, socialism and communism.

Robert Owen and the Birth of Utopian Political Economy

Sensing that something fundamental was intrinsically wrong with laisser-faire (i.e. the market mechanism), New Lanark (Scotland) Mills owner and manager Robert Owen proposed a new form of economic organization, one based not on markets, but on a form of planning, one that would lay the intellectual foundations for the Chartist movement, and ultimately, Utopian political economy in general.[3]

The failure of markets, Owen explained, owed to their inherent inability to create the wherewithal (i.e. money income) to purchase the new, higher level of output. Potential output chronically exceeded actual output. However, not only did higher productivity not lead to greater wealth, but it also led to falling wages and a general worsening of living conditions, a paradox according to Owen. Consider, for example, the following passages taken from *The Report to the County of Lanark*, where he extols the effects of "scientific improvements and arrangements."

> *It is well known that, during the last half century in particular, Great Britain, beyond any other nation, has progressively increased its powers of production, by*

a rapid advancement in scientific improvements and arrangements, introduced, more or less, into all the departments of productive industry throughout the empire.

The amount of this new productive power cannot, for want of proper data, be very accurately estimated; but your Reporter has ascertained from facts which none will dispute, that its increase has been enormous;—that, compared with the manual labour of the whole population of Great Britain and Ireland, it is, at least, as forty to one, and may be easily made as 100 to one; and that this increase may be extended to other countries; that it is already sufficient to saturate the world with wealth and that the power of creating wealth may be made to advance perpetually in an accelerating ratio.

(Owen 1820, 246)

It must be admitted that scientific or artificial aid to man increases his productive powers, his natural wants remaining the same; and in proportion as his productive powers increase he becomes less dependent on his physical strength and on the many contingencies connected with it.... That the direct effect of every addition to scientific, or mechanical and chemical power is to increase wealth; and it is found, accordingly, that the immediate cause of the present want of employment from the working classes is an excess of production of all kinds of wealth, by which, under the existing arrangements of commerce, all the markets of the world are overstocked.

(Owen 1820, 247)

Getting in the way of increased wealth and welfare, however, was the problem of insufficient income, or simply underincome. Society's capacity to produce had increased; income and thus expenditure had not.

Having taken this view of the subject, your Reporter was induced to conclude that the want of beneficial employment for the working classes, and the consequent public distress, were owing to the rapid increase of the new productive power, for the advantageous application of which, society had neglected to make the proper arrangements. Could these arrangements be formed, he entertained the most confident expectation that productive employment might again be found for all who required it; and that the national distress, of which all now so loudly complain, might be gradually converted into a much higher degree of prosperity than was attainable prior to the extraordinary accession lately made to the productive powers of society. Cheered by such a prospect, your Reporter directed his attention to the consideration of the possibility of devising arrangements by means of which the whole population might participate in the benefits derivable from the increase of scientific productive power; and has the satisfaction to state to the meeting, that he has strong grounds to believe that such arrangements are practicable.

> *His opinion on this important part of the subject is founded on the following considerations:*
>
> *First.—It must be admitted that scientific or artificial aid to man increases his productive powers, his natural wants remaining the same; and in proportion as his productive powers increase he becomes less dependent on his physical strength and on the many contingencies connected with it.*
>
> *Second.—That the direct effect of every addition to scientific or mechanical and chemical power is to increase wealth; and it is found, accordingly, that the immediate cause of the present want of employment for the working classes is an excess of production of all kinds of wealth, by which, under the existing arrangements of commerce, all the markets of the world are overstocked.*
>
> *Third.—That, could markets be found, an incalculable addition might yet be made to the wealth of society, as is most evident from the number of persons who seek employment, and the far greater number who, from ignorance, are inefficiently employed, but still more from the means we possess of increasing, to an unlimited extent, our scientific powers of production.*
>
> *Fourth.—That the deficiency of employment for the working classes cannot proceed from a want of wealth or capital, or of the means of greatly adding to that which now exists, but from some defect in the mode of distributing this extraordinary addition of new capital throughout society, or, to speak commercially, from the want of a market, or means of exchange, co-extensive with the means of production.*
>
> (Owen 1820, 248)

To address these problems, Owen, in his report to the *Committee of Gentlemen of the Upper Ward of Lanarkshire*, proposed a "radical" reorganization of distribution, and, to a lesser extent, production, both for agriculture and industry, the main feature of which was a new standard of value. Specifically, money as a unit of account would be replaced by human labor, which he defined as the "combined manual and mental powers of men called into action."

> *Already, however, the average physical power of men as well as of horses (equally varied in individuals), has been calculated for scientific purposes, and both now serve to measure inanimate powers.*
>
> *One the same principle the average of human labour or power may be ascertained; and as it forms the essence of all wealth, its value in every article of produce may also be ascertained, and its exchangeable value with all other goods fixed accordingly; the whole to be permanent for a given period.*
>
> (Owen 1820, 251)

A similar argument can also be found in the writings of Swiss political economist Jean-Charles Léonard Simonde de Sismondi and Thomas Malthus. Firms, they argued, minimize costs, which, in turn, minimizes aggregate, overall monetary income, resulting ultimately in deficient demand and macroeconomic stagnation.

> *Le vendeur n'a pas par lui-même aucun moyen détendre son débit, qui ne réagisse sur ses confrères; il leur dispute une quantité donnée de revenu qui doit remplacer son capital; et plus, il réussit en garder pour lui même; moins il en laisse pour les autres. Il ne dépend nullement du producteur d'augmenter les revenus de la société, ou du marché qu'il sert de manière qu'ils puissent s'échanger contre une augmentation de produits .... Entre commerçants, on regarde comme une mauvaise action de se séduire réciproquement ses pratiques; mais la concurrence que chacun exerce contre tous ne présente point une idée aussi précise; et un commerçant n'a pas moins d'empressement d'étendre son débit aux dépens de ses confrères qu'à le proportionner à l'accroissement des richesses, lorsque celles-ci lui offrent l'échange d'un nouveau revenu. Jusqu'ici dans l'un ou l'autre cas, la découverte d'un procédé nouveau a causé une grande perte nationale, une grande diminution de revenu, et par conséquent, la consommation.*
>
> *(Simonde de Sismondi 1819, 345)*

Translated, Simonde pointed to the fact that firm cannot, individually, increase money income (debit), framing the problem as one of coordination and of a coordination failure. Thomas Malthus, in *Principles of Political Economy Considered with a View to their Practical Applications*, also made reference to this problem, viewing it as a problem of distribution, distribution in this case referring to the creation of income, and not the functional distribution of income.

> *We have seen that the powers of production, to whatever extent they may exist, are not alone sufficient to secure the creation of a proportionate degree of wealth. Something else seems necessary in order to call these powers fully in action. This is effectual and unchecked demand for all that is produced. And what appears to contribute most to the attainment of this object, is, such a distribution of produce, and such an adaptation of this produce to the wants of those who are to consume it, as constantly to increase the exchangeable value of the whole mass... In the same manner, the greatest stimulus to the continued production of commodities, taken altogether, is an increase in the exchangeable value of the whole mass, before a greater value of capital has been employed upon them.*
>
> *(Malthus 1827, 361)*

Could businessmen, acting individually, bring such a situation about? Could they, playing what essentially amount to Nash wage and price strategies, resolve the underlying coordination failure? As it turns out, Owen placed little confidence in the for-profit economy, which led him, in characteristic *Owenesque* fashion, to propose an alternative, in this case, to reorganize British society around the concept of communes—in short, a return to the organization of yore, of early civilizations, from Sumer to Assyria, to Egypt, to Rome, to pre-industrial Great Britain. Economic activity would be coordinated (hierarchically), for the good of all.

While instrumental in the rise of radical/utopian political economy, these writers did little to advance the formal study of income distribution, owing in large measure to the absence of a well-developed theory of production. While most advocated higher wages, few concrete reasons were provided. Which is not surprising given their modus vivendi, namely raising overall money income and aggregate demand.

Robert Owen's work is a case in point. As mentioned, he advocated replacing money with labor certificates (in an amount equal to the value of potential output). These certificates would then be distributed to the workers, who he argued were the source of all value.[4] Clearly, this was opportunistic on his part. Specifically, maintaining that labor was source of all value legitimized his theory of distribution. There can be little doubt that he was well aware of the fact that the steam engine had transformed labor from a source of energy, supervision and information, into a simple supervisory (read: organizational) input, one that was no longer physically productive.

Karl Marx

The first 19th-century political economist to formally delve into the "theory" of income distribution was Karl Marx. Like Owen, he was drawn to political economy by the shortcomings of industrialization, notably by the business cycle and the poverty, misery and hardship that resulted. In short, Great Britain had failed to make the transition to the new, higher growth path, defined by the widespread use of the steam engine. In the place of unlimited wealth for all was abject poverty and suffering, especially in the industrialized North. Paradise had been lost.

Unlike Owen, Marx was more forthcoming. The business cycle and the resulting misery and suffering were, in his eyes, the result of class conflict. In his view, the owners of capital were playing a game with workers, one aimed at increasing profits–what he referred to as "surplus value." The end result was the business cycle, unemployment, lower wages and widespread poverty. Whereas Owen had suggested that labor was the source of all value, Marx made it the cornerstone of his work. The Marxian "labor theory of value" holds that labor is the source of all value. In other words, labor is the only physically productive factor input, and consequently, is legally and morally entitled to all of the spoils (wealth). Anything less amounts to theft.

In many regards, Marx's work was a radicalized version of Owen's earlier writings. Whereas Owen attributed the business cycle to the lack of private incentives to raise wages, Marx went further and invoked a motive, namely the presence of class-based conflict, or a form of class economic warfare. Out of this came a radicalized form of utopian thought, namely Marxism.

That Marx chose to radicalize what was a decades-old debate over the business cycle is a subject matter for further research. What is important, in so far as the question of income distribution is concerned, is the fact that the labor theory of value stands as the first formal theory of income distribution in an industrial setting. What is also important to note is the fact that the labor theory of value is based, in large measure, on classical production theory as developed by Adam Smith and David Ricardo. Recall that according to classical production theory, only labor is physically productive. Capital or machinery alters labor productivity without being physically productive itself.

In hindsight, the lack of intellectual (read: scientific) rigor on the part of the early classical political economists had come back to haunt them – with a vengeance. Marx's *Labor Theory of Value* was unassailable from the Classical point of view as it was based on the writings of Smith and Ricardo.

The Radicalization of Income Distribution Theory

The Labor Theory of Value altered forever the debate over income distribution, moving it away from science, over to rhetoric. The fallout was immediate. Classical political economy found itself in a bind. Not only had Marx become a threat, but also he was right, at least according to classical production theory according to which capital was not physically productive.

The radicalization of the question of income distribution was unfortunate from a scientific point of view. Labor was elevated to production royalty, a fact that belied its new, more subordinate role in industrial production processes. No longer a source of power/force, it had been reduced to a supervisory role managing machines, a fact that explains the increasing use of women and children in factories. Human and animal brawn had been rendered redundant for the most part.

This raises the question: was this contradiction not apparent to Marx? Was he not perspicacious enough to realize that far from being the source of all value, labor's role in production had been marginalized – or trivialized – by the introduction of machinery?[5] There is evidence that would indicate that he was aware of these changes. Consider, for example, the following passage taken from Chapter 15 of *Das Kapital*, which describes the role of tools and power in "heterogeneous" and "serial manufactures," the former being a reference to the domestic system, and the latter, to the newly instituted factory system.

> *Mathematicians and mechanicians, and in this they are followed by a few English economists, call a tool a simple machine, and a machine a complex tool. They see no essential difference between them, and even give the name of machine to the simple mechanical powers, the lever, the inclined plane, the screw, the wedge, etc. As a matter of fact, every machine is a combination of those simple powers, no matter how they may be disguised. From the economic standpoint, this explanation is worth nothing, because the historical element is wanting.*

> *Another explanation of the difference between tool and machine is that, in the case of the tool, man is the motive power, while the motive power of a machine is something different from man, is, for instance, an animal, water, wind. and so on. According to this, a plough drawn by oxen, which is a contrivance common to the most different epochs, would be a machine, while Claussens circular loom, which, worked by a single labourer, weaves 96,000 picks per minute, would be a mere tool. Nay, this very loom. though a tool when worked by hand, would, if worked by steam, be a machine. And, since the application of animal power is one of mans earliest inventions, production by machinery would have preceded production by handicrafts. When in 1735, John Wyalt brought out his spinning machine and began the industrial revolution of the eighteenth century, not a word did he say about an ass driving it instead of a man. and yet this part fell to the ass. He described it as a machine to spin without fingers.*
>
> *All fully developed machinery consists of three essentially different parts, the motor mechanism, the transmitting mechanism, and finally the tool of working machine. The motor mechanism is that which puts the whole in motion. It either generates its own motive power, like the steam engine, the caloric engine, the electro-magnetic machine, etc., or it receives its impulse from some already existing natural force, like the water-wheel from a head of water, the windmill from wind, etc. The transmitting mechanism, composed of flywheels, shafting, cogwheels, pulleys, straps, ropes, bands, pinions, and gearing of the most varied kinds, regulates the motion, changes its form where necessary, as, for instance, from linear to circular, and divides and distributes it among the working machines. These two parts of the whole mechanism are there solely for putting the working machines in motion, by means of which motion the subject of labour is seized upon and modified as desired. The tool or working machine is that part of machinery with which the industrial revolution of the eighteenth century started. And, to this day it constantly serves as such a starting point whenever a handicraft, or a manufacture, is turned into industry carried on by machinery.*
>
> *(Marx 1867, 181)*

What is notable and noteworthy about this excerpt and indeed all of Chapter 15 is the breadth of his understanding and appreciation of classical mechanics and thermodynamics, and to put it mildly, his understanding was astounding, especially when considered in light of the labor theory of value. Clearly, he understood the basic physics of steam engine-based mechanization. Just why he would turn a blind eye to the implications for distribution is a question for future research.

According to the underlying physics of mechanization as described in Chapters 2 and 3, neither labor nor capital is physically productive. Both are organizational inputs, one defining and the other overseeing inanimate-energy-powered material processes. There can be little doubt that Marx was aware of this, but chose to ignore it for what, we suspect, were strategic reasons. After all, the problem of underincome and the resulting business cycle is what brought him to political economy. It was imperative to increase wage income in the hope of making a successful transition to the new, higher equilibrium growth path – in short, of realizing the potential unleashed by the steam engine.

The Classical Response: Neoclassical Production Theory

Radical utopian thought constituted the first serious challenge to the newly established order. It provided a convenient and convincing diagnosis of the problems that ailed Great Britain, as well as a well-articulated solution in the form of communism/socialism – in short, a call for the return of a hierarchical communication and coordination strategies (CCS). Labor felt empowered, as did workers in general.

Classical political economy was, by far, its greatest victim. After all, its theoretical foundation, the *Labor Theory of Value,* was based on the writings of Adam Smith and David Ricardo. As capital was not physically productive, then how could profits (roughly 30 percent of national income) be justified, theoretically and legally? In short, classical political economy found itself at a crossroads of sorts.

How did it respond? How did it defend itself? How did it set out to defend the established order? To answer this question, we shall chronicle the work of British classical political economist, William Stanley Jevons whose writings personify the many challenges political economy in general, and classical political economy in particular faced in the mid-19th century. Among these was the perennial problem of understanding the new technology that was the steam engine.

In 1865, two years prior to the publication of Marx's *Das Kapital*, he published *The Coal Question; An Inquiry Concerning the Progress of the Nation and the Probable Exhaustion of Our Coal Mines*, where he examined the role of coal in an industrial economy, and more importantly, the state of coal reserves in Great Britain. Consider, for example, the following passage taken from the *Introduction* in which he extolled the virtues of coal, going as far as attributing England's new-found wealth to its abundant supply.

> *Day by Day it becomes more evident that the Coal we happily possess in excellent quality and abundance is the mainspring of modern material civilization. As the source of fire, it is the source at once of mechanical motion and of chemical change. Accordingly, it is the chief agent in almost every improvement or discovery in the arts which the present age brings forth.... And as the source especially of steam and iron, coal is all powerful. This age has been called the Iron Age, and it is true that iron is the material of most great novelties. By its strength, endurance, and wide range of qualities, this metal is fitted to the fulcrum and lever of great works, while steam is the motive power. But coal alone can command in sufficient abundance either the iron or the steam; and coal, therefore, commands this age—the Age of Coal.*

> *Coal in truth stands not beside, but entirely above all other commodities, it is the material source of the energy of the country—the universal aid—the factor in everything we do. With coal almost any feat is possible or easy; without it we are thrown back into the laborious poverty of early times. With such facts familiarly before us, it can be no matter of surprise that year by year we make larger draughts upon a material of such myriad qualities—of such miraculous powers. But it is at the same time impossible that men of foresight should not turn to compare with some anxiety the masses yearly drawn with the quantities known or supposed to lies within these islands.*
>
> *(Jevons 1865, 2)*

With the benefit of hindsight, it is clear that by this time, Jevons was moving toward a more physics-based formalization of production, one based on energy and one that was consistent with both classical mechanics and the emergent field of thermodynamics. In his words, coal is "the mainstream of modern material civilization." He explains "it is the material source of the energy of the country, the factor in everything we do." From a scientific point of view, his account of material processes in the industrial era rivals those of Charles Babbage and Karl Marx. Clearly, he understood the prominent role played by energy in general, and coal in particular in wealth creation.

Again, with the benefit of hindsight, it could be argued that classical political economists were moving in the "right" direction, incorporating energy/coal into their analysis. In short, there was hope that a more scientific theory of wealth was around the corner. As it turned out, however, any and all such hope was short lived. With the publication of *Das Kapital* in 1867, classical political economy (and the established order) found itself under siege. How did it respond? Quite simply, by decreeing *ex-cathedra* that capital was physically productive. With one stroke of the fountain pen/quill, profits were legitimized. The owners of capital were not thieves, appropriating 30 percent of wealth. Tools and equipment were de facto physically productive. Take, for example, William Stanley Jevons, who in Chapter VII of *The Theory of Political Economy*, entitled "The Theory of Capital," declared:

> *In considering the nature and principles of capital, we enter a distinct branch of our subject. There is no close or necessary connection between the employment of capital and the process of exchange. Both by the use of capital and by exchange we are enables vastly to increase the sum of utility which we enjoy; but it is conceivable that we might have the advantage of capital without those of exchange. An isolated man like Alexander Selkirk might feel the benefit of a stock of provisions, tools and other means of facilitating industry, although cut off from traffic, with other men. Economics, then, is not solely the science of exchange or value; it is also the science of capitalization.*
>
> *(Jevons 1871, 225)*

To Jevons, capital is output increasing as evidenced by the following passage in which he compares spinning in Cashmere and in Great Britain.

> *In the first place, labour will be required to till the land which is to bear the cotton plants, and probably two years at least will elapse between the time when the ground is first broken and the time when the cotton reaches the mills. A cotton mill, again, must be a very strong and durable structure, and must contain machinery of a very costly character, which can only repay its owner by a long course of use. We might spin and weave cotton goods as in former times, or as it is done in Cashmere with a small use of capital; but then the labour required would be enormously greater in proportion to the produce. It is far more economical in the end to spend a vast amount of labor and capital in building a substantial mill and filling it with the best machinery, which will then go on working with unimpaired efficiency for thirty years or more. This means that in addition to the labour spent in superintending the machines at the moment when goods are produced, a great quantity of labour has been spent from one to thirty years in advance. This expenditure is repaid by an annuity of profit extending over those thirty years.*
>
> *(Jevons 1871, 228)*

Capital, according to him, increases overall output, in return for which its owners receive an annuity of profit. Alfred Marshall echoed Jevons' views. In *Principles of Economics*, published in 1890, he referred to capital as aiding labor – labor being the key or prime productive factor. Income distribution, he argued, was determined by the principle of marginal service—in short, marginal product.

> *The net aggregate of all commodities produced is itself the true source from which flow the demand prices for all these commodities and therefore for the agents of production used in making them. Or, to put the same thing in another way, this national dividend is at once the aggregate net product of, and the sole source of payment for, all the agents of production within the country: it is divided up into earnings of labour; interest of capital; and lastly, the producers surplus, or rent, of land and of other differential advantages for production.*
>
> *(Marshall 1890, 445)*

What's more, capital and labor were now seen as complementary in so far as productivity was concerned, standing in stark contrast to Marx who saw them as substitutes, capital displacing labor, and, more importantly, contributing to its plight (lower real wages, unemployment, etcetera).

> *In studying the influence which increased efficiency and increased earnings in one trade exerts on the condition of others, we may start from the general fact*

> *that, other things being equal, the larger the supply of any agent of production, the farther will it have to push its way into uses for which it is not specially fitted; the lower will be the demand price with which it will have to be contented in those uses in which its employment is on the verge or margin of not being found profitable; and in so far as competition equalizes the price which it get in all uses, this price will be its prices for all uses. The extra production resulting from the increase in that agent of production will go to swell the national dividend, and other agents of production will benefit thereby: but that agent itself will have to submit to a lower rate of pay.*
>
> *(Marshall 1890, 446)*

The implications for income distribution were self-evident. The radical view was, according to Jevons and Marshall, flawed. Like labor, capital was physically productive. Profits were not a form of theft but rather legitimate payment for services (physically productive services) rendered. And so was born, neoclassical production theory and its corollary, neoclassical distribution theory. Ironically, at a juncture in the history of material processes (i.e. production technology) where neither labor nor capital was physically productive, mainstream political economy put both at the center of their analysis. This ranks as one of the greatest ironies of the history of economic thought.

What is important to note here is the fact that by the end of the 19th century, political economy in general and the question of income distribution, were less about science per se, and more about legitimizing the established order. Socialism and communism posed a real and present danger to "capitalism." Nowhere is this more obvious than in the writings of American neoclassical theorist, John Bates Clark, who in a series of writings in the 1870s, formally outlined neoclassical distribution theory.

Motivating and indeed fueling his interest in the question of income distribution were a number of factors, not the least of which was the ongoing threat of communism and socialism. In a series of articles published in *New Englander* and *Yale Review*, Bates addressed what he saw as the real and present danger that was socialism and communism (Clark 1878, 1879). These include: "How to Deal with Communism," 1878, *New Englander and Yale Review* and "The Nature and Progress of True Socialism 1879," *New Englander and Yale Review*. Consider the following passage, which captures the essence of Clark's ideological bias.

> *It is necessary to dissociate from the meaning of the term socialism, as I intend to use it, the signification of lawlessness and violence which is apt to be attached to it. I do not mean by socialism a certain rampant political thing which calls itself by that name, and whose menacing attitude at present is uniting well-meaning men against it. The socialism which destroys property and arms itself to resist law is rather socialistic Jacobinism, or communism of the Parisian type. Political socialism, even when moderate and law-abiding, has no right to the*

exclusive use of the generic term; it is a part only of a very general movement, the signs of which are to be seen in other things than communistic newspapers and Lehr-und Wehr-Vereins. I mean by socialism, not a doctrine, but a practical movement, tending not to abolish the right of property, but to vest the ownership of it in social organizations, rather than in individuals. The organizations may be private corporations, village-communities, cities, states, or nations, provided only that working men be represented in them. The object of the movement is to secure a distribution of wealth founded on justice, instead of one determined by the actual results of the struggle of competition. Wherever numbers of men unite in the owning of capital, as they already do in the performing of labor, and determine the division of the proceeds by some appeal to a principle of justice, rather than by a general scramble, we have a form of socialism.

(Clark 1879, 556)

Clark's *magnum opus*, *The Distribution of Wealth: A Theory of Wages, Interest and Profits*, published in 1899, formalized the neoclassical theory of factor income distribution, one based on marginalist principles, notably, the marginal product of capital and labor. In Chapter 17 entitled "How the Efficiency of Final Increments of Producers Wealth is Tested," he outlined the marginalist approach.

We are now ready to apply to the fixing of wages and interest the principle which we may term that of analytical valuation. Everywhere does the market have a marvelous power of resolving concrete things into their elements, and of measuring separately the efficiency of each element. Consumers wealth and producers wealth alike it treats in this way. If we are to understand its procedure in fixing prices, we must seek out and identify not, as a rule, certain whole commodities, but certain elements in commodities; and so, if we are to understand the adjusting of interest, we must find in instruments of production, in a like way, certain elements that are in a strategic position and control the gains of all capital.

The earning power of capital is fixed by the productivity of the final increment of it; and this final increment of capital does not, as a rule, consist of instruments of production in their entirety. It consists of elements in such instruments. Just as we add to our consumers wealth by procuring for personal use better articles than those which we have been using, so we add to our producers wealth by procuring better instruments of production. When, for a machine that has worn itself out, we substitute one that is by a single point more efficient and more costly, we are adding a final increment to our capital. It is final increments of capital, as such, the productive power of which fixes the rate of interest. As entrepreneurs, we must pay for any capital that we hire what a final increment of it will produce; and that is what we and others can get, as a net addition to our products, by making our buildings by one degree larger or more substantial, our machines by one degree more rapid or more nearly automatic, our engines

> *or our water-wheels by one degree more powerful, our raw materials by one grade finer, etc.*
>
> (*Clark 1899, 220*)

What is particularly ironic about Clark's writings is the numerous references to science. In a paper published in 1889 in the *American Economic Review*, entitled "Possibility of a Scientific Law of Wages," he described his work as scientific, wanting like his fellow neoclassical theorists to (i) avoid normative analysis and (ii) deflect any and all criticism. Ironically, no references to classical mechanics, thermodynamics or the physics of material processes were provided.

As we shall see, the economic, social and political turmoil of the 19th century had failed to resolve the debate over income distribution, as evidenced by its recurrence in the early 20th century. With the coming of the electric power age (second industrial revolution) came renewed debate over the question of income distribution.

CAPSULE: THE PARETO DISTRIBUTION AND ITS ORIGINS IN 19TH-CENTURY INCOME DISTRIBUTION

While it is typically the case that a field like economics will draw from that tributary fields like statistics, there are cases in which the reverse is true, namely that economics has contributed to statistics. This is the case of Pareto distribution, named in honor of French political economist, Wilfred (Vilfredo) Pareto. The distribution is shown in Figure, where the cumulative density function is shown for five quintiles. What he wanted to show is that the top 20 percent of the population held 80 percent of the wealth – this case the land. This is analogous to the current literature on the one percent, where it is alleged that the top one percent of the population earns 9–11 percent of income, and the top ten percent earns 50 percent.[6]

The Second Industrial Revolution

Roughly two decades after Alfred Marshall's *Principles of Economics*, the commercial development of the electro-magnetic motor renewed early 19th-century optimism. More flexible in its uses, and more amenable to energy-deepening (i.e. higher throughput rates-speeds) than steam power, electric power held out the promise of unlimited riches. According to Chicago power magnate, Martin J. Insull:

> As a consequence of the added power which invention has contributed to industry, the forty-five and one-half million workers in the United States have

achieved an output equivalent to from six-hundred million to nine-hundred million workers before the power era.

Matthew Sloan, president of the New York Edison Company, described the effects of electric power on productivity in the following terms:

> *Mr. Sloan compared this age which he termed the new industrial revolution with the industrial revolution of the eighteenth century, when the steamboat and the locomotive came into use. As steam brought in the machine era, electricity, he said, has brought in the era of mass production which has so greatly affected the general economic situation and social conditions. Thus, electricity, he said, is responsible for our present production. With all its attendant circumstances of lowered unit costs, lowered prices, increased wages, intensified merchandising, wider markets, higher standard of living. Electricity-motivating machinery has multiplied the working power of the nation many times, he said, and the generating stations of the country now have a capacity of 35,000,000 horsepower, or the ability to do the work of about 35,000,000 men. In 1900, the generating capacity was only 3,000,000 horsepower.*
>
> *(New York Times, February 15, 1929)*

To some, like MIT-trained economist Stuart Chase, the problem was no longer scarcity, but, rather, abundance, specifically, the problem of achieving the new-found potential.

> *Two men are lost on a great desert. One has a full bottle of water, the other a bottle quarter filled. As they move wearily onward, hoping for an oasis, justice demands that they pool the water supply and share it equally. Failure to do so will undoubtedly result in a fight. Now let us transport these two men to a row boat on Lake Superior. Again, they are lost, and again, one has a full bottle of water, and one a bottle quarter full. The full bottle man refuses to share and a battle ensues. Maniacs! There is plenty of fresh water over the side of the boat. The Desert is the Economy of Scarcity; the lake, the Economy of Abundance. The choice between sharing or fighting is chronic in the former, pointless in the latter. Today, throughout western civilization, men in boats are fighting, or preparing to fight, for fresh water. They do not know they are in boats; they think they are still on camels. The lake, as we have seen in the previous chapter, is not limitless, but nobody need go thirsty.*
>
> (Chase 1934, *51)*

As had been the case in the early 19th century, the introduction of a new technology raised the problem of income distribution for what were essentially the same reasons, namely the problem of under income and the problem of underconsumption – in short, the failure to produce at the new capacity. A number of political economists, from Thorstein Veblen to Rexford Tugwell to Paul Douglas, maintained that the failings of the US economy in the 1920s, and ultimately, in the 1930s owed to the failure of real wages (nominal and real) to keep pace with productivity. Electrification, like the steam engine a century earlier, had increased the US economy's overall ability to generate wealth; however, the failure of income and expenditure to increase commensurately had stymied growth, resulting in recession, and ultimately in a full-blown depression.

Wanting to extend what had until then been a theoretical debate into the statistical realm, University of Chicago economist Paul Douglas, a student of John B. Clark, took it upon himself to estimate the two key neoclassical output elasticities (labor and capital), the values of which formed the cornerstone of modern distribution theory. This was an epic development, moving the problem of distribution away from ideology over to the realm of science.

Combining his efforts with those of Smith College mathematician Charles Cobb, Douglas presented his results in a 1928 *American Economic Review* article entitled "A Theory of Production," in which the first-ever numerical estimates of the marginal product of labor and capital are presented. Accordingly, labor was entitled to 75 percent of overall wealth with the remainder (25 percent) going to capital (see Table 4.1). For the first time, the profession appeared to be on solid scientific grounds, regardless of what one thought of the resulting estimates. In fact, in his 1947 American Economic Association Presidential Address, Paul Douglas intimated that he and his associates had discovered the "laws of production" (see Douglas, 1948). For the first time, ideology and heuristics appeared to be absent, although not entirely.

While Cobb and Douglas' estimates of the output elasticities for labor and capital (0.75 and 0.25, respectively) have become the rule of thumb in contemporary micro and macroeconomics, more recent results have cast considerable doubt on their findings. In a review of Cobb and Douglas's results, Iain Fraser using their data re-estimated these two output elasticities using more-sophisticated time-series methods. Table 4.2 reports the results, where we see that the labor output elasticity

TABLE 4.1 Cobb and Douglas's 1928 Estimates of Output Elasticities

Among function with these properties, let us make a definite choice and examine the consequence of that choice, reserving the right to make other choices if we wish. Let us choose the function.

$P' = bL^{k}C^{1-k}$

And find such numerical values of b and k that P' will "best" approximate P in the sense of the Theory of Least Squares. Then relative to the indices and the period, we have the norm.

$P' = 1.01L^{3/4}C^{1/4}$

Source: Cobb and Douglas (1928).

TABLE 4.2 Iain Fraser's Least Squares Estimation Cobb-Douglas Functional Form with Technical Change

Parameters	*USA*	*Mass*	*NSW*	*VIC*	*NZ*
α	2.84	1.983	−0.15	−2.175	−2.0513
	(1.362)	(0.29)	(0.5)	(1.536)	(1.13)
δ	0.048	0.0267	−0.0013	−0.0248	−0.013
	(0.021)	(0.0028)	(0.0055)	(0.0176)	(0.005)
β1	0.913	0.631	0.697	0.799	0.403
	(0.134)	(0.064)	(0.113)	(0.335)	(0.119)
β2	−0.54	−0.111	0.343	0.697	0.904
	(0.34)	(0.045)	(0.106)	(0.369)	(0.139)
R^2	0.9622	0.9882	0.993	0.9297	0.9262
F	195.929	1001.848	1188.83	110.14	84.649
F-Test	4.37	50.52	0.11	1.97	3.63

Fraser (2002), 51.

(β1) 0.913–0.403, and his capital output elasticity (β2), from −0.54 to 0.904. In short, only the New South Wales data and to a lesser extent the New Zealand data yield results that appear to be consistent with those of Cobb and Douglas.

The Rise of Scientific Production Theory: The Technocracy Movement

As it turned out, the Great Depression was a catharsis of sorts for the science of production and distribution, the main impetus coming from the engineering profession in the form of the Technocracy movement. Inspired by the writings of Thorstein Veblen, and founded by Columbia University engineering professors Walter Rautenstrauch and Howard Scott, *The Continental Committee on Technocracy* (Technocracy) rejected outright mainstream economics, especially mainstream production theory, on scientific grounds, pointing to its many contradictions (with the pure and applied sciences) and omissions. In its place, they proposed a theory of material processes based on energy. Energy, they argued, was the only physically productive factor input, one that had been ignominiously ignored by mainstream economics. Consider, for example, the following excerpt from Howard Scott's *Introduction to Technocracy*, published in 1933:

> *A century ago these United States had a population of approximately 12,000,000 whereas to-day our census figures a total of 122,000,000—a tenfold increase in the century. One hundred years ago, in these United States, we consumed less than 75 trillion British thermal units of extraneous energy per annum, whereas in 1929, we consumed approximately 27,000 trillion British thermal units an increase of 353 fold in the century. Our energy consumption now*

> *exceeds 150,000 kilogram calories per capita per day; whereas in the year 1800 our consumption of extraneous energy was not less than 1600 or more than 2000 kilogram calories per day.... The United States of our forefathers, with 12,000,000 inhabitants, performed the necessary work in almost entire dependence upon the human engine, which, as its chief means of energy conversion, was aided and abetted only by domestic animals and a few water wheels. The United States to-day has over one billion installed horsepower. In 1929, these engines of energy conversion, though operated only to partial capacity, nevertheless had an output that represented approximately 50 percent of the total work of the world. When one realizes that the technologist had succeeded to such an extent that he is to-day capable of building and operating engines of energy conversion that have nine million times the output capacity of the average single human being working an eight hour day, one begins to understand the acceleration, beginning with man as the chief engineer of energy conversion and culminating with these huge extensions of his original one-tenth of a horse power. Then add the fact that of this 9,000,000 fold acceleration, 8,766,000 has occurred since the year 1900.*
>
> *(Scott et al 1933, 42)*

Stuart Chase, in *The Economics of Abundance*, referred to the new-found abundance in terms of the following propositions.

1. *A condition where the bulk of the economic work is performed not by men, but by inanimate energy, drawn from coal, oil and water power. Such a condition was reached in the United States toward the close of the 19th century, circa 1880.*
2. *A point at which living standards per capita reach an average which is, at least potentially, twice as high as ever obtained under scarcity conditions. Reached circa 1900.*
3. *A point at which the curve of invention, following, as it does, a geometric increase, becomes the dominant factor in economic life precisely as the Nile was the dominating factor in the economic life of Egypt. Circa 1870.*
4. *A point at which the scientific method supersedes the use and want of the craftsman in the production of most material goods. Circa 1900.*
5. *A point where output per man hour becomes so great that total productive labor must thereafter decline, even as output grows. A point at which labor ceases to be a measure of output as it always has been in preceding ages. Circa 1920.*
6. *A point at which overproduction carries a more serious threat to the financial system than shortage. Circa 1880.*
7. *A point at which specialization has destroyed all practicable local self-sufficiency and made economic insecurity for all classes latent, growing, and*

ultimately intolerable, given no change in financial methods. Circa 1900, with the closing of the American frontier.

8 *A point at which consumption becomes a greater problem than production. Circa, 1920. Our economy, says F.L. Ackerman, is so set up that it produces goods at a higher rate that it produces income with which to purchase them.*

9 *A point at which the industrial plant is, substantially, constructed, requiring relatively smaller outlays for capital goods in the future, and where pecuniary savings are not only unnecessary in their old volume, but seriously embarrassing, Circa, 1925.*

10 *A point where, due to the presence of the technical arts, costs, prices, interest rates, debts, begin a descent with zero as their objective. Circa 1920. (Chase 1934, 12)*

Technocracy rejected neoclassical distribution theory on scientific grounds, arguing that neither capital nor labor was physically productive. In their view, energy and energy alone was physically productive. However, capital and labor had appropriated and continued to appropriate the rents (energy rents = value of output less the cost of energy) from energy use. Such were the theoretical underpinnings of Technocratic distribution theory. The ramifications were straightforward, at least in the eyes of Walter Rautenstrauch, Howard Scott, R. Marion Hubbard, and others. Energy rents ought to be distributed equitably across individuals and classes.

On this basis our distribution then becomes foolproof and incredibly simple. We keep our records of the physical costs of production in terms of the amount of extraneous energy degraded. We set industrial production arbitrarily at a rate equal to the saturation of the physical capacity of our public to consume. We distribute purchasing power in the form of energy certificates to the public, the amount issued to each being equivalent to his pro rata share of the energy-cost of the consumer goods and services to be produced during the balanced-load period for which the certificates are issued. These certificates bear the identification of the person to whom issued and are nonnegotiable. They resemble a bank check in that they bear no face denomination, this being entered at the time of spending. They are surrendered upon the purchase of goods or services at any center of distribution and are permanently cancelled, becoming entries in a uniform accounting system. Being nonnegotiable, they cannot be lost, stolen, gambled, or given away because they are invalid in the hands of any person other than the one to whom issued. If lost, like a bank checkbook, new ones may be had for the asking. Neither can they be saved because they become void at the termination of the two year period for which they are issued. They can only be spent.

> *Contrary to Price System rules, the purchasing power of an individual is no longer based upon the fallacious premise that a man is being paid in proportion to the so-called value of his work (since it is a physical fact that what he receives is greatly in excess of his individual effort) but upon the equal pro rata division of the net energy degraded in the production of consumer goods and services. In this manner the income of an individual is in nowise dependent upon the nature of his work, and we are then left free to reduce the working hours of our population to as low a level as technological advancement will allow, without in any manner jeopardizing the national or individual income, and without the slightest unemployment problem or poverty.*
>
> *The period of work required of each individual, once the reconstruction following the transition from the old system to the new is complete, need be no longer than about 4 hours per day, 164 days per year, from the ages of 25 to 45. The income of each individual, however, will continue without interruption until death. Hence the insecurity of old age is abolished and both saving and insurance become unnecessary and impossible.*
>
> *Such a mechanism of distribution simply renders all forms of trade and commerce obsolete, and at the same time, because of the abolition of money, makes them impossible. The entire social mechanism then becomes one unit organization with as many branches as there are industrial and social functions to perform. This organization, the Technate, comprises all members of the population.*
>
> *(Scott et al 1933, 43)*

Interestingly, Scott alluded indirectly to the notion of "energy rent":

> *Contrary to Price System rules, the purchasing power of an individual is no longer based upon the fallacious premise that a man is being paid in proportion to the so-called value of his work (since it is a physical fact that what he receives is greatly in excess of his individual effort) but upon the equal pro rata division of the net energy degraded (i.e. energy rents) in the production of consumer goods and services.*

Technocracy should as such be seen as the culmination of over two centuries of work on material processes in general, and a century of progress in the field of thermodynamics, the science of heat. More specifically, it should be seen as the logical continuation of the 19th-century insights of Charles Babbage, Karl Marx and William Stanley Jevons. It was science at the service of economics, material wealth seen through the prism of universal scientific principles.

Unfortunately, but not surprisingly, it was unceremoniously dismissed as a form of quackery by the profession, not unlike the fate that had befallen Robert Owen a century earlier. Take, for example, University of Chicago economics professor Aaron Director's (Milton Friedman's father-in-law) *The Economics of*

Technocracy, published in 1933, which rebutted its many elements. To begin, he summarized Technocracy in six points:

> 1 *The* importance of energy*: "Through the expenditure of energy we convert all raw materials into products that we consume and through it operate all the equipment that we use." This, of course, has always been familiar to us, except that it was stated in terms of work, and not of energy. The great merit of the latter term is the possibility of dragging in the Law of Conservation of Energy and this marrying physics to the social mechanism.*
> 2 *Energy can be measured, and the unit of measurement is always the same, while the dollar varies from time to time.*
> 3 *The chief distinction between our society and that of all previous societies is the much greater amount of energy which can be generated. This has always been recognized by the designation of our civilization as the machine era.*
> 4 *With every increase in the amount of mechanical energy the need for labor decreases.*
> 5 *The present depression marks the end of an era, since the increase in mechanical energy has at last become so great that, regardless of what happens, the need for human labor will rapidly decline.*
> 6 *Does it follow, therefore, that the price system must break down, and that only the engineers can run a mechanical civilization.*
>
> (Director 1933, 8)

He then proceeded to re-examine each one of these from a neoclassical point of view. In keeping with the 19th-century tradition of equating energy with machinery, he spoke in terms of "technical progress," and not of energy deepening. This was then followed by a Ricardian-inspired analysis of the effects of "technical progress" on costs, wages and prices. Competition, he argues, is a sufficient condition for full employment.

> *On the other hand, the technocrats imply that a more scientific utilization of existing equipment would result in a much larger product. It is only necessary to insist that the number of engineers in industry far outweigh the number of economists, and if these engineers are to run industry in the future, they should be competent to point out methods of improving efficiency. It is not enough to hide behind a barrage of words. It should be patent to the most critical observer that the one thing which the individual enterprise under competitive conditions does strive for is to reduce its cost, regardless of the consequences on employment.*
>
> *(Director 1933, 16)*

Having concluded that "technical progress was not incompatible with full employment," he proceeded, in Chapter VII, to debunk the view of the Great Depression as resulting from energy-based technological change. This, metaphorically speaking, is where the gloves came off. First, he, in the tradition of Jean-Baptiste Say and David Ricardo, ruled out underincome, *ex cathedra*. Output, he argued, is identically equal to income, whether in the form of money (i.e. money income) or in kind.

> *If there were no commercial banking system, the national income would be distributed for consumption goods and the production of additional equipment in accordance with the desires of the community. The output of industry is equal to the income of the laborers employed in it and of the property owners whose capital is invested in it. Clearly, if entrepreneurs borrowed funds directly from the income receivers, they could not continue to produce capital equipment in excess of the amount which income receivers were willing to save.*
>
> *(Director 1933, 21)*

In short, according to Aaron Director, Technocracy offered nothing new, and, more importantly, was riddled with the most elementary of oversights and errors. Energy was nothing new, and, as such, presented no particular challenge to mainstream political economy. Technological progress, in this case, electric drive, increased, in a commensurate fashion, income, wages and profits. The causes of the Great Depression, he argued, lie elsewhere, notably in "the war, the resulting debts, and tariffs" without being more specific.

The economic profession's response to Technocracy, in combination with John Maynard Keynes' *The General Theory of Employment, Interest and Money*, combined to spell the death knell for what in hindsight was a truly scientific approach to material processes and income distribution, one that was light years ahead of its time.

A Hypothetical Scientific Theory of Distribution

Thus far, we have seen that none of the existing theories of distribution, from the classical to that of Marx, to the neoclassicals, is scientifically sound as each violates the laws of physics. This then begs the question, what would a scientific theory of income distribution look like? In this section, we outline the rudiments of just such a theory.

First, consider the legal aspects. The cornerstone of distribution theory from the start is the Western notion of property rights. Specifically, each agent has an inalienable right to his/her property. IN other words, if through my effort, I produce something of value, then I have a right to that something.

Second, according to classical mechanics, the only physically productive factor input is energy as it and only it is capable of work. This is an undeniable and inalienable fact.

Third, because conventionally defined labor and capital are both organizational factor inputs, not being sources of energy, it follows that neither is directly responsible for wealth. However, as organizational factor inputs are also energy-based, it follows that both are indirectly productive as they define the context or framework in which energy performs work.

This then points to three possible options, namely that either the owners of the energy used directly in production are entitled to all of the spoils-that is, are entitled to the product. This is analogous to the implications and/or predictions of neoclassical distribution theory.

The second possibility is that distribution be based on a comprehensive energy standard. That is, using any of a number of standards (i.e. calories, *kwhs*, joules, *btus*), distribution is based on each factor's energy input. For example, if machine operatives consume 700 calories in their shift, then they would be entitled to a fraction, 700 total calories worth, of the output.

The third possibility and the one that come closest to mimicking the current functional distribution of income is one in which the owners of broadly defined energy and broadly defined organization bargain over (viz. share) energy rents which are defined by the value-product of energy (i.e. the total value of output) net of the cost of producing the energy in question. We refer to this as the bargaining outcome. As in all bargaining situations, the outcome will depend, in large measure, on each factor's relative bargaining power. For example, the greater is labor's bargaining power vis-a-vis capital, the greater their share of these rents.

This theory was presented in *Energy Rents: A Scientific Theory of Income Distribution*, published in 2005, and thus will not be presented here. Suffice it to say that unlike the neoclassical approach, it is consistent with the laws of physics and is amenable to testing. Further, it provides a compelling explanation of the evolution of wages over the course of the past two centuries – in short, in the industrial era. The upshot is that most of what today constitutes wage and profit income is, in actual fact, an energy rent that was apportioned among the owners of non-physically productive organizational inputs.

The Bargaining Approach to Income Distribution

The 1920s and 1930s were marked by the growing realization that wages were lagging behind productivity, the latter increasing as the result of the introduction of the new, power-drive technology that was electric unit drive. This led to a number of changes, including the increased unionization of the work force. The National Industrial Recovery Act of 1933 and the National Labor Relations Act of 1935 both had clauses, which encouraged, via new labor-related statutory rights, collective bargaining as a means to close the gap. In the aftermath of WWII, many European countries, including the Nordic countries, Great Britain, France and Germany adopted a form of bargaining known as *tripartism* consisting of tripartite agreements, which were agreements entered by corporations, unions and governments.

In many regards, it was an admission of sorts that the unfettered labor market was flawed and in need of an alternative. Harvard University economics professor John Kenneth Galbraith referred to this development as countervailing power, the idea being that large unions had emerged in response to large corporations. Wages and working conditions would, as such, be determined by a bargaining process.

Income Distribution in the Productivity Slowdown Era (1980–Present)

As pointed out in Chapter 3, the massive productivity gains of the post-WWII period were divvied up between workers and investors in the form of higher wages and greater profits. As such the functional distribution of income in this period remained relatively constant with workers receiving roughly 65–70 percent and investors 30–35 percent.

The Productivity Slowdown however marked the beginning of a fundamental change as workers' share of national income declined monotonically, while investors' share increased. Among the purported causes were (i) increased factory automation, (ii) declining unionization and (iii) off-shoring. The 1980s and 1990s witnessed the increased use of computers and computer-based control systems. In short, worker-based supervision of material processes was being replaced by control systems that operated autonomously. The result is known as smart manufacturing, where most of the material processes were self-regulating. The second factor was declining unionization, a phenomenon that has its roots in post-productivity ideology. Many, including US President Ronald Reagan, pointed the finger of blame for the slowdown on unions, arguing that they were an impediment to innovation and thus, to long-term growth. Unionization, as measured by the percentage of manufacturing workers that were unionized, declined markedly in this period, reaching all-time lows in the 1990s.

The third factor was off-shoring as US and European companies seized the opportunity made possible by trade liberalization and the China's new foreign policy to invest massively in off-shore manufacturing, taking advantage of low wages. As a result, inequality increased throughout this period. Investors' share of income increased as did managerial salaries. For the most part, these developments were welcomed by governments wanting to restore growth rates to post-WWII levels. Lower wages and greater profits would portend to greater investment, greater innovation and ultimately, greater growth. In fact, many Western governments, wanting to accelerate the level of investment and innovation, lowered taxes on corporations and the wealthy, again all in the name of growth (i.e. trickle-down).

Theoretical Developments in the Productivity Slowdown Era

This period witnessed few theoretical developments in so far as income distribution was concerned. The neoclassical approach continued to dominate despite its many shortcomings, not the least of which was the fact that workers or labor in general were/was being eliminated in manufacturing, being replaced by smart manufacturing

Perhaps the most important development, however, was the publication in 2013 by French economist Thomas Piketty of his best-selling work entitled *Capital in the 21st Century*, which moved the debate over income distribution in the Productivity Slowdown era forward, showing that income of the top ten percent of income earners evolved steadily throughout the 20th century, falling in the post-WWII period, and increasing throughout the 1980s, 1990s and 2000s, highlighting the growing inequality in this period.

According to Piketty, this owed in large measure to two factors, namely slow growth and the rise of *supermanagers.* Using a growth model akin to that of Roy Harrod and Evsey Domar, he argued that when the rate of profit is greater than the rate of growth of the economy, the share of income paid to investors and thus the top ten percent of income earners, as a fraction of overall income, would increase. Exacerbating this trend, according to Piketty, was the emergence of *supermanagers*, managers who were paid 200–300 times the average wage in their companies, often totaling tens of millions of dollars. As pointed out above, these developments were sanctioned and in fact encouraged by most governments as a precondition of sorts for a return to the high growth rates of the post-WWII period. These findings became the basis for his policy prescriptions, which focus on taxation as a means of decreasing inequality.

In essence, the Piketty approach is a variant of neoclassical distribution theory, based in large measure on neoclassical production theory. That is, he assumes that labor and capital are physically productive. The upshot is that income inequality has increased owing to high rates of return to capital relative to the overall rate of growth of the economy. While he also focuses on the role of supermanagers, their exact role in wealth creation is not specified.

The Theory of Income Distribution: Timeline

TABLE 4.3 Income Distribution: Timeline Summary

Year	*Theoretical Development*
1776	The Wage Fund
1819	Robert Owen's Labor Certificates
1867	Marx's Labor Theory of Value
1872	Marginal Productivity of Capital
1894	Wicksteed's Neoclassical Theory of Income Distribution
1928	Charles Cobb and Paul Douglas' Estimates of Output Elasticities
1945	Bargaining Approaches to Income Distribution
2014	Thomas Piketty's Capital in the 21st Century

TABLE 4.4 Distribution Theory: Ideology or Science?

Principle/Hypothesis/Theory	*Ideology or Science*	*Justification*
Wage Fund	Ideology	NT
Surplus Value	Ideology	NT
Neoclassical Distribution Theory	Ideology	VLPW

Distribution Theory: Ideology or Science?

The state of knowledge in the field of income distribution is one best described by the adage, *if the foundation isn't solid, the whole structure will won't be.* In other words, because production theory is, for the most part, non-scientific, it stands to reason that distribution theory, specifically neoclassical distribution theory, cannot be anything but non-scientific. The idea that wages are based on/reflect the value of labor's marginal physical product in a world in which labor is not physically productive is preposterous. Ibid for capital.

This critique also applies to the Marxian surplus-value approach according to which labor is the source of all value. Clearly, radical distribution theory, best associated with the writings of Karl Marx, was and remains scientifically invalid. At the time of writing (i.e. 1867) of *Das Kapital*, labor had been reduced, for the most part, to a supervisory or operative role in machinery-dominated material processes.

In short, there is little one can salvage in distribution theory other than the lessons learned. Further, the only credible theory of income distribution would start with the affirmation that energy and energy alone is productive, making for a situation in which payments made to labor and capital would be apportioned from the earnings of energy – energy rents. As earnings would not be based on any metric (i.e. physical productivity), it stands to reason that bargaining power would figure prominently in such a theory.

Summary and Conclusion

As was shown in this chapter, the problem of income distribution has been and continues to be inextricably linked to the problem of modeling (and understanding) material processes (Chapter 2). Given both the history of, and current state of the latter, it should come as little surprise to find the problem of income distribution to be equally troublesome, especially in so far as its scientific underpinnings are concerned. Today, neoclassical distribution theory constitutes the accepted dogma, despite its many problems and challenges. Among these are:

1 Its apparent contradictions with classical mechanics, applied physics, and thermodynamics.
2 The fact that both capital and labor are not physically productive.
3 Its disregard for the central role played by energy in material processes.

4 The inability to deal adequately with increasing automation (i.e. the disappearance of labor from the equation).
5 Rationalizing the increasing managerial remuneration of the past four decades.

Discussion

1 Why was the problem of distribution virtually non-existent in the pre-industrial period?
2 The Neoclassical Approach to Income Distribution is based on a productivity standard. Explain what is meant by a "productivity standard."
3 The Labor Theory of Value equates relative values/prices to relative labor content. In your view, is this a good way to describe the process of price determination in 19th century, industrial Great Britain? Why? Explain.
4 What were the ideological and political ramifications of the Labor Theory of Value in the mid-19th century?
5 In your view, why has the theory of income distribution not evolved in the 20th century despite major advances in our understanding of material processes?
6 Does *Smart Manufacturing* and *Factory Automation* pose a threat to the neoclassical theory of income distribution? Why?
7 Why has CEO remuneration gone from 30X the average wage in the corporation to 300X over the past three decades? Explain.

Directions for Future Research

1 A scientific theory of income distribution that is consistent with the laws of physics.
2 A theory that is general enough to explain a worker-less (*aka* intelligent) production processes.
3 An empirically consistent model of manager remuneration.
4 An empirically consistent model of worker-machine operative remuneration.
5 An empirically consistent model of service-based labor-work.

Notes

1 As such, slaves were not and are not productive per se, but rather transformed and transform the calories from food consumption into work.
2 This had percolated to the literature of the day in titles such as *Paradise Found, Paradise Lost* by John Milton.
3 Chartism was a large working-class movement for political reform in Great Britain that erupted from 1838 to 1857 and was strongest in 1839, 1842 and 1848. It was fiercely opposed by government authorities who finally suppressed the movement. It took its name from the People's Charter of 1838 and was a national protest movement, with particular strongholds of support in Northern England, the East Midlands, the Staffordshire Potteries, the Black Country and the South Wales Valleys. Support for the movement was at its highest when petitions signed by millions of working people were presented to

the House of Commons. The strategy employed was to use the scale of support, which these petitions and the accompanying mass meetings demonstrated to put pressure on politicians to concede manhood suffrage. Chartism thus relied on constitutional methods to secure its aims, though some became involved in insurrectionary activities, notably in South Wales and in Yorkshire.

4 Hence, he was classical in his view of labor's role in industrial processes.

5 For example, if we abstract from breakage and control, workers were no longer needed as evidenced today by workerless plants.

6 The analogy stems from the fact that in an agrarian society, wealth is increasing in the net surplus from land (i.e. net of the subsistence wage). Hence, a skewed distribution of wealth is the equivalent to a skewed distribution of income.

References

Chase, S. (1934) *The Economy of Abundance*, New York: The John Day Company.

Clark, J.B. (1878) How to Deal with Communism, *The New Englander and Yale Review*, 37, pp. 533–542.

Clark, J.B. (1879) The Nature and Progress of True Socialism, *The New Englander and Yale Review*, 38, pp. 565–581.

Clark, J.B. (1899) *The Distribution of Wealth: A Theory of Wages, Interest and Profits*, New York: Macmillan.

Cobb, C. and P. Douglas. (1928) A Theory of Production, *American Economic Review*, 18(1), pp.139–165.

Director, A. (1933) *The Economics of Technology*, Chicago, IL: University of Chicago Press.

Douglas, P. (1948) The Laws of Production, *American Economic Review Papers and Proceedings*.

Fraser, I. (2002) The Cobb-Douglas Production Function: An Antipodean Defense, *Economic Journal,* 7(1), pp. 39–58.

Jevons, W.S. (1865) *The Coal Question*, London: MacMillan and Co.

Jevons, W.S. (1871) *The Theory of Political Economy*, London: Macmillan and Co.

Malthus, T. (1827) *Principles of Political Economy Considered with a View of Their Potential Application*, New York: Augustus M. Kelley.

Marshall, A. (1890) *Principles of Economics*, London: Macmilllan.

Marx, K. (1867) *Das Kapital*, Hamburg: Verlag von Otto Meisner.

New York Times, February 15, 1929.

Owen, R. (1820) Report to the County of Lanark.

Piketty, T. (2013) *Capital in the 21st Century*, Cambridge, MA: Harvard University Press.

Ricardo, D. (1817) *The Principles of Political Economy and Taxation*, New York: Everyman's Library, 1965.

Scott, H. et al. (1933) *Introduction to Technocracy*, New York: The John Day Company.

Simonde de Sismondi, J.C.L. (1819) *Nouveaux Principes d'Économie Politique*, Paris: Calmann-Lévy.

5
MACROECONOMICS

Introduction

The macroeconomic problem per se can best be defined in terms of the aggregate *Industrial Exchange Sequence* (IES) presented in Chapter 2. Specifically, aggregate, multistage, system-wide (in short, macroeconomic) equilibrium can be described as a state in which the sum of projected wealth (vision stage) is equal to the sum of trade credit (finance stage) is equal to the sum of GDP (the production stage) is equal to the sum of national income (variable factor input stage and the fixed factor input stage) is equal to aggregate, economy expenditure (the expenditure stage). In short, macroeconomic equilibrium requires the presence of four, pairwise sub-equilibria. If any of these fails to hold, the economy will no longer be in macroeconomic equilibrium.

For example, for a given level of projected wealth (vision stage), the amount of available credit may be insufficient, forcing firms to revise downward their projected levels of output. Or, for given and equal levels of projected aggregate wealth, credit and output, the resulting level of income may be insufficient, resulting in unsold goods and ultimately, a downwardly revised projected aggregate level of output. Lastly, consider the case in which for given and equal levels of aggregate projected wealth, credit, output and income, aggregate expenditure is insufficient, resulting once again in unsold goods and ultimately, in a reduction in the projected aggregate level of output.

The macroeconomic problem can as such be defined as the presence of one or more of these IES pairwise disequilibria. It can be either transitional or conjectural in nature. By transitional, it should be understood a disequilibrium that results from an output-increasing technology shock, and by conjectural, it should be understood all other macroeconomic disequilibria. For example, a technology

DOI: 10.4324/9781003527060-5

shock, by increasing potential output, would *ceteris paribus* result in transitional disequilibria as trade credit, national income and expenditure would be insufficient (e.g. underincome), thus preventing the economy from achieving a successful transition to the new, higher equilibrium level of GDP. As pointed out in Chapters 3 and 4, these were the very concerns of Adam Smith, Robert Owen, Jean-Charles-Léonard Simonde de Sismondi and Karl Marx, not to mention Paul Douglas and the Technocrats.

A conjectural macroeconomic disequilibrium describes cases in which any of the other components in the IES either increases or decreases. For example, suppose that the nation's trade credit decreases. This would result in a decrease in overall output, income and expenditure. Or expenditure may increase or decrease, with the purported decrease in investment expenditure in the 1930s being the most famous. The study of these disequilibria will constitute our definition of the field of macroeconomics.

This chapter examines macroeconomic disequilibria in two distinct time periods, namely the 19th century and the 20th century. The approach is similar to the previous chapters. To begin with, the various macroeconomic disequilibria that characterized the century are documented, which is followed by a description of the corresponding history of macroeconomic thought (i.e. hypotheses and theories). As was the case in Chapters 3 and 4, an attempt will be made to draw parallels between the events of the two centuries and the corresponding theorizing.

What You Will Learn in This Chapter

In this chapter, you will:

- Learn about the origins of the macroeconomic problem in pre-industrial Europe, owing in large measure to dearth of specie in France.
- Learn about the underlying transitional nature of macroeconomic disequilibria in the 19th and 20th centuries. The Great Depression is a case in point.
- Learn about the role of ideology in the study of macroeconomic disequilibria.
- Learn about the role of monetary institutions in both transitional and conjectural disequilibrium.
- Learn about the unsettled and unresolved nature of macroeconomics throughout the 19th and 20th centuries.
- Learn about the role institutions play in macroeconomic equilibria. Specifically about the centuries-old debate over the role of markets and government in resolving the business cycle.

By the End of this Chapter, You Should Understand

- How major technology shocks have been a key cause of macroeconomic disequilibria in the industrial era (1800–present).

- How the inability of private, market economies to make the transition to the new equilibrium growth path in response to technological change resulted in major downturns, including the Great Depression.
- How macroeconomic analysis, from Keynes on (1936), has focused on the production and expenditure stages of the Industrial Exchange Strategy as opposed to all six stage equilibria.
- How macroeconomics in general and the causes of macroeconomic fluctuations in particular are currently in a state of flux, not having a basis in.

Pre-industrial Macroeconomic Disequilibria

The macroeconomic problem as defined here subsumes the existence of trade, which, in turn, subsumes the existence of large-scale specialization and exchange. In other words, owing to its aggregate, systemic nature, it cannot arise in situations in which economic agents are self-sufficient. Put differently, it is by its very nature a trade-related problem, a medium-of-exchange-intermediated trade-related problem.

It therefore stands to reason that the absence of large-scale specialization and trade-based gains will preclude the very possibility of the macroeconomic problem. Only in countries where significant gains to trade (and specialization) exist and have been exploited will it arise.

In this section, the focus will be on two cases of pre-industrial macroeconomic disequilibria. The first is 18th-century France where it was believed that the supply of money was insufficient, resulting in under-production and under-consumption. The second is the 16th-century inflow of gold (specie) from the New World.

18th-Century France

As pointed out, large-scale specialization and exchange requires money (a medium of exchange), money to intermediate the various welfare-increasing trades. A dearth of money will, of course, have important consequences, specifically in terms of wealth and well-being. In the early 18th century, it was generally believed that the French economy was underperforming. In other words, welfare-increasing trades were not taking place owing to a dearth of money. The basic argument was simple. Were there more specie, there would be more trade, and with more trade would come higher government revenues.

In 1705, Scottish political economist John Law published a pamphlet entitled *Money and Trade Consider'd with a Proposal for Supplying the Nation with Money*. In it, he argued that money, or the lack thereof, was the chief impediment to exploiting a country's potential.[1] In short, he argued that countries had underperformed and continued to underperform, relative to their potential, owing to the lack of money (i.e. the finance stage in the IES). As shall be shown, this is a common theme running through centuries of macroeconomics.

Law was one of the first political economists to understand that money was a medium of exchange, a means to an end, and not an end in and of itself. While real wealth (via specialization and trade) depended on money, money was not a form of wealth per se. According to Law, it would be in the interest of an underperforming nation to somehow increase its supply of money, and in the process, increase wealth and well-being. At the time, trade credit was limited by the amount of precious metals a country had in its possession.

Cognizant that credit notes would have to be backed by real assets to ensure acceptance, but knowing that trade credit was not wealth per se, he devised a system whereby credit notes would be based on foreign assets, in this case, the consolidated value of the French government's trading companies in the Mississippi River valley (La compagnie du Mississippi). With the benefit of hindsight, Law had anticipated present-day fiat currency.

CAPSULE: THE HUGUENOT DIASPORA, DEPRESSED CONDITIONS IN FRANCE AND JOHN LAW

It could be argued that the Mississippi and South Sea Bubbles had their origin in one of the most defining events of the 17th century, namely the Revocation of the Edict of Nantes in 1685, which led, ultimately, to the exodus of hundreds of thousands of Huguenot refugees from France. As it turned out, most were from the upper echelons of French society. As they left, they liquidated their assets in return for specie, which was then transferred to host countries (England, the Netherlands, Switzerland and Germany).

This acted as a de facto drain on French specie and thus on the French money supply, resulting in a slowdown in economic activity. Add to this the loss of its most enterprising and industrious citizens, Louis XIV's France fell into depression.

It therefore was not surprising that he would be receptive to John Law's proposal for what was essentially a fiat currency, based on an unknown, but promising asset, namely the riches of the Mississippi.

That France was slow to recover from the loss of species raises the question of price adjustments, or price flexibility. Clearly, according to the quantity theory of money, prices should fall, thus increasing the real money supply. However, this appears to not have been the case in the late 17th/early 18th century, which would explain his openness to Law's ideas and schemes.

The idea pleased King Louis XIV at the time, for obvious reasons. Greater national wealth would mean greater government revenues, and greater royal expenditure. Law's plan seemed water tight, or so it was thought. The government could issue notes backed by the value of shares in the Mississippi company. As the demand increased, so too would the price. As a result, trade credit (read: money) would increase, as would overall economic activity.

However, for this scheme to be successful, the value of the underlying asset had to be stable and predictable. The inevitable, however, occurred. Louis XIV, in his grandiosity increased the supply by 100 percent, touching off a run as noteholders attempted to convert them into specie, at which point, the so-called bubble burst.

While history has been less than kind to John Law, the Banque Générale de France and the Mississippi Company, the fact remains that this experiment in central banking anticipated developments in the 19th and 20th centuries, notably the creation of the Bank of England and the Federal Reserve, and ultimately, the creation of fiat currencies.

In many ways, Law is to be considered the father of modern-day macroeconomic policy. He believed steadfastly that, owing to various circumstances, economies (Scotland and France) underperformed relative to their potential. As Controller General, he instituted many beneficial reforms (some of which had lasting effect, others of which were soon abolished). For example, he tried to break up large land-holdings to benefit the peasants; he abolished internal road and canal tolls; he encouraged the building of new roads, the starting of new industries (even importing artisans but mostly by offering low-interest loans), and the revival of overseas commerce – and indeed industry increased 60 percent in two years, and the number of French ships engaged in export went from 16 to 300.

16th-Century Europe

The previous case focused on a dearth of currency and its ramifications for wealth and well-being. Here, the opposite case is examined, namely one of specie abundance relative to the level of wealth (i.e. the level of trade activity). The story here begins with the Spanish conquest of Meso-America (Mexico, Peru, Columbia), and the influx of the plundered specie into Europe by way of Spain and Portugal. The result was there for everyone to see. The supply of money exceeded the demand for money, itself based on the existing level of trade activity, resulting in a "conjectural macroeconomic disequilibrium." As specie from the New World made its way into the Spanish and Portuguese economies, nominal prices began to rise, prompting an increase in foreign trade, specifically imports. Soon, prices throughout Europe began to rise, prompting a case of generalized price inflation.

Pre-industrial Macroeconomic Theory

Other than a handful of references to the relationship between gold (specie) and prices, this period was relatively uneventful. Among the most prominent were the aforementioned John Law, Jean Bodin and David Hume. The discussion, for the most part, centered around two questions, namely the effect of species on prices and, in the case of John Law, the role of government in the regulation of commerce. The former anticipated the well-known *Quantity Theory of Money*, while the latter, as pointed out, anticipated the current fiat currency system.

The crux of the matter can be understood in terms of a single basic question, namely does an increase in the medium of exchange (gold) lead to an increase real wealth, or does it simply increase prices? Writers in this period were divided on the issue. Jean Bodin and David Hume argued that it would simply result in higher prices, a result formalized in terms of the quantity theory of money according to which the supply of money times its velocity of circulation is equal to nominal GDP. Hence, when real GDP is equal to potential GDP (level of trade), then increases in the nominal money supply will result in an increase in prices, and hence the price level. It is important, however, to note that this is a steady-state, long-run result. That is, in the absence of any unrealized trades, increasing the level of species will have no effect whatsoever on output, but will only serve to increase nominal prices. Put otherwise, it will decrease the goods price of money.

The Early Quantity Theory of Money

In its modern form, the quantity theory builds upon the following definitional relationship.

$$MV = PY \tag{5.1}$$

where:

M is the total amount of money in circulation on average in an economy during the period, say a year.

V is the transactions velocity of money, that is the average frequency across all transactions with which a unit of money is spent. This reflects availability of financial institutions, economic variables, and choices made as to how fast people turn over their money.

P and Y are the price level associated with transactions for the economy during the period and the index of the real value of aggregate transactions, respectively.

As an example, it might represent currency plus deposits in checking and savings accounts held by the public, real output (which equals real expenditure in macroeconomic equilibrium) with the corresponding price level, and the nominal (money) value of output. In one empirical formulation, velocity was taken to be "the ratio of net national product in current prices to the money stock."

Thus far, the theory is not particularly controversial, as the equation of exchange is essentially an identity. A theory requires that assumptions be made about the causal relationships among the four variables in this one equation. There are debates about the extent to which each of these variables is dependent upon the others. Without further restrictions, the equation does not require that a change in the money supply would change the value of any or all of P, Y or V. For example, a ten percent increase in could be accompanied by a ten percent decrease in, leaving unchanged. The quantity theory postulates that the primary causal effect is an effect of M on P.

John Law

John Law, the 17th-century financier and political economists, held the opposite view, namely that an increase in the nation's money supply could increase its output. As he argued in his *magnum opus,* the *Money and Trade Consider'd with a Proposal for Supplying the Nation with Money*, the lack of money (exchange medium) acted as a constraint on trading and hence on output and income. Insufficient specie, as such, limited the level of exchange and thus, the level of overall wealth. Unlike quantity theorists Bodin and Hume, Law felt that at any given point in time, not all profitable trade opportunities had been exploited, owing to the absence of sufficient circulating medium. Thus, in his view, an increase in specie (money) would increase output and wealth.

And so was born a debate that would go on to characterize macroeconomics for centuries, namely could money be scarce to the point of limiting trade activities and the generation of wealth in general? Or, in the presence of unrealized output and trade, would prices fall sufficiently, increasing the real quantity of money, thus de facto solving the problem altogether. John Law argued the former, which of course has important policy implications. The quantity theorists (Hume in particular) dismissed this argument, pointing out that over the long run, prices will adjust either downward or upward, this ensuring the appropriate real quantity of money. In other words, Law's argument is a non-issue in the presence of perfectly flexible prices.

Ideology or Science?

To what extent was the quantity theory of money debate scientific? The answer is unequivocal: neither school (Bodin and Hume, Law) was scientific in its method. Both were essentially descriptive/impressionistic, outlining what they considered to be the problem of the day. Despite the lack of rigor, the predictions of each were born out in the data. For example, as pointed out, overall economic activity in France increased 60 percent under Law's rule as *Controller*. The question, however, is whether this owed to an increase in money, or to any of the many additional reforms he instigated. As for the quantity theory, it too was borne out by the generalized increase in prices observed throughout Europe in the 16th and 17th centuries in Europe.

This being said, the key issue, in so far as the quantity theory was concerned, was whether nominal prices would actually fall in economic slowdowns? Or would economic activity (read: trade) simply slow down as trading diminished – that is, quantities would adjust in lieu of prices. If so, then real money balances (M/P) would fail to increase, thus invalidating the quantity theory argument.

History of 19th-Century Macroeconomic Disequilibria

The 19th century marked the beginning of what could be referred to as the industrial-based macroeconomic "problem" per se. The source of the "problem" was the most celebrated technological development of all time, namely the steam engine. By tapping into the earth's reserve of carbon-stored solar radiation, the millennia-old energy constraint was lifted. As shown in Chapter 2, no longer would *Homo sapiens sapiens* be constrained by contemporaneous solar radiation (i.e. source of food), but now would be able to tap into the world's seemingly limitless reserves of fossil fuels.

Potential output soared. As pointed out in Chapters 2 and 3, estimates in the order of 40 to 1, to 100 to 1 abounded. The world would never be the same again, or so it was believed. To most, utopia was within reach. The problem, however, was getting there, and once there, staying there.

In a simple, autarkic setting, the effects of output-increasing technological change will be instantaneously and immediately. The result is greater output and wealth. Such, however, is generally not the case in a modern, exchange-based, monetary economy. According to the IES (Chapter 2) an increase in potential output is but one of a series of necessary conditions to ensure a successful transition to the new, higher equilibrium growth path. More to the point, the visions, finance, income and expenditure stages have to adjust to the new, higher productivity and potential GDP. Bank credit, money income and expenditure have to increase commensurately. In short, firms have to have the incentives/will to exploit the new technology to its fullest.

As shall be shown, while the steam engine contributed to raising potential GDP in the UK, the other macroeconomic aggregates, notably credit, money income and expenditure failed to rise in step. Which resulted in a conundrum. If the adoption of the new power technology that was the Watt steam engine (especially the reciprocating, dual-action engine) was conditional on firms' expectations of future sales (the expenditure stage), then there arises the distinct possibility that the transition to the new higher output could be aborted.

Adam Smith was the first to raise this issue. His now infamous adage in the *Wealth of Nations* that "specialization is determined by the extent of the market," is a direct reference to it. In other words, the extent of the market (or future sales) would affect the firm's decision to specialize (i.e., adopt the technology). Without an increase in the extent of the market, specialization, or the adoption of the steam engine, would simply not occur. This being said, other factors will also enter the firm's decision, notably the desire to reduce costs. For example, replacing costly labor with a steam engine could theoretically be a profit-increasing proposition.

The 1820 Recession

The first sign that the UK was experiencing the effects of a "transitional macroeconomic disequilibrium" came in 1820 by way of Robert Owen, the owner of New Lanark Mills in New Lanark, Scotland. In his report to the County of Lanark, he pointed out:

> *Having taken this view of the subject, your Reporter was induced to conclude that the want of beneficial employment for the working classes, and the consequent*

public distress, were owing to the rapid increase of the new productive power, for the advantageous application of which, society had neglected to make the proper arrangements. Could these arrangements be formed, he entertained the most confident expectation that productive employment might again be found for all who required it; and that the national distress, of which all now so loudly complain, might be gradually converted into a much higher degree of prosperity than was attainable prior to the extraordinary accession lately made to the productive powers of society. Cheered by such a prospect, your Reporter directed his attention to the consideration of the possibility of devising arrangements by means of which the whole population might participate in the benefits derivable from the increase of scientific productive power; and has the satisfaction to state to the meeting, that he has strong grounds to believe that such arrangements are practicable.

His opinion on this important part of the subject is founded on the following considerations:

First.—It must be admitted that scientific or artificial aid to man increases his productive powers, his natural wants remaining the same; and in proportion as his productive powers increase he becomes less dependent on his physical strength and on the many contingencies connected with it.

Second.—That the direct effect of every addition to scientific or mechanical and chemical power is to increase wealth; and it is found, accordingly, that the immediate cause of the present want of employment for the working classes is an excess of production of all kinds of wealth, by which, under the existing arrangements of commerce, all the markets of the world are overstocked.

Third.—That, could markets be found, an incalculable addition might yet be made to the wealth of society, as is most evident from the number of persons who seek employment, and the far greater number who, from ignorance, are inefficiently employed, but still more from the means we possess of increasing, to an unlimited extent, our scientific powers of production.

Fourth.—That the deficiency of employment for the working classes cannot proceed from a want of wealth or capital, or of the means of greatly adding to that which now exists, but from some defect in the mode of distributing this extraordinary addition of new capital throughout society, or, to speak commercially, from the want of a market, or means of exchange, co-extensive with the means of production.

(Owen 1820, 248)

In short, scientific power had increased the UK's ability to create wealth. Wages and thus wage income, however, had not increased commensurately, resulting in stagnation and unemployment. Owen was not alone. Others felt that something was amiss, that the transition to the new, higher equilibrium growth path had stalled. Among these were Swiss political economist, Jean-Charles-Léonard Simonde de

Sismondi, who spent considerable time in Great Britain in the early 19th century studying the process of industrialization, and British political economist, Thomas Malthus. In *Principes d'économie politique*, published in 1819, Simonde described the problem of insufficient income or "underincome," and, more importantly, alluded to the underlying game-theoretical (strategic) aspects, specifically, the absence of private incentives on the part of firms to increase income in response to a process-based technology shock.

> *Le vendeur n'a pas par lui-même aucun moyen d'étendre son débit, qui ne réagisse sur ses confrères; il leur dispute une quantité donnée de revenu qui doit remplacer son capital; et plus, il réussit à en garder pour lui même; moins il en laisse pour les autres. Il ne dépend nullement du producteur d'augmenter les revenus de la société, ou du marché qu'il sert de manière qu'ils puissent s'échanger contre une augmentation de produits .... Entre commerçants, on regarde comme une mauvaise action de se séduire réciproquement ses pratiques; mais la concurrence que chacun exerce contre tous ne présente point une idée aussi précise; et un commerçant n'a pas moins d'empressement d'étendre son débit aux dépens de ses confrères qu'à le proportionner à l'accroisement des richesses, lorsque celles-ci lui offrent à l'échange d'un nouveau revenu. Jusqu'ici dans l'un ou l'autre cas, la découverte d'un procédé nouveau a causé une grande perte nationale, une grande diminution de revenu, et par conséquent, la consommation.*
>
> *(Simonde 1819, 345)*

Translated, producers have no private incentives to increase wages in response to technological change (i.e. the introduction of the steam engine) as higher wages have no bearing whatsoever on his revenue (or little) but increase his costs. Thomas Malthus, in *Principles of Political Economy Considered with a View to their Practical Applications*, described the problem in the following terms:

> *We have seen that the powers of production, to whatever extent they may exist, are not alone sufficient to secure the creation of a proportionate degree of wealth. Something else seems necessary in order to call these powers fully in action. This is effectual and unchecked demand for all that is produced. And what appears to contribute most to the attainment of this object, is, such a distribution of produce, and such an adaptation of this produce to the wants of those who are to consume it, as constantly to increase the exchangeable value of the whole mass... In the same manner, the greatest stimulus to the continued production of commodities, taken altogether, is an increase in the exchangeable value of the whole mass, before a greater value of capital has been employed upon them.*
>
> *(Malthus 1827, 361)*

CAPSULE: JEAN-CHARLES-LÉONARD SIMONDE DE SISMONDI, FATHER OF MACROECONOMIC MODELING

$$y(t) = w(t-1) \tag{5.2}$$

The gist of Simonde de Sismondi's argument can be reduced to Equation 5.2 where output in time t, y(t) is a function of income in time t – 1, w(t – 1). In the steady state, income equals output (full-employment level). However, a technology shock will increase potential output without increasing income, which leads to the downturn.

The Birth of Radical Political Economy

These contributions mark the beginnings of radical political economy, a school of thought, which maintained that the for-profit economy was characterized by a fundamental flaw, namely its inability to make the transition to the new, higher output in response to technological change. Throughout the 19th century, it would evolve in a number of ways, including Friedrich Engels and Karl Marx's reformulation based on class conflict. In other words, failed macroeconomic transitions owed to a fundamental conflict between the owners of capital and the owners of labor. Others referred simply to the absence of private incentives for firms to increase wages in response to productivity-increasing technological change (steam engines, steam turbines, etc.). The upshot was straightforward: private, decentralized economies appeared to suffer from a fundamental flaw in making the transition to higher aggregate output levels.

The Classical Response

Allegations that private, decentralized economies could not spontaneously make the transition to the new, higher equilibrium growth path in response to the massive technology shock that was the steam engine did not sit particularly well with classical political economists. However, what raised their ire was the proposed solution, namely, the abandonment of open, free markets in favor of hierarchical (read: government) governance. For example, Robert Owen, having dismissed the "for-profit" economy as unable to make the transition to the new, higher equilibrium growth path, advocated a form of communal or government intervention. As Simonde de Sismondi had pointed out, firms have no strategic interest to raise wages in times of technological change.

To the classical political economists, the proposed cure was worse than the disease. A response, a rejoinder was in order. After all, the future of a market-based economy was in the balance. As it turns out, the classical response came from

French political economist Jean-Baptiste Say, by way of what is today known as "Say's Law." Reacting to late 18th-century arguments that an increase in supply does not necessarily create a comparable increase in demand, he proposed his famous *Loi des débouchées* according to which supply de facto creates its own demand. In other words, insufficient demand was logically impossible.

As it turned out, Say had reduced the problem of macroeconomic equilibria to one of simple barter. At its most basic level, it amounted to a tautology where the very act of putting oneself in an exchange position (i.e. supplying a good/service) implied an equivalent demand for another good/service. Absent from the analysis were the defining features of an advanced, market-based economy, namely the financing stage and the two income stages (variable and fixed factor).

The 1835 Recession

While the 1820 recession produced the first bona-fide macroeconomic debate, the 1837 recession in the UK witnessed the beginning in earnest of what could be referred to as a macroeconomic debate. For example, it was responsible for (i) launching the debate on the role of money in the "business cycle," (ii) with further radicalizing radical political economy and with (iii) bringing the debate over free trade to its logical conclusion.

Having dismissed underincome and underexpenditure as possible causes of the earlier downturns, classical political economists found themselves without a credible account of the forces which led to the severe downturn in the late 1830s. Soon, they turned their attention to money in general, and the money supply in particular, arguing that the "business cycle" was, in essence, a "credit cycle," caused by over-zealous bankers. And so was born the currency school, which attributed the business cycle to monetary forces. Unlike the various "radical" schools, it believed that private, for-profit economy was inherently stable, but that bankers and their zeal were largely responsible for the business cycle.

The second major development was in the field of radical political economy, notably the contribution of Friedrich Engels and Karl Marx. Whereas Robert Owen had simply raised the problem of underincome, attributing it to the inherent nature of a "market" economy, Engels and Marx went further, invoking a somewhat malevolent motive. Specifically, underincome and the ensuing underexpenditure were not spontaneous occurrences, but rather were the result of a sociological class-based dialectic, one between the owners of capital and the owners of labor. The former's ultimate objective consisted of increasing the rate of surplus value. The means was the labor-saving technology shock-induced business cycle. By investing massively in labor-saving devices (i.e. steam engine-powered machinery), firms decreased both their and overall demand for labor, resulting in a glut and consequently, lower wages and higher profits. In short, Engels and Marx had taken the debate out of the realm of the purely spontaneous, and into the realm of class conflict.

The third development was the final adoption, by the British Houses of Commons and Lords in 1846, of free-trade, by way of the wholesale revocation of the Corn Laws.[2] For many, free trade was seen as a means whereby unsold goods/merchandise could be find a market abroad. Again, this was consistent with the view that the business cycle was somehow related to the problem of insufficient demand.

19th-Century Macroeconomic Theory

By macroeconomic theory, it should be understood the systematic representation of macroeconomic aggregates and phenomena in a systematic manner, one that is ultimately amenable to testing empirically. Unfortunately, based on this standard, most 19th-century writings came up short. Instead of formal treatises, what one finds are poorly developed notions, vague definitions and vague imputations regarding causality.

Owen's Theory of Underincome

Owen, like most of his 19th-century contemporaries, was first and foremost a man of action, a doer of sorts. To his way of thinking, little was to be gained by studying in depth the problem of insufficient wage income. In his view, the cause of transitional macroeconomic disequilibria was obvious, namely the market mechanism, which kept wages low. There was no incentive for employers to raise wages, despite higher productivity.

Having established this, he would spend the rest of his life advocating an alternative form of economic and social organization, namely the industrial/company commune. Accordingly, the market would give way to an internal form of governance and a new form of money based on labor (labor certificates). As it would be controlled by the commune, its level could easily be adjusted in line with the level of potential output. Implicitly, he felt that the market could not move the UK economy on to the new, higher equilibrium growth path defined by the new power technology that was the steam engine. His views were neither ideological, nor class-conflict based, nor spurious, but rather, based on what could be described as a keen sense of observation.

Say's Law

Say's Law was one of the more important theoretical developments to come out of this period. However, it was more tautology than law (Say, 1809). It held that in the case of barter, the very act of supplying/offering a good implied, by definition, a corresponding demand – that is, for another good. Hence, there could be no such thing as insufficient demand. It made as little sense to Say as insufficient supply. Demand was simply the flip side of supply.

Say's Law should be seen for what it, namely the first line of defense on the part of classical political economists to allegations, by radical political economists, that market-based economies were unable to make successful transitions to new, higher equilibrium growth paths in response to technological change. It was neither scientific, nor logically consistent. Instead of setting in a highly complex, multi-good, multi-factor industrialized economy, it focused on Robinson Crusoe-based barter, where it became a tautology of sorts. Subsequent work has all but invalidated it, relegating it to the status of disproven hypothesis, and theoretical anomaly.

The Currency School and the Business Cycle

Recurrent recessions (business cycles) had pushed classical political economists outside of their comfort zone. After all, if markets could "no sooner produce business cycles as a man could give birth to a baby," then why were they increasing not only in frequency but also in intensity? David Ricardo and others pointed in the direction of the money supply, specifically the Gold Standard. The result was the currency school view of the business cycle according to which an increase gold inflows would lead to an expansion of credit, to the point that demand would exceed supply, leading to inflation and eventually to a downturn as firms would have overextended themselves. And so would begin the downward spiral.

In short, it attributed the business cycle to the banking sector, notably to its speculative and thus instable nature. Gold inflows and outflows were seen as the culprits, leading to a series of expansions of bank credit. Lower interest rates led to higher investment, which in turn led to overinvestment and eventually, a recession. In short, bankers were what Robert Shiller of Yale University refers to as "irrationally exuberant." To rectify the situation and thus prevent recurrent business cycles, it advocated third-party control of the banking sector.

As it turned out, this did not sit particularly well with banks and the banking sector. Not only did they feel unfairly targeted, but also they rejected its main premise, namely that the business cycle was the result of imprudent behavior on their part. And so was born the Banking School of monetary thought, which invoked the Real-Bills doctrine according to which if the maturity of the outstanding credit bills is within reason (not more than 60 days), then bank credit cannot be inflationary, and hence, cannot be the cause of the business cycle.

Their reasoning was simple. In short, bank credit (bills of exchange) is extended to entrepreneurs on the basis of projected/planned real economic activity (e.g. planned output/value added). This refers to the finance stage in the IES (Chapter 2). For example, an entrepreneur will demand credit in the amount of his/her projected output or a fraction thereof. Thus, for every dollar or pound of credit issued, there will exist a dollar/pound of real output. Thus, the notion of "real" bills – or put differently, each bill has its equivalent in real output, wealth-wise.

The debate between the currency school and the banking school was never resolved. That is, from a scientific point of view. The real bills doctrine continued to hold sway as did the principles underlying the currency school. As such, neither can be viewed as truly scientific. Despite this, the government of Prime Minister Robert Peel, in its 1844 Bank Charter Act, adopted the currency school view, giving credence to the view that the business cycle was monetary in its origins. This historic piece of legislation (1st-ever comprehensive central banking law) effectively limited the amount of credit banks could issue. Furthermore, it limited individual banks' ability to issue money, imposing a unique currency in the form of Bank of England notes.

The Business Cycle According to the Currency School

Proponents of the Currency School believe that a sustained period of low interest rates and excessive credit (exchange bills) creation from fractional reserve banks result in a volatile and unstable imbalance between saving and investment. According to the theory, the business cycle unfolds in the following way: low interest rates from fractional reserve banks tend to stimulate borrowing, which lead to an increase in capital spending funded by newly issued bank credit. Proponents hold that a credit-sourced boom results in widespread malinvestment. A correction or credit crunch, commonly called a "recession" or "bust," occurs when the credit creation has run its course. The money supply then contracts (or its growth slows), causing a curative recession and eventually allowing resources to be reallocated back toward their former uses.

Marx's Theory of the Business Cycle

Karl Marx was perhaps the first 19th-century political economist to develop a complete theory of the business cycle. Its essence consisted of the owners of capital or capitalists' unrelenting desire to increase the rate of surplus value, defined as total value less the wage bill, divided by the latter. This desire set in motion a series of actions and events that led invariably to boom and bust. By investing in new, labor-saving technology, the entrepreneur/capitalist contributed to increasing the army of surplus workers, thus lowering wages and raising the rate of surplus value (profit).

Factually, this line of reasoning appeared to be factually correct or consistent, both early in the 18th century and in the 1830s, when the downturns were preceded by massive investments in steam-power-driven machinery. This led to massive layoffs (as productivity per worker increased), and a depressed labor market. Thus, in many ways, his account of the business cycle is consistent with that of Owen and Simonde de Sismondi. Where it differs, however, is in terms of intent. To Marx, the downturn is not only planned but also desired as a means to the ultimate end of increasing the rate of surplus value. Owen and Simonde de Sismondi simply attributed it to incentives and market failure.

Ideology or Science?

How is this body of 19th-century work to be judged, which can be referred to as proto-macroeconomics? As science or ideology? Strictly speaking, it fails the test of science as it amounts to little more than a series of plausible, but unproven hypotheses. For example, Robert Owen made no attempt to substantiate his claims, relying instead on his sense of observation and inference. The same holds for Simonde de Sismondi, Engels, Marx and others. None of their theories and predictions were ever tested. This leaves us with but one conclusion, namely that 19th-century macroeconomic theory consisted overwhelmingly of ideology.[3]

19th-Century Macroeconomics: Summary

The 19th century began with a bang but ended with a whimper. By the 1870s, the problems that had confronted the British economy had all but subsided. Overall, energy consumption in the form of increasing steam-based horsepower per worker had leveled off, which had important implications for macroeconomics. Specifically, the source of transitional macroeconomic disequilibria had, for all intents and purposes, disappeared.

With it went interest in the macroeconomic problem. By the end of the century, the debate over the causes of the business cycle had become less of an issue. That the British and World economies had not known a major downturn in the later part of the century was seen as proof that markets did work, and that the fears raised by the radicals were unsubstantiated.

What is noteworthy about 19th-century macroeconomics is its close relationship with growth theory as evidenced by the fact that most of its contributors also involved in describing wealth and growth. This was not a coincidence, but rather the result of the fact that to many, the macroeconomic problem constituted an important constraint on attaining the potential wealth defined by the new power-drive technologies of the 19th century. In fact, one could argue that were it not for the macroeconomic problem, the field of economics would have evolved more slowly. Put differently, had specialization not been determined by the extent of the market, but been automatic (i.e. a sufficient condition for growth), *then The Wealth of Nations* may never have been written.

We now turn our attention to the 20th century, which like the 19th century presented its share of challenges. As shall be shown, many of these paralleled those described above, especially with regard to the cause.

20th-Century Macroeconomic History

As far as macroeconomic disequilibria are concerned, the 19th century pales in comparison to the 20th century. Not only would a new power transmission technology replace the steam engine, the leitmotiv of 19th-century growth, but also it would usher in a new way of life, known as modernity, defined by electricity, household appliances, the automobile and mass communication. Wealth levels soared beyond imagination. The very nature of living changed, from what was a daily struggle for survival to a nirvana of sorts.

But as had been the case in the early 19th century, the path to nirvana would not be without incident. Once again, the ability of a market-based economy to make the transition to the new higher equilibrium growth path would be called into question. In short, the issues that had occupied the thoughts of Owen, Simonde de Sismondi, Engels and Marx would, once again, rear their heads.

The introduction in the United States of a new power-drive technology in the form of electric unit drive would have dire consequences for the UK. Electric unit drive gave America a non-negligible cost advantage in virtually all sectors of the economy. Moreover, the goods that are commonly associated with modernity (e.g. household appliances, electric lighting, automobiles, radios) were decidedly American. The fallout was devastating as the UK economy slid into the worse depression of its history, one from which it would never truly recover.

Given the richness of the 20th-century experience, the century will be divided into three distinct sub-periods, namely 1900–1945, 1945–1975 and 1975–present. The first is marked by boom and bust, by high rates of growth and employment and by the greatest recession/depression of all times, namely the Great Depression. The second is best described as one of stability. Growth rates are high, unemployment is low and governments, now an integral part of the economy, balance their budgets. The third and last is characterized by low growth (Productivity Slowdown), high inflation and unemployment and fiscal decline.

1900–1945 Macroeconomic Disequilibria

This is, by the far, the most important period of the 20th century. The reasons are many and include (i) the fact that it witnessed the first-ever decline of an industrial and economic behemoth, namely Great Britain; (ii) the rise of a new industrial and economic behemoth, namely the United States; (iii) an unprecedented technology shock both in breadth and magnitude, namely electricity and electrification and (iv) commensurate with the former, an unprecedented economic depression in the form of the Great Depression. Together, they would yield the greatest of paradoxes. One such paradox was the Great Depression, the greatest and severest industrial downturn in history. The richest and mightiest country on the face of the earth found itself in the throes of unprecedented stagnation, poverty and suffering. As had been the case in early 19th-century Great Britain, paradise had been found, then lost.

This section will be organized as follows. To begin with, the rise to industrial and economic supremacy of the United States and the fall of Great Britain, two nations on diametrically opposed paths, will be chronicled. This will then be followed by a look at the problems than plagued both. Specifically, of the massive unemployment in post-WWI Great Britain, and of the Stock Market Boom and Crash, and subsequent

Great Depression in the United States. This will then be followed by the developments in macroeconomic theory, both in Great Britain and in the United States.

As will become apparent, the macroeconomic "problem" differed across country. The problems facing Great Britain were qualitatively and quantitatively different from those facing the United States. Great Britain was in the throes of industrial and economic decline as it technology (i.e. the steam engine) had been "creatively destroyed" by the introduction of the electric motor. Its failure to respond had dire consequences as it slipped from first to third place in the ranking of world powers, behind the United States and Germany.

The Fall of Great Britain and the Rise of America

For over a century, Great Britain reigned supreme in so far as industrial, economic and military might was concerned, owing in large measure to the steam engine which, as shown in Chapter 3, catapulted it to the summit of the world economy. Its costs were the lowest, making it's the largest exporting nation on the face of the planet. "The sun never sets on the British Empire," as the saying went. Its textiles were exported to all corners of the planet, as were its manufactured goods. Industrial dominance translated into financial supremacy as its banks and financial institutions (insurance companies) dominated world trade. City of London, the central business district in London, was the center of the world finance. Its currency, the pound, was the world currency, the equivalent of today's US dollar.

However, all of this came to an ignominious end with the introduction of a new power-transmission technology, one that promised even greater machine speeds, higher productivity and lower costs. One that would extend the power revolution to the realm of consumer goods, and one that would usher in a new era in human history, namely the individual electric motor (see Chapter 3). By lowering costs on the existing products, electric unit drive catapulted US firms ahead of their British counterparts, offering lower prices and, oftentimes, higher-quality goods.

However, in addition to providing a cost-based comparative advantage (vis-a-vis Great Britain), electricity and the electric motor ushered in a host of intermediate inputs and goods (and services) that would revolutionize life as we know it. These include the petrochemical industry with its myriad new materials, electric lighting, electrical appliances (refrigerators, washers, dryers, vacuum cleaners, radios, cinema and TVs), automobiles and airplanes. In short, what sociologists labeled modernity. And it all started in the United States.

In little time, US firms came to dominate world trade, not unlike British firms had done in the 19th century. However, unlike the British, the US presence abroad would extend beyond simple exports, to the realm of investment, specifically direct investment. Throughout the early 20th century, large US firms established branch plants throughout the world, exporting a new way of producing and a new way of life. Among these are the Ford Motor Company, General Electric, Westinghouse and Standard Oil.

The Aftermath of WWI

The story begins in the aftermath of WWI, or what until WWII was known as the Great War. Trade and war are not, in general, good bedfellows. Like all other major conflicts, trade is one of the first victims of war. Exports typically fall as nations muster all of their resources with one goal in mind, namely victory. Another victim is the Gold Standard, as inflation ravages a nation's gold reserves. WWI was no exception. However, in the aftermath, Great Britain found itself in a conundrum, namely high wages and prices, high unemployment and faltering exports.

This prompted a debate in Britain, specifically at the Bank of England and the Treasury, over the very cause(s) of its decline. Montagu Norman, the Governor of the Bank of England, cast an accusatory finger at the breakdown of the gold standard and the ensuing opportunistic post-WWI behavior on the part of Great Britain's trading partners, notably France which it accused of strategically devaluing its currency. Others, however, pointed to its failure to change with the times – in short, to follow the United States and Germany. More specifically, its failure to "electrify" and move into the 20th century. Leading the charge was David Lloyd-George, who in the 1924 *Coal and Power Report*, pleaded with his fellow countrymen to abandon steam in favor of electro-magnetic power and electric unit drive. And so was born, one of the first macroeconomic debates of the 20th century. Was Great Britain's decline due to the breakdown of the gold standard, or to its failure to "electrify."

Meanwhile, in the United States, the 1920s were a heyday of sorts, referred to as the Roaring Twenties. Growth had reached dizzying heights as mass production techniques spread across industries, raising productivity and productive capacity. US firms were busy investing overseas, opening up branch plants-in short, dominating the world economy in terms of its exports of goods and services as well as branch plants. Wall Street had usurped City of London as the center of world finance with the US dollar becoming the international currency.

However, by the late 1920s, there were signs that growth was stalling, that the roar was faltering. Unemployment began rising despite record productivity and capacity growth. Some pointed an accusing finger at wages and wage income, arguing that they had not kept pace with productivity growth. Among these were the likes of Henry Ford, who invited his fellow businessmen to follow his example of doubling wages in 1914 as a means to increase overall expenditure and the US economy in line with potential output.

Government Policy Responses

Meanwhile, across the Atlantic, the Bank of England and the Treasury were adamant: Britain's decline owed, in large measure, to the breakdown of the gold standard and post-WWI opportunistic behavior on the part of its trading partners. Countries like France and Italy had strategically devalued their currency, thus increasing their exports – at Great Britain's expense. According to Montagu Norman, the Governor of the Bank of England, the problem was systemic. And the solution would have to be fit the problem. In short, he envisaged nothing less than a return to the Gold Standard at pre-WWI parities (i.e. exchange rates) for Great Britain and for the rest of the World. To this end, in 1925, Great Britain acted and unilaterally restored the gold standard at pre-WWI parities, specifically with the US dollar. The value of the pound was set at $4.86. The thinking was simple: return to the gold standard and thereby force the rest of the world back to pre-WWI parities (exchange rates), thus setting the stage for a return to glory as the first-rate nation it was.

Not everyone agreed, however. Pre-WWI parities would require pre-WWI price levels, both in the UK and abroad. Inflation, however had hit harder in the UK than in the United States, making the pre-WWI value of the pound of $4.86 somewhat dubious. Among the most vocal critics was a young Cambridge-educated statistician by the name of John Maynard Keynes, whose estimates of the relative purchasing power parity between the United States and the UK convinced him that a $4.86/pound was overvalued. According to his estimates, based on the notion of purchasing power parity, the pound's true value was somewhere in the vicinity of $4.20. His prediction: Great Britain would run a current account deficit, forcing it to either devalue its currency, or suspend the Gold Standard.

CAPSULE: HOW THE AFTERMATH OF WWI PUT MARSHALLIAN ECONOMICS TO THE TEST

WWI was a costly war for Great Britain and the United States. As a result of the Bank of England and the Federal Reserve's decision to finance the war with credit, prices increased significantly in both countries – roughly 200 percent in England and 100 percent in the United States. Like most countries, both suspended the gold standard.

Given Great Britain's desire to restore latter at pre-WWI parities, it was clear that prices (and wages) would have to fall significantly. Newly minted Marshallian price theory predicted that prices and wages would fall in the face of excess supply of goods and labor, making a return to pre-WWI parities possible.

However, this did not occur. Despite record levels of unemployment, wages remained relatively constant, casting a pall over economics, specifically Marshallian price theory. John Maynard Keynes headed the resistance, arguing that markets were flawed, or at the very least, did not behave according to price theory. In many regards, the debate that followed was internecine as it pitted two Cambridge scholars, Keynes and Marshall with Keynes being the ultimate victor.

Things were decidedly different in the United States. With the roar of the twenties faltering, the US government, specifically the governing Republican party, set its sights on an upward tariff revision in the hope of securing a larger share of the market for its firms. By restricting access to its market, the hope was to increase capacity utilization rates, hopefully eliminating the problem of growing excess capacity.

The 1928 general election was thus fought over the question of tariffs. The Republican party, under the leadership of Senator Reed Smoot of Utah and presidential candidate Herbert Hoover, proposed an upward revision of tariff rates. Elected in November 1928, the Republicans tabled the Smoot-Hawley Tariff Bill in the House of Representatives in May 1929. Investors reacted favorably, bidding up the price of shares as the proposed, tariff-based higher capacity utilization rates foretold of greater earnings and profits.

CAPSULE: THE SMOOT-HAWLEY TARIFF ACT AS MACROECONOMIC POLICY[4]

Tariffs have a long and illustrious history in the United States, going back to the early days of the newly found Republic. Throughout the 19th century, no less than 30 tariff laws were passed, each more restrictive than the last. In most cases, they sought to raise the price of imports (from Great Britain) in the hope of stimulating domestic production, a policy known as import substitution.

However, in the Roaring Twenties, with the United States riding atop the Western world, a new objective appeared, namely closing a growing output gap. Technological change, specifically electric unit drive and public utility provided electric power, had increased the rated capacity of the US economy, opening up a gap between actual and potential output.

Senator Reed Smoot of Utah proposed two upward tariff revisions in the hope of closing the gap. The Fordney-McCumber Tariff Act of 1922 and the Smoot-Hawley Tariff Act of 1930 were designed to further restrict virtually all imports and in the process, deliver a larger share of the market to the now more productive-efficient US firms.

The promise of higher sales and profits fueled the stock market boom in 1928 and 1929. In its legislative journey, however, it suffered a catastrophic defeat in October, when the Republican party splintered, with 13 Insurgents voted with the Democrats to lower, not raise, tariffs.

The Stock Market Crash of 1929 and the Great Depression

On October 23 and 29, the US stock market lost a third of its value as prices collapsed. This cataclysmic event was known as the Stock Market Crash of 1929. It marked the beginning of the severest industrial downturn of all times, namely the Great Depression which saw output fall by as much as 50 percent, and unemployment rise to 30 percent. Falling share prices were soon followed by falling investment levels. Private investment in the United States virtually dried up in the aftermath. And the surprising thing was that no one knew why.

In little time, economic activity began to decline, as did exports and imports. Soon, what was initially a US phenomenon spread to Europe and the rest of the World, making it universal in nature. What was to become the greatest economic depression in history had begun. By 1933, US GDP had been halved and employment had fallen by a third.

Government Responses

As with previous downturns, most governments responded timidly, the idea being that the business cycle would run its course, and employment and output would turn up. US President Herbert Hoover reassured Americans that the economy was fundamentally sound. Ibid for presidents and prime ministers throughout the world. However, by 1932, the optimism had turned to pessimism. Output and employment continued its downward slide, with no end in sight. Investment, a leading indicator, remained virtually flat. The public grew increasingly wary.

Responding to a demand for action, the US Democratic party, under the leadership of New York Governor Franklin D. Roosevelt, called for fundamental changes in the US economy as a whole and in business behavior in particular. According to him, low wages and insufficient purchasing power were among the chief causes of the downturn. Productivity had risen, but wages had failed to keep pace, resulting in underincome and underconsumption, not unlike what had happened in the 19th century. To correct this, Roosevelt proposed the National Industrial Recovery Act of 1933 which (i) called for higher wages (ii) introduced a large-scale government spending program (three years before Keynes) (iii) gave workers the right to bargain collectively and (iv) reinvented wage and price setting. The British government also responded timidly, doing little, other than to abandon the gold standard (again).

Macroeconomic Theory: 1900–1945

As shown, the early 20th century was rich in developments. Great Britain was in free fall. The United States was ascending to stratospheric heights atop the world economy. The stock market boomed and crashed. Output both in the United States and abroad collapsed in the early 1930s. The problem, however, is that all of this occurred against what was essentially a theoretical void in so far as macroeconomics was concerned. Great Britain's decline was a mystery as was the stock market boom and bust, not to mention the subsequent Great Depression. However, as nature abhors a void, this period witnessed a flurry of intellectual activity, the upshot of which was the establishment of macroeconomics as a legitimate sub-field in economics.

Great Britain

It is important to understand, from the start, that the problems afflicting Great Britain were fundamentally different from those afflicting the United States. The UK economy was in decline, and wages and prices were, according to Treasury and Bank of England officials, too high. Throughout the 1920s, unemployment remained high at one million workers.

CAPSULE: WHO WAS JOHN MAYNARD KEYNES?

John Maynard Keynes was a British scholar trained at the University of Cambridge in statistics and philosophy who waded into the debate over Britain's return to the gold standard in the mid-1920s, arguing that a return to the pre-WWI parity of $4.86 pound was not warranted by relative prices in the two countries (i.e. purchasing power parity would be violated).[5] In short, it would be overvalued, leading to a balance of payments deficit, and either adjustment or the eventual suspension of the gold standard.

He was not, however, an economist per se, having no formal training in the subject matter. His degrees were in statistics and philosophy. This stood him in good stead when it came to establishing the purchasing power parity rate of exchange, it being based on statistical price indexes.

This led, ultimately, to his interest in prices and price adjustment, with an emphasis on wage and price stickiness. In other words, why had prices in the UK not adjusted downward in the face of massive unemployment? The seeds of Keynesian macroeconomics had been sowed. How do markets work when prices are sticky, especially downward.

John Maynard Keynes

Analytically, John Maynard Keynes was the first in England to measure purchasing power parity. He did this by creating price indexes for Great Britain and comparing them with similar indexes for other countries, notably the United States. These comparisons are what led him to oppose Britain's return to the gold standard at the pre-WWI parity value of $4.86. However, this was only the beginning.

A $4.86 pound was, in his eyes, overvalued owing to what he felt were abnormally high wages and prices in Great Britain. A decade after the end of WWI, wages and prices had failed to return to their pre-war levels, raising what was to become his greatest contribution to macroeconomics in particular and economics in general, namely sticky wages and prices, and the notion that such a state of affairs could, rather than be seen as a temporary disequilibrium, be seen as an equilibrium. For unknown reasons, markets had not, and apparently, could not perform their primary function of coordinating economic behavior. Wages remained high despite massive unemployment, while prices remained high despite generalized excess supply. The presence of sticky wages and prices was at the very root of his opposition to the Bank of England's decision to return to the gold standard at pre-WWI parity.

Given these circumstances, he advocated what would become the staple of early macroeconomic policy, namely government expenditure programs aimed at relieving short-term unemployment. In other words, given the failure of wages and prices to adjust and markets to clear, governments could move the economy to full employment by increasing expenditure. To justify his position, he coined the now celebrated phrase, "in the long run, we are all dead," when confronted with market-clearing arguments.

It bears reminding that few took heed, and that most dismissed his arguments, including Bank of England governor Montagu Norman. His break came, however, in 1932 when Great Britain was ultimately forced to abandon the gold standard, yet again, something he had predicted in 1925. Not surprisingly, he became an overnight sensation, an economic prophet of sorts. And so began Keynes' rise to scientific prominence, not to mention celebrity. Sticky wages and prices, deficient demand and equilibrium disequilibrium were his calling cards.[6]

The United States

Thorstein Veblen

Economic decline was not an issue in the US in the 1920s. On the contrary, problems associated with precipitous growth plagued the US economy. Capacity seemed to be outpacing income and expenditure. Enter US economist Thorstein Veblen who, despite being a classically trained economist (and faculty member at the University of Chicago), broke with tradition, arguing as had Robert Owen, Jean Charles-Léonard Simonde de Sismondi, Karl Marx and others in the 19th century, that what ailed the US economy was insufficient income and expenditure. Like Owen before him, he laid the blame squarely on the profit motive-in short, on the workings of a decentralized market economy. Companies, he argued, responded to technological change by cutting employment and purchasing power, "sabotaging" the transition to the new, higher equilibrium growth path (defined by the new technology). The profit motive, he argued, was to blame. Instead of maximizing purchasing power, managers collectively minimize it, thus sabotaging progress.

> *Without some salutary restraint in the way of sabotage on the productive use of the available industrial plant and workmen, it is altogether unlikely that prices could be maintained at a reasonably profitable figure for any appreciable time. A businesslike control of the rate and volume of output is indispensable for keeping up a profitable market, and a profitable market is the first and unremitting*

condition of prosperity in any community whose industry is owned and managed by business men. And the ways and means of this necessary control of the output of industry are always and necessarily something in the way of retardation, restriction, withdrawal, unemployment of plant and workmen-whereby production is kept short of productive capacity.

(*Veblen 1921, 8*)

Like 19th-century radicals, he proposed a wholesale reorganization of society around a new set of institutions, referred to as technocracy. As pointed out in Chapters 3, industry would be run by a new elite composed of engineers and scientists, the modus operandi of which would be to maximize, not minimize, output. Maximize purchasing power so as to make judicious use of the nation's productive capacity.

Veblen's call for a new institutional framework was heeded by a group of engineers at Columbia University. The result was a new paradigm in economics, notably *The Economics of Abundance* and *Technocracy*. Among the leading authors – and there were many – were Stuart Chase and Howard Scott. Defining the economics of abundance were (1), the role of energy in general, and electric power in particular in production processes, and consequently in early 20th century US economic growth, (2) the purported flawed nature of the for-profit economy, distribution system, and/or money supply process, and (3) the call for change, whether it be in the conduct of business or government regulation. Regarding the role of energy, nearly every publication begins by extolling the virtues of the new "power age." Consider, for example, the following excerpt from Howard Scott's *Introduction to Technocracy*, published in 1933:

A century ago these United States had a population of approximately 12,000,000 whereas to-day our census figures a total of 122,000,000—a tenfold increase in the century. One hundred years ago, in these United States, we consumed less than 75 trillion British thermal units of extraneous energy per annum, whereas in 1929, we consumed approximately 27,000 trillion British thermal units—an increase of 353 fold in the century. Our energy consumption now exceeds 150,000 kilogram calories per capita per day; whereas in the year 1800 our consumption of extraneous energy was not less than 1600 or more than 2000 kilogram calories per day.... The United States of our forefathers, with 12,000,000 inhabitants, performed the necessary work in almost entire dependence upon the human engine, which, as its chief means of energy conversion, was aided and abetted only by domestic animals and a few water wheels. The United States to-day has over one billion installed horsepower. In 1929, these engines of energy conversion, though operated only to partial capacity, nevertheless had an output that represented approximately 50 percent of the total work of the world. When one realizes that the technologist had succeeded to such an extent that he is to-day capable of building and operating engines of energy conversion that have nine million times the output capacity of the average single human being working an eight hour day, one begins to understand the acceleration, beginning with man as the chief engineer of energy conversion and culminating with these huge extensions of his original one-tenth of a horse power. Then add the fact that of this 9,000,000 fold acceleration, 8,766,000 has occurred since the year 1900.

(Scott et al 1933, 42)

Another good example is the following excerpt taken from Chapter 1 of Stuart Chase's *The Economics of Abundance*, entitled "Forty to One"

Suppose that the thirteen million people living in the United States in 1830 had awakened on the morning of January 1, 1831, with forty times the physical energy they had gone to bed with the night before. An active picture meets the mind's eye; a very active picture. A lumberman can fell forty times as many trees in a week, a housewife sweep forty times as many square feet of floor; forty barns can be built in the time hitherto required for one—and forty chests and forty chairs. Porters can transport forty times their accustomed load in a day; weavers ply their shuttles forty times as fast—if the shuttles can brook the strain; and children raise forty times their normal rumpus.

Assuming no increase in the invention of labor-saving devices—and where would be the point with such an exuberance of labor available—what might we logically expect in the way of economic changes in a culture essentially handicraft? From an economy of scarcity, with barely enough to go around, the young republic would almost immediately enter an economy of abundance.

(Chase 1934, 1)

This is eerily similar to statements made by Robert Owen and David Ricardo in the early 19th century regarding the overall effect of the steam engine or mechanization on Great Britain's capacity to produce wealth. In the same chapter, Chase defines "Abundance" in terms of the following series of propositions.

1 A condition where the bulk of the economic work is performed not by men, but by inanimate energy, drawn from coal, oil and water power. Such a condition was reached in the United States toward the close of the 19th century, circa 1880.
2 *A point at which living standards per capita reach an average which is, at least potentially, twice as high as ever obtained under scarcity conditions. Reached circa 1900.*
3 *A point at which the curve of invention, following, as it does, a geometric increase, becomes the dominant factor in economic life – precisely as the Nile was the dominating factor in the economic life of Egypt. Circa 1870.*
4 *A point at which the scientific method supersedes the use and want of the craftsman in the production of most material goods. Circa 1900.*

5 *A point where output per man hour becomes so great that total productive labor must thereafter decline, even as output grows. A point at which labor ceases to be a measure of output—as it always has been in preceding ages. Circa 1920.*
6 *A point at which overproduction carries a more serious threat to the financial system than shortage. Circa 1880.*
7 *A point at which specialization has destroyed all practicable local self-sufficiency and made economic insecurity for all classes latent, growing, and ultimately intolerable, given no change in financial methods. Circa 1900, with the closing of the American frontier.*
8 *A point at which consumption becomes a greater problem than production. Circa, 1920. "Our economy," says F.L. Ackerman, "is so set up that it produces goods at a higher rate that it produces income with which to purchase them."*
9 *A point at which the industrial plant is, substantially, constructed, requiring relatively smaller outlays for capital goods in the future, and where pecuniary savings are not only unnecessary in their old volume, but seriously embarrassing, Circa, 1925.*
10 *A point where, due to the presence of the technical arts, costs, prices, interest rates, debts, begin a descent with zero as their objective. Circa 1920.*

(Chase 1934, 12)

The economics of abundance should be understood as a reaction to mainstream economics and its overriding emphasis on scarcity. Technology and technological change had rendered scarcity virtually obsolete. The economic problem, it maintained, consisted of managing abundance – in short, of realizing the potential that had been unlocked by new power-drive technologies.[7] Income and expenditure should be brought in line with potential output.

Rexford G. Tugwell

Rexford G. Tugwell was a University of Pennsylvania-trained economist who taught at Columbia University and who played a key role in President Franklin Roosevelt's *Brains Trust*.[8] He was of the view that the US economy in the 1920s was increasingly characterized by generalized excess capacity, the result of a number of key innovations. Foremost among the "technical causes" of increased productivity, he argued, was "the bringing into use of new and better power resources more suited to our technique, more flexible and less wasteful; and continued progress in the technique of generating and applying power" (Tugwell 1927, 180) – in short, the electrification of the US industry.

The electrification of industry has now progressed to the extent of between 55 and 60 per cent completion. So widespread an adoption of this new flexible means of moving things cannot have taken place without numerous secondary

> *results in lowered costs, improvements in quality, and a heightened morale among workers. For the new power is not only cheaper to use; it is also cleaner, more silent and handier. On the whole, the electrification of industry must be set down as the greatest single cause of the new industrial revolution.*
>
> *(Tugwell 1927, 182)*

According to Tugwell, wage income, and income in general, had lagged behind potential output, leading to stagnation in the late 1920s, and generalized depression in the 1930s. This view would become the theoretical underpinning of Roosevelt's *New Deal*. In short, the cause of the Great Depression was structural/transitional, not conjectural.

The National Industrial Recovery Act of 1933, the first New Deal, called for across-the-board wage increases, massive government expenditure, and a strengthening of labor legislation, the latter intended to increase workers' bargaining power vis-à-vis employers.

CAPSULE: WAS THE STOCK MARKET BOOM AND CRASH OF 1929 DUE TO IRRATIONAL EXUBERANCE?

The stock market boom and crash of 1929 was a watershed-like event, an event that changed the course of the world economy as well as casting more-than-a-shadow of a doubt over the stability of market economies. Was it a bubble, a rare occurrence where investors, through their behavior, spontaneously create a boom, which eventually turns into a crash. Were the banks complicit?

Surprisingly, this debate has never been resolved. There are two schools of thought, the fundamentals view and the instability view. The former, held by Irving Fisher and more recently, by Ellen McGrattan and Nobel laureate, Edward Prescott, alleges that the boom was based on fundamentals, notably on technological change. The instability view is found in the writings of Robert Shiller at Yale University (McGrattan and Prescott, 2004) and Hyman Minsky (Minsky, 1986). Both maintain that the stock market is prone to recurrent crises.

The problem, however, is the lack of conclusive evidence. Because the sample and population consists of a single data point, it is virtually impossible to test either view. As such, ideology as manifested in schools of thought (Irrational Exuberance versus Minsky-like instability).

Keynes' General Theory of Employment Interest and Money

In 1936, John Maynard Keynes published what was to become the bible of the nascent field of macroeconomics, namely *The General Theory of Employment, Interest and Money.* Having been a witness to the downturn in Great Britain in the 1920s and the Great Depression in the United States in the 1930s, he had set his sights on a general, overriding theory or understanding of downturns. While having no formal training in economics, he nonetheless provided an account of downturns based in large measure on three concepts or principles, namely the dynamics of employment in the presence of fixed or sticky wages and prices, the determinants of the marginal propensity to invest and the role of monetary policy in financial markets.

By general, it should be understood a theory that was broad enough to explain the UK and US case, which admittedly is a limited sample. Not making matters easy was the fact that the two downturns differed markedly, time-wise and content-wise. As shown above, the UK found itself in the midst of a structural decline in the post-WWI period, while the United States found itself reeling in the wake of an unprecedented structural boom, an economic heyday of sorts (i.e. the Roaring Twenties). While wages and prices appeared to be sticky in the UK, they were anything but in the United States. In fact, Presidents Herbert Hoover and Franklin Roosevelt adopted policies that were explicitly aimed at putting an end to the wage and price chiseling that characterized the first few years of the Depression. *The Codes of Fair Competition*, the key policy instrument of the New Deal, explicitly targeted wage and price chiseling – in short, they called for stable product prices and higher nominal wages – in short, for an end to competition and the beginning of cooperation. Also, the weak marginal propensity to invest noted by Keynes was a feature of the depression in the United States, but not in the UK. As for the celebrated liquidity trap, expansionary monetary policy under the Roosevelt Administration (e.g. the suspension of the gold standard and a depreciation of the dollar) led to marked decreases in interest rates.

It should be pointed out that the "general" in *The General Theory of Employment, Interest and Money* had no bearing whatsoever to what in science is a general theory. For example, there is no discussion of markets when wages and prices are not fixed/sticky. There is no discussion of the role of technology in investment decisions. There is no discussion of the structural underpinnings of the crises in the UK and the United States. There are, however, vague references to underconsumption theories, which, unfortunately, are devoid of any mention of technological change.

Regardless of its analytical shortcomings, it did have one distinct advantage, namely of offering a ready-made solution to both problems, namely an increase in government expenditure. This, however, was not particularly novel as the Roosevelt Administration's National Industrial Recovery Act of 1933 (thus, three years before *The General Theory*) called for an increase in government expenditure of roughly $2 billion as a short-term, stop-gap measure and numerous make-work programs. However, the focus of the act was correcting the structural imbalance, something Keynes was unaware of.

The Alleged Cyclicality of Crises

In addition to spawning a new field in the form of macroeconomics, it prompted a number of questions regarding cyclicity of GDP in the early 20th century prompted

TABLE 5.1 Cyclical Theories of Expansion and Contraction Cycles

Cycle	*Periodicity*	*Cause(s)*
Kondratieff	45–60 years	Technological change
Juglar	7–11 years	Variations in fixed capital
Kitchin	3–5 years	Time lags

an interest in long- and short-term waves, inspired in large measure by developments in electromagnetism (field theory).[9] One such question was the apparent cyclicality of large-scale crises. By the end of WWII, a number of writers pointed to what appeared to be a cycle of sorts. The mid-1800s had witnessed a major crisis, as had the 1930s. Despite the paucity of data/occurrences, writers began to speculate.

The first such writer was Nicolai Kondratieff, a Russian statistician, who posited the existence of a 45–60 year cycle or wave. In short, the underlying dynamics of capitalism were such that every half century, a major crisis occurs. Within such cycles were shorter ones with periodicity of 7–11 years (Juglar) and 3–5 years (Kitchin).

Eugen Slutsky and the Stochastic Cyclicality of the Business Cycle

Developments in electromagnetics and differential calculus, in combination with the apparent randomness of GDP shocks, seemed to suggest that there was something decidedly stochastic and recurrent going on. In other words, could the cyclicality of macroeconomic aggregates be explained by the randomness of its parts? Moreover, could a purely stochastic view of say investment or consumption expenditure mimic the business cycle?

In the 1920s, Eugen Slutsky was to first to show that it was mathematically possible for apparently cyclical behavior to emerge as the result of random shocks to the economy if the latter were modeled using a random numbers and moving averages.[10]

Slutsky was a Russian mathematician who worked at the Conjuncture Institute of Moscow under the direction of Nikolai Kondratieff. What is important to note is that the events of the early 20th century in conjunction with data from the 19th century had given rise to a stochastic approach to the business cycle, one that would be reinvented in the 1980s in the form of Real Business Cycle analysis, where random technological shocks would drive the cyclicality of macroeconomic aggregates.

G.B. Shackle and Kaleidic Economics

The failure to truly understand the underlying dynamics of the business cycle had a profound effect on macroeconomics. Randomness became the name of the game. In other words, investment expenditure, the apparent lead variable in cycles, was seen as stochastic. Some went as far as to attribute these variations to "animal spirits," totally unpredictable and stochastic.

G.S. Shackle, a British economist formalized the randomness in what he referred to as *Kaleidic Economics*. In other words, the economy in general and investment expenditure in particular were akin to a kaleidoscope, always changing, never the same.

A Dark Day for Macroeconomic Thought?

Animal Spirits, randomness, kaleidics, etc. were increasingly popular in the post-Stock Market Crash and Great Depression era. It could be argued that this owed ultimately to the inability of the profession to understand investment expenditure and of the economy as a whole. Put differently, randomness was the best the profession could come up with as it endeavored to understand the events of the 1930s and the business cycle in general.

It could be argued that this was a dark day for macroeconomics as a scientific endeavor as it attributed the lion's share of variation to purely random factors. There was no rhythm nor rhyme to the collective behavior of investors, a fact that profound implications for policy. Specifically, if investment was indeed largely random, then a case could be made for large-scale, recurrent government intervention in the form of public spending or investment. As will be shown in the next section, it constituted the main underlying motive for the full employment acts that popped up in most industrialized nations in the post-WWII period.

The Post-WWII Period: 1945–1975

WWII had a salutary effect on the US and World economies, increasing expenditure – in fact, doubling it – and restoring full employment. While the Great Depression remained a mystery, the World economy came out of the war with a renewed vigor, a renewed optimism armed in large measure with the belief that government could solve any and all macroeconomic problems. This would manifest itself in the passing, in most industrialized nations, of employment and full-employment legislation and laws, mandating government to use fiscal and monetary policy in order to maintain full employment.

Macroeconomic History: 1945–1975

WWII was both a military and macroeconomic watershed. In 1939, US GNP stood at $209.4 billion (constant 1958 dollars). By 1944, it had reached $361.3 billion, a 73 percent increase. Metaphorically speaking, the war had unleashed the potential that had been building throughout the early part of the century, putting the US economy squarely on a new, considerably higher growth path. The challenge, according to President Harry Truman, was staying on it. In his 1945 budget speech to the new Congress, he referred repeatedly to the country's "productive capacity," implicitly referring to the gap between actual and potential output:

> *The American people have learned during the war the measure of their productive capacity, and they will remember the experience in the peace to come. It is the responsibility of business enterprise to translate market opportunities into employment and production. It is the responsibility of the Government to hold open the door of opportunity and assure sustained markets. Then and only then can free enterprise provide jobs.*
>
> *(Senate Congressional Record, January 7, 1945)*

The result was a series of measures, including *The Employment Act*, which institutionalized and *de jure* legalized macroeconomic policy as a legitimate instrument and obligation of the state. From then on, governments had the legal-and moral-obligation to intervene. Among the policy instruments available were (i) government expenditure and (ii) monetary policy.

While WWII had "put" the United States and world economies onto the equilibrium growth paths defined by the new power-drive technology that was electric unit drive, it had not eliminated the business cycle. The post-WWII period was characterized by peaks and troughs, by rising and falling unemployment, and by rising and falling investment expenditure.

The Post-WWII Business Cycle

However, macroeconomic fluctuations were reduced considerably. Prior to 1945, the amplitude of cyclical changes in real GNP were twice as important as after. This owed, in large measure to the judicious and timely use of fiscal and monetary policy. Economic slowdowns were met with a combination of fiscal and monetary stimuli, while periods of economic expansion were moderated by the presence of progressive income taxes and other fiscal measures that limited expansion/growth.

In general, growth rates in this period were historically high, averaging 5 percent. Unemployment was generally low, hovering in the four to five percent range. Today, this period is referred to as an economic heyday of sorts as it combined high, persistent growth with low unemployment and inflation. Many refer to it as a "golden age," a heyday of sorts of capitalism.

It was an era that witnessed the emergence of the welfare state as it exists today. Vast bureaucracies emerged in virtually all Western industrialized countries, overseeing all aspects of policy (social, economic, political). Government expenditure increased markedly, as did government revenues. Outstanding government debt, however, remained surprisingly low (relative to today).

History of Macroeconomic Thought: 1945–1975

Surprisingly, this period which was characterized by relative economic stability was rich in developments and innovations in so far as macroeconomic theory is concerned. This owed, in large measure, to two factors, namely the Great Depression and the emergence of institutionalized macroeconomic policy. While Keynes had provided the West with a short-term solution to what at the time was a crisis of epic proportions, his work remained incomplete. Questions remained. For example, why did investment activity fall precipitously in the early 1930s? Was monetary policy to blame? Were wages and prices as sticky as he contended? And, secondly, the emergence of post-WWII institutionalized macroeconomic policy raised a series of questions regarding the efficacy of both fiscal and monetary policy.

Theorizing about the Great Depression

It goes without saying that the Great Depression was a traumatic, if not cataclysmic event. Never before had the world found itself in a state of economic, social and political despair. Ironically, at a time of great potential wealth (owing to the emergence of a new technology), the world found itself at the brink. WWII ended the Great Depression. Wartime expenditure levels increased output and employment, ending a decade of stagnation and depression. However, it had not provided answers to important questions, including what is perhaps the most important question, namely what triggered the Great Depression. Here, various theories are examined.

Monetarist Theories of the Great Depression

The New Deal had taken the United States and indeed the World by storm. The general consensus at the time was that private, market economies were prone to crisis and depression, and that government was the solution. However, not all were convinced. Those on the right of the political spectrum were particularly skeptical. One such case was that of economist Milton Friedman who with Anna Schwartz set out to provide an alternative narrative. Specifically, they argued, using historical data, that far from being the solution, government was the problem – specifically, the Federal Reserve. In *A Monetary History of the United States*: 1867–1960, they argued that the business cycle was largely determined by a credit/money cycle, with causality running from the latter to the former. As for the Great Depression, they argued that what was a minor economic downturn was transformed by the actions – or lack thereof – of the Federal Reserve into a major depression. In short, at a time when the Federal Reserve should have been increasing liquidity to the banking system, it did the exact reverse, removing high-powered money (monetary base). By reducing the money supply, the Federal Reserve contributed to the conditions of price deflation which characterized the 1930s.

This view has been the object of much debate within the profession. Economic historian Peter Temin, in "Did Monetary Forces Cause the Great Depression," tested the theory and found it wanting. More specifically, he found no evidence to the effect that the Federal Reserve willingly reduced liquidity to the banking system, thus rejecting the monetarist approach. According to Temin, the demand for credit had decreased, bringing with it the supply of credit and thus, of the money supply.

Clifford Douglas and the Social Credit Movement

Like Friedman and the monetarists, Scottish economist Clifford Douglas believed that recessions and depressions owed in large measure to the lack of a sufficient level of credit in the economy.[11] More specifically, he believed that the economy was fundamentally sound, except for the banking sector, which was monopolized, resulting in recurrent situations of insufficient back credit. As such, actual output was systematically below potential output, making for recessions and depressions.

To rectify the situation, he proposed the creation of social credit, a de facto substitute for private credit. Hence, in periods of unemployment and recession, the government should issue social credit as a means of stimulating overall expenditure and employment.

Its underlying premise, however, was never proven. Douglas was never able to provide sufficient evidence to show that private credit was in short supply.

Secular Stagnation

The theory of secular stagnation maintained that with time, potential output would exceed overall expenditure as consumption expenditure would level off, owing to a form of saturation. The underlying argument was simple, namely that consumption expenditure would, at some income level, level off. In other words, there was an upper limit to consumption, beyond which all income will be saved. This, of course, has dire consequences for investment and for overall expenditure. Specifically, as per capita income increases, consumption expenditure will not follow, making it increasingly difficult for firms to sell their products, which will have consequences for investment expenditure and overall economic activity. In short, Western industrialized nations will have a tendency to stagnate owing to consumer satiation.

Animal Spirits and Kaleidic Economics

"When all else fails, then resort to chance, to the unknown, to the arcane." This describes that school of thought in macroeconomics which attributes the business cycle to extraneous, unknown forces. With a tradition that extends back to William Stanley Jevons who invoked sunspots as the underlying cause of the business cycle, this school includes the likes of Joan Robinson and John Maynard Keynes who, at a loss to explain business investment behavior, alluded to animal spirits, or in the case of human beings, hormonal (testosterone, estrogen, progesterone) fluctuations. Another contributor to this literature was G.S. Shackle who argued that there was no rhyme or reason behind the business cycle – instead, the economy behaved much like a kaleidoscope, ever changing, ever different.

Macroeconomic Analysis

The Standard Keynesian Model

By fixing prices and wages (hence removing the notion of market equilibrium), Keynes examined the out-of-equilibrium behavior of economic aggregates (GDP, consumption, investment and government expenditure). The result was perhaps the most celebrated macroeconomic model of all time, namely the simple Keynesian model (sometimes referred to as the Keynesian Cross).

While considered by most to be a model, it was, in actual fact, little more than an exercise in macroeconomic accounting. It is mechanistic, with causality running from its aggregate expenditure (I, G, X, and M), to GDP. Other than the multiplier, it cannot be tested empirically as it makes no predictions. The key contribution is the notion of multiple macroeconomic equilibria, most of which are inefficient – due to unemployment. All the points along the 45-degree line are de facto equilibria in the sense that there are no forces at work pushing the economy in either direction.

The IS-LM Model: Increasing the Dimensionality

By the 1950s, it was felt that the simple Keynesian model was incomplete. Lacking was a more complete account of the different markets affecting macroeconomic equilibria. In short, the Keynesian model focused solely on the Production and Expenditure stages of the IES presented in Chapter 2. As investment was assumed to depend, in large measure on the interest rate, it was imperative to integrate the financing stage into the analysis.[12]

Responding to this need, John Hicks proposed what would become the IS-LM (investment-saving, liquidity money) model, which extends the simple Keynesian model to include monetary equilibrium. By explicitly modeling the demand and supply for money, it provided a more complete account of macroeconomic phenomena. Movements in GDP could result from either a change in "real" factors, or "monetary" factors.

Moreover, the IS-LM model provided a convenient framework in which to understand the Great Depression. Keynes, for example, by invoking the presence of a liquidity trap (horizontal-segment of the LM curve), argued in favor of fiscal policy as the only option to increase output and employment. The monetarists, in the other hand, argued that the LM curve was nearly vertical, making output and variations in output, a monetary phenomenon – that is, resulting from variations in the interest rate.

Friedrich Von Hayek versus John Maynard Keynes: The Return of the Austrians.

As it turned out, John Maynard Keynes did more than pen editorials in British newspapers and journals the mid-1920s against the proposed return to the gold standard at pre-WWI parities, he wrote one of the most influential monographs of all times, one that changed the economics discourse away from Marshallian and neoclassical concepts to disequilibrium ones. In a nutshell, the markets (i.e. the market ICS) that were the cornerstone of the industrial era, the pride of classical and neoclassical thought were deemed to be inherently flawed as was capitalism itself.

Not surprisingly, this did not sit well with the defenders of the established order. Recall that Carl Menger and Eugen Bohm-Bawerk had staunchly defended capitalism in the face of the Marxism in the 1880s, founding what is known today as the Austrian School. In the post-WWII period, in what was the heyday of Keynesian economics, it reappeared in the person of Friedrich Von Hayek, an Austrian political economist. The essence of his approach is best described by the title of his magnum opus, *On the Road to Serfdom*, in which he warned of the impending dangers of the rise of government, or put differently, Keynesianism.

In his view, the business cycle resulted from what was essentially a credit cycle, with monetary policy being the underlying cause. In short, the private, for-profit economy was stable. What was unstable was the state and the banking sector over-extending itself. In many regards, this was nothing more than a variation on the British *Currency School* that argued in favor of full convertibility of all notes in order to avoid crises

Foremost among Von Hayek's concerns was freedom in general, and freedom to innovate, to change, to adopt new ways of seeing and doing things. Another well-known Austrian with similar interests and views was Joseph A. Schumpeter whose work revolved around the theme of innovation and change (i.e. creative destruction).

Taken as a whole, it could be argued that the views expressed by the Austrian School were very much autobiographical in that they were a reaction to the inertia of Austrian society – in comparison with that of the Anglo-Saxon world (i.e. the UK and the United States).

1975–Present

Macroeconomic Developments: 1975–Present

The post-WWII period, from 1945 to 1975, was a heyday of sorts for macroeconomics. The Keynesian approach with its multiple macroeconomic unemployment equilibria dominated the field. And its policy prescriptions dominated the public discourse. Governments around the world took heed and established ministries or departments whose mandate it was to regulate macroeconomic activity. Statistical departments/agencies were established and/or enlarged.

For the first time in its history, economics and economists themselves were relevant. Problems were met with more than simple 19th-century rhetoric. The business cycle could be and was in fact controlled. Unemployment could be reduced. With all of this came a sense of pride and accomplishment. Economists in general were held in high esteem by the population.

Unfortunately, all of this changed in the mid-to-late 1970s. As pointed out in Chapter 3, economic growth had slowed down to a trickle, as had productivity growth. This would prove to be catastrophic for economics in general and for macroeconomics in particular.

To understand why, it is important to appreciate the role of growth in post-WWII macroeconomics. Throughout the post-WWII period, potential output increased at a rate of four-to-five percent. With the benefit of hindsight, the goal of macroeconomics consisted of maintaining actual output at its potential. As such, fiscal and monetary policy throughout this period were about maintaining overall expenditure growth in line with output growth which, as pointed out, was growing at a brisk pace.

The growth slowdown wreaked havoc on what had been, for three decades, a winning combination. Potential output was no longer growing at the same rate. Governments, however, maintained expenditure levels, increasing them as unemployment increased. The Vietnam War and two oil crises pushed prices up against a backdrop pf lower output and productivity growth.

However, the death knell, in so far as Keynesian economics was concerned, was its seeming inability to restore growth to post-WWII levels. As pointed out, throughout the post-WWII period, government expenditure had fueled growth – or its realization. Now, with lower productivity growth, government expenditure only served to fuel price inflation and rising debt levels against a backdrop of anemic growth. Clearly, the end was in sight. Keynesian-style macroeconomics had run out of, surprisingly, productivity growth. As potential output was no longer growing, expenditure increasing policies were of little to no use.

And so began a new chapter in macroeconomics, one whose emphasis would no longer be on using expenditure-based policies to realize potential output but rather one that would focus on increasing potential output itself, specifically on increasing growth whether via investment, research and development, deregulation, or free trade. This became known as supply-side economics and macroeconomics. Policies in general focused on the supply side. That is, raising productivity, lowering regulatory constraints, opening up new markets, lowering prohibitive taxation etc.[13]

History of Macroeconomic Thought: 1975–Present

The Phillips Curve and Rational Expectations

The 1970s witnessed to a new macroeconomic phenomenon, namely double-digit, non-wartime price inflation. Never before in peacetime had inflation become a chronic problem, extending over years if not decades.[14] As it turned out, this posed a problem for Keynesian macroeconomics as the Keynesian Cross framework as well as the IS-LM framework assumed fixed prices and wages. How would macroeconomic aggregates behave in times of inflation and hyperinflation?

Enter New Zealand economist A.W. Phillips, whose work in the 1960s pointed to the existence of an inverse relationship between price inflation and unemployment. Higher prices, he argued, were associated with lower unemployment.

Subsequently, the underlying mechanics were worked out, in large part by Canadian economist Richard Lipsey. The gist was simple, namely that higher prices resulted in lower real wages, which given a downward sloping demand for labor curve, implied higher employment/lower unemployment. In little time, expectations were incorporated into the analysis (Phelps-Friedman), with the result that the Phillips curve was no longer stable in time.

The upshot of the resulting analysis was relatively simple, namely that if expectations were anything but rational (correct on average), higher inflation could indeed lower unemployment. However, in the case in which expectations were rational (Lucas), the long-run tradeoff disappeared, undermining Keynesian-style macroeconomic policy.

The Unit Root Controversy

The final nail in the Keynesian coffin, however, came from econometricians who in the early 1980s made a startling discovery, namely that contrary to the accepted wisdom of the day, macroeconomic time-series did not and do not revert to their mean values. That is, when GDP is shocked (either via fiscal or monetary policy), it does not – as was thought – revert back to its mean value. The latter is referred to as mean reversion.

Instead, they found that macroeconomic time-series behaved in a random fashion, known as random walks. Which is to say, they exhibit a unit root. As it turned out, this was disturbing for macroeconomics at the time as it implied that supply factors, specifically technological change (shocks), not demand conditions (fiscal and monetary policy) were driving most macroeconomic time series. For example. The business cycle was not primarily a demand-side phenomenon, but rather was a supply-driven one, closely tied to technological change (both positive and negative).

Real Business Cycles

This finding had important implications for macroeconomics. Keynesian-style models were out, and technology-based models were in. The pioneers in this nascent brand of macroeconomics were Nobel Prize laureates, Finn Kydland and Edward Prescott, whose 1982 paper, *Time-to-Build and Aggregate Fluctuations*, set the stage for real business cycle (RBC) models, which attribute innovations in

GDP to positive and negative technology (real) shocks. Hence, the business cycle is real in its origins.

While RBC theory enjoyed much success in the 1990s and early 2000s, it lost much of its shine in the aftermath of the Financial Meltdown of 2008 which, most agreed, had its origins in the financial sector, a sector which is ignored altogether in RBC analysis. This has resulted in a flurry of RBC with financial frictions models intended to capture the gist of the crisis itself. Financial frictions are, to put it simply, imperfections in financial markets that have real effects.

Macroeconomics: Timeline Summary

TABLE 5.2 Macroeconomics: Timeline Summary

Year	*Historical Development*	*Theoretical Development*
1819	Recession in the UK	Technological Theory of Downturn
1840	Recession in the UK	Banking versus Currency School Debate
1927	Debate of Causes of Downturn	Say's Law
1936	Great Depression	Keynesian Macroeconomics
1937	Great Depression	IS-LM Model
1950	Great Depression	Harrod-Domar Growth Model
1955	Great Depression	Solow-Swan Growth Theory
1960	Inflation	Phillips Curve
1963	Great Depression	Monetary Theory of Great Depression
1977	Stagflation	Phelps-Friedman Expectations-Augmented Phillips Curve
1978	Stagflation	Rational Expectations
1982	Stagflation	Unit Root Hypothesis
1979	Stagflation	Real Business Cycle Theory

20th Century Macroeconomics: Summary and Conclusions

Macroeconomics put economics on the map, so to speak. The Great Depression transformed what was a fledging social science into a premier scientific discipline. So, it comes as somewhat of a surprise, not to mention deception, that all the bulk of 20th century macroeconomics is non-scientific in the sense that it is either not testable, or has been found to be false. For example, Real Business Cycle theory is not testable given the absence of a theory of real shocks (aggregate). As such, shocks are residuals, much like in growth theory. Which explains, to a certain degree, the continued existence of schools of thought or ideologies (e.g. Real Business Cycles, Neo-Keynesian, Monetarist and Radical).

The fact that events that took place decades ago are still not understood with any certainty reflects poorly on the field. Among these are the Stock Market Boom and Crash of 1929, the Great Depression, the Productivity Slowdown and the Financial Meltdown of 2008.

TABLE 5.3 Macroeconomics: Ideology or Science?

Principle/Hypothesis/Theory	*Ideology or Science*	*Justification*
Say's Law	Ideology	NT
Quantity theory of money	Tautology	
Real Bills Doctrine	Ideology	NT
Stock Market Bubble (1929)	Ideology	NEMPCON
Animal spirits	Ideology	NT
Monetary theory of the Great Depression	Ideology	NEMPCON
Secular stagnation	Ideology	NEMPCON
Real business cycle theory of the Great Depression	Ideology	NT
Real business cycle theory	Ideology	NT
Unit root hypothesis	Science	EMPCON

20th-Century Macroeconomic Theory: Ideology or Science?

As was the case in the previous chapters, the inevitable question is one of relevance, of scientific relevance. To what extent is the body of knowledge known as 20th-century macroeconomics ideology or science? Put differently, how much of it is has been tested and proven empirically?

Start with the Great Depression. Is there a proven theory of the Great Depression? After all, it occurred roughly a century ago. The answer unfortunately is no. There are myriad hypotheses and theories, but no proven theory. As a result, schools of thought (ideology) have come to characterize the debate with real theories on the one hand, and monetary theories on the other. This has made for the current situation in which there is no consensus as to the causes, nearly a century after the event. Instead, what remains is a shouting match between Keynesians and Von Hayekians, of those who believe that the private, for-profit economy is inherently unstable and in need of a third-party, and those who disagree and point an accusing finger at government.

As it turned out, this was problematic in the aftermath of the 2008 Financial Meltdown when comparisons to the Great Depression abounded. For example, Federal Reserve Board chairman Ben Bernanke, an economic historian by profession, compared the banking crisis to that of 1930–1933, a comparison that motivated the board's decision to purchase over $4 trillion in private bank's assets. The fear was that not doing so would lead to a repeat of the Great Depression.

Next, is there a proven theory of price inflation in the 1970s and 1980s? Once again, the answer is no. Is there a proven theory of the post-productivity slowdown business cycle? No. Is there a proven theory of the 2008 financial crisis, known as the Financial Meltdown? No.

In short, very little of contemporary macroeconomics can be considered to be scientific. Most of it consists of unsubstantiated hypotheses and theories, which explains, to a certain extent, the presence – in fact, dominance – of ideology-based schools of thought, including the monetarist school of thought (monetarism) according to which the business cycle is always and everywhere a monetary phenomenon, the Keynesian-New Keynesian school, which focuses on shocks in the presence of nominal rigidities and the Real Business Cycle school which attributes it to random real shocks, without however being able to identify them.

All of this points to one important fact, namely that in the absence of science, ideology comes to dominate, and so intergenerationally. The Marxian-Menger-Bohm-Bawerk debate of the 1880s simply metamorphosized itself into the post-WWII Keynesian-Monetarist debate, and the current real versus monetary causes of the business cycle and crises (e.g. the Financial Meltdown).

Questions for Discussion

1. Compare 20th-century macroeconomics with the proto-macroeconomics of the 19th century.
2. What do the UK Bank Charter Act of 1844 and the Federal Reserve Act of 1913 have in common?
3. Was the Great Depression in the UK comparable with that of the US? If so, how; if not, why not?
4. Are there institutional reasons why Milton Friedman's brand of macroeconomics took root at the University of Chicago? Why?
5. What are "real bills" and how are they part of the money supply? Which of the Banking School or the Currency School was right, in your opinion?
6. Compare growth theory with real business cycle theory from a scientific point of view?
7. Were wages and prices actually rigid in the 1930s?
8. Has a consensus emerged in the field of macroeconomics over the causes of major downturns and the business cycle? Why?
9. Could the Productivity Slowdown be responsible for verticalizing the Phillips Curve?
10. Who ultimately is responsible for determining the level of money income in an industrial economy?
11. To what extent was the macroeconomic problem tied to the growth problem in the 19th century?
12. Montagu Norman and the UK Treasury attributed the England's fall from economic supremacy to the breakdown of the gold standard. In your view, was he right? Why?

Notes

1 In many regards, his Banque générale de France was similar conceptually to the many 17th-century land-bank proposals, notably by William Patterson, one of the founders of the Bank of England in 1694. Others include the Darien scheme, which was based on land in central America, specifically the isthmus of Panama. In these cases, paper currency would be backed by assets in the New World.

2 The Corn Laws were a series of tariffs and other restrictions imposed on imported cereals (wheat, oats, barley) by the House of Lords (property owners) in the early 19th century.

3 This would continue well into the 20th century (and 21st century) for essentially the same reasons, namely poor science, specifically the lack of any fact-based evidence.

4 It could be argued that another of Reed Smoot's forays into macroeconomic-motivated tariff policy was the 1922 Fordney-McCumber Tariff Act that doubled tariff rates on imports.

5 Purchasing power parity is the notion that exchange rates should equalize domestic and foreign price levels. That is, the price level in Country A multiplied by the exchange rate should be equal to that of Country B).

6 He also dismissed the view that the UK's plight owed to its antiquated power-driven technology – in short, to real factors. In fact, he disparaged David Lloyd George, referring to him as the "Welsh Witch."

7 In fact, this is analogous to Adam Smith whose ultimate purpose in penning *The Wealth of Nations* was to create the market conditions such that Great Britain could realize the potential from the steam engine.

8 In fact, he was the only trained economist in the Brains Trust.

9 Electromagnetic Spectrum.

10 Specifically, he started with a long string of random numbers which was then transformed by a ten-item moving average, yielding a series which resembled macroeconomic time series.

11 Analytically, Douglas developed the $A+B \neq C$ theory according to which wages and profits (i.e. A+B) were insufficient to purchase C, overall GDP. He attributed this to insufficient credit, itself the result of the banking system being monopolized by a few firms. To remedy the situation, the government was to issue "social" as opposed to "private" credit.

12 The upshot of the IES framework is that macroeconomic equilibria is multi-dimensional. Few, if any, models today are able to capture this feature.

13 One could argue that macroeconomics had metamorphosized into growth economics.

14 WWI witnessed double-digit inflation over a period of four years as the Bank of England suspended convertibility (in specie) as did the Federal Reserve, resulting in a marked increase in credit and prices.

References

Chase, S. (1934) *The Economy of Abundance*, New York: The John Day Company.

Law, J. (1705) Money and Trade Consider'd with a Proposal for Supplying the Nation with Money.

Lloyd-George, David. (1924) *Coal and Power*, London: Hodder and Stoughton.

Malthus, T. (1827) *Principles of Political Economy Considered with a View of Their Potential Application*, New York: Augustus M. Kelley.

Owen, Robert. (1820) Report to the County of Lanark.

Say, Jean-Baptiste. (1809) Principes d'économie politique.

Scott, H. et al. (1933) *Introduction to Technocracy*, New York: The John Day Company.
Senate Congressional Record, January 7, 1945.
Shiller, R.J. (2000) *Irrational Exuberance*, Princeton, NJ: Princeton University Press.
Simonde de Sismondi, J.C.L. (1819) *Nouveaux Principes d'Économie Politique*, Paris: Calmann-Lévy.
Tugwell, R.G. (1927) *Industry's Coming of Age*, New York: Columbia University Press.
Tugwell, R.G. (1933) *The Industrial Arts and the Governmental Arts*, New York: Columbia University Press.
Veblen, Thorstein. (1921) *The Engineers and the Price System*, New York: B.W. Huebsch.

6

PRICE THEORY

Introduction

Prices lie at the very heart of exchange, defining the ratio at which goods (and money) trade at. Since exchange is an integral part of all economic institutions and because these same institutions are one of the two cornerstones of the science of wealth, it stands to reason that an understanding of prices is essential to every aspect, every field and sub-field of economics. Again, it is important to note that prices are not an end, but rather a means to an end, the end being exchange and ultimately, overall welfare.[1] This chapter examines the history of price theory, paying particular attention to science. Classical and neoclassical price theory asserts that free markets lead to the best possible outcome. That is, they maximize overall welfare. This raises a number of questions, not the least of which is, where's the proof? Has this proposition been tested scientifically? Other than anecdotal references to the superiority of Western industrialized nations over command-based economies, there does not appear to be any hard evidence of this proposition.

Like the previous chapters, this chapter will be organized chronologically. To begin with, the developments of the 19th century, the century that witnessed the emergence of free markets, will be surveyed. Of particular interest are two questions, namely the price setting mechanism and secondly, the associated welfare implications. In other words, is there evidence that the resulting free markets outperformed other coordinating strategies (institutions). It is important to remember that command-based, hierarchical trade-related institutions characterized most of civilization, with markets being a fairly recent development.

This will be followed by a look at 20th-century developments, many of which raised serious questions about 19th-century price theory. For example, the 20th century witnessed the emergence of giant firms which dominated their respective

DOI: 10.4324/9781003527060-6

markets and appeared to set prices independently of market conditions. While the 19th century was the century of perfect competition, it will be shown that the 20th century was the century of imperfect competition. This raises the obvious question: Did welfare suffer as a result? After all, classical and neoclassical price theory maintains that overall social welfare is decreasing in market concentration. Yet, the evidence shows that the 20th century witnessed the greatest levels of wealth and welfare ever recorded in history. Can these two facts be reconciled?

Definition

By price theory, it should be understood the set of theoretical constructs that describe the formation of prices in an exchange setting. Also included are the resulting welfare implications.

What You Will Learn in This Chapter

In this chapter, you will:

- Learn about the critical role prices played in the pre-industrial and industrial eras, and the transition between the two.
- Learn about the morality of prices, from Thomas Aquinas' notion of the just price to contemporary anti-trust legislation.
- Learn about the role of morality in Adam Smith's endorsement of the Physiocratic notion of free markets.
- Learn about how distribution-related and macroeconomic issues profoundly altered price theory in the mid-to-late 1800s.
- Learn how marginal cost pricing came to dominate the field, despite having no basis in either fact or the data.
- Learn about the history of anti-trust policy and the important role of energy-related developments.
- Learn why price theory, despite its elegance and mathematical sophistication, is more art than science.

By the End of This Chapter, You Should Understand

- The moral principles behind Adam Smith's endorsement of economic freedom and the invisible hand.
- The role of energy-related developments in shaping the theory of factor prices.
- The role of the popular uprisings in Europe in the mid-19th century in price theory in general and in the profession's interest in general equilibrium.
- The crisis in price theory provoked by the emergence of the vertically integrated, multinational giant firm.

- That despite two centuries of work, economics is still without a proven theory of prices.

The Pre-industrial Era

History of Wages and Prices in the Pre-industrial Era

Prices are an integral part of any and all trade-based societies from the very primitive to the most sophisticated. As our species *Homo sapiens* is decidedly social in its behavior, it stands to reason that prices or exchange ratios would play and do play an important role in primitive societies (i.e. pre-Neolithic) and an integral role in early civilizations (i.e. Mesopotamia).

Price Theory in the Pre-industrial Era

As pointed out, prices are simple numbers, simple numbers that convey rates at which agents are willing to trade – that is, goods for goods. Accordingly, an increase in price implies that one has to give up more of a good to get another good. And conversely, as far as the suppliers are concerned, they will now receive more in return for their product.

As trade is one of the key characteristics of our species (*Homo-sapiens sapiens*), it stands to reason that prices have been around for at least 200,000 years.[2] This then raises the question, when and why did they become the subject of discussion and debate? In other words, when did they become important?

As it turns out, prices entered the public debate in times of crisis, mostly in urban areas. Famines, wars and diseases brought the question of prices into the public discourse. And, not surprisingly, the debate focused on the question of morality, or put differently, the question of the just price. In times of crisis, was it morally acceptable to raise prices?

> *It is in the interest of buyers to seek the lowest price and of sellers to seek the highest price. Buyers and sellers negotiate and settle on a price agreeable to each side: the market price. For Thomas, then, the market price is the just price if the buyer and seller are honest and not trying to take advantage of each other. The ethical problem arises most commonly when there are dishonest participants, especially when the civil law allows or encourages such dishonesty.*
>
> *A just price should reflect the worth or value of a good or service. How is such value determined? Usually quite subjectively, which is why haggling over prices takes place. Economists distinguish between value in use and value in exchange to explain why something useful but plentiful like water costs much less than something rare but useless like diamonds. (Economists are not particularly concerned with beauty!) They also distinguish between the total utility of all of one's possessions and the marginal utility of an additional unit of a*

> *particular good, with the latter, not the former, determining what the buyer is willing to pay.*
>
> (*Jayabalan 2019, 3*)

A related question pertained to borrowing and the "just" rate of interest. Many writers questioned the legitimacy of interest rates. Could a high interest rate charged to someone in need be morally justified?

> *The basic idea of just price holds that there should be equality or fairness in economic transactions. The doctrine has its roots in Aristotle's conception of corrective justice and was given shape by various medieval scholars starting in the twelfth century. For every sale of goods or services, these authors held, there was a just price (typically a range) that would ensure that neither party to the exchange was able to exact unfair gains at the expense of the other. The overarching concern was to prevent coercion or compulsion in economic relationships. When markets could not be trusted to ensure that goods and services traded at their just price, various types of regulation, formal and informal, were called upon to correct or fix prevailing prices and align them with the just price.*
>
> (*Boyd 2018, 34*)

Prices in the Classical World

It is important to remember that throughout the Classical era (Greece and Rome), economies were essentially agricultural, with few cities and little industry (specialization). As such, most individuals were autarkic, and thus were not involved in market activity. Such was not the case in cities where specialization and exchange were a key part of civic life.

In general, prices in cities, regions and even countries were set by government. For example, in Rome prices were set by the Senate and/or Emperor. By fixing prices by decree, possible usury and other forms of exploitation could be controlled. Furthermore, the government could raise certain prices in an attempt to generate revenue – essentially the equivalency of an excise tax.

Prices, Price Setting and the Underlying View of Homo oeconomicus

The one important take-away from the pre-industrial era is the notion of morality in price setting. Prices were seen as more than just a rate of exchange, more than just a number. In fact, the ability to set prices was akin to power, one's power over another. In short, in the very nature of one's behavior vis-a-vis another.

In short, in most pre-industrial economies, prices were set by governmental decree, mostly to avoid usury, exploitation, as well as to ensure government revenues. Nowhere is this best understood than in the "Classical" social hierarchy, where government, lawyers, doctors and artists were at the top of the social hierarchy and merchants and thieves at the bottom.

Conclusion

Other than a handful of writings on the question of price, with the focus being squarely on the issue of a just or equitable price, the pre-industrial period was devoid of what could be referred to as price theory per se. This owed to two things, namely technological and institutional stasis, and second, the near absence of free markets. From the beginnings of civilization in Mesopotamia to the 18th century, little had changed. Innovations were few and far between. As shown in Chapter 3, the level of wealth remained more or less constant throughout this period. Ergo, there was little reason to enquire into prices given that they were, for the most part, fixed or regulated by the state.

The 19th Century

History of Wages and Prices in the 19th Century

Price Theory

As pointed out in earlier chapters, the industrial revolution brought new challenges to the West. Suddenly, countries like Great Britain had the possibility of what appeared to many to be unlimited wealth, of an *unbound prometheus*. As shown in Chapters 2 and 3, artisanal production techniques were replaced with industrial ones, based largely on greater machine speeds, and thus greater productivity per unit of capital/labor.

This new technology would not only increase the capacity of countries to produce the existing set of goods (and lower their price) but also witness the introduction of new goods, new consumer goods. However, as shown in Chapters 2 and 3, the problem was one of getting to the promised land, to the industrial nirvana. While the steam engine and other technological advances created a potential for vastly increased wealth, the problem was one of realizing the potential. In short, of making the transition from what was a Neolithic-based economy to an industrial one.

Steam and the Path to Wealth: From the Visible to the Invisible Hand

Enter Adam Smith and his two most celebrated works, namely *The Theory of Moral Sentiments* 1759, and *An Inquiry into the Nature and Causes of the Wealth of Nations* 1776. As pointed out in earlier chapters, *The Wealth of Nations* was, first and foremost, a critique aimed in large measure at the inability of market economy (read: competitive economy) to move spontaneously to the new, higher level of wealth (GDP) defined by the new technology.

In his view, not only would new markets need to be found but also resources would have to be allocated to what, for lack of a better term, was the new economy. Recall that in the mid-1700s, most European countries were command economies, by which it should be understood that prices and quantities were set in large measure by government decree.

Smith saw this an impediment to the transition to the new economy. Without a will on the part of the British House of Lords, the upper chamber, to move from what was a Neolithic to an industrial economy, England could fail to capitalize on its new-found power-drive technology, one capable of increasing output manifold.

Labor Theory of Value (General Theory of Prices)

The earliest theory of value – and of relative prices – was the labor theory of value. Historians believe that the concept was not new to the early 19th century, but rather had a long history, one that dated back to Antiquity. Thomas Aquinas in *his Summa Theologiae* expressed the view that "value can, does and should increase in relation to the amount of labor which has been expended in the improvement of commodities."

That the early political economists would have subscribed to such a theory is a question worth exploring. After all, the prices and values that they sought to understand and explain were the product of the industrial age, where labor had been reduced to a supervisory input, overseeing production processes. If anything, labor, while a cost, had a marginal role to play in early 19th-century industry.

The reason is twofold, namely that Adam Smith and David Ricardo were not scholars (in the current sense of the word), but rather pamphleteers, and secondly, the question of industrial prices (as opposed to resource prices) was not foremost in their mind – that is, it did not advance the cause(s) they championed. A pamphleteer was someone who used his pen, his wit, his logic, his command of history to affect or influence a public debate. Neither was a scholar in the current tradition (i.e. employing the scientific method). Smith's *The Wealth of Nations* and Ricardo's *The Theory of Political Economy and Taxation* were de facto calls for expanding the extent of the market (read: freedom) so as to allow firms to adopt the new power-drive technology that was the steam engine (i.e. specialization). Ricardo's interest in agricultural prices stemmed from his view that high corn (i.e. cereal) prices led to higher wages that, in turn, were growth decreasing as they lowered profits, savings and investment, and ultimately economic growth, thus preventing the UK from realizing its newfound, steam-engine-based potential.[3]

Karl Marx, Wages and Prices

As pointed out in Chapter 3, Karl Marx subscribed to the labor theory of value, taking the argument to its logical conclusion, arguing that labor was entitled to all of the value that it produced. According to him, the rate of surplus value was defined as ratio of what essentially were profits to value. Labor-saving devices, he argued, would increase this rate (by increasing constant capital), while increases in wages would decrease it.

Fundamental Contradiction of Capitalism

As rate of surplus value increases, the chances that the system will eventually collapse increase. Wage payments fall, decreasing purchasing power leading to a decrease in consumption, an increase in poverty and misery, and ultimately to the implosion of capitalism. It goes without saying that this scenario was troublesome, not only for workers but also for political economy and society in general. After all, Marx's analysis was founded on the postulates of classical political economy, making it virtually unassailable.

CAPSULE: IS ECONOMICS REALLY ABOUT SCARCITY?

Most students of economics are familiar with the view that economics is about scarcity, about unlimited wants and needs set against limited resources, about how society allocates these resources, and about the resulting overall level of welfare. But is it?

After all, the modern discipline of economics had its roots in the most abundant period and country in the history of mankind, namely 19th-century Great Britain, a period which is unmatched in so far as the level of and growth of material wealth are concerned. Early political economists estimated the steam power-based increase to be in the order of 40–100 times.

In the 1920s and 1930s, in what was the second industrial revolution, abundance once again reared its head. However, as had been the case in the early 19th century, a number of factors militated against the realization of the promised wealth (see Chapters 3 and 5). In the midst of this, a number of economists turned the problem on its head, arguing that, in actual fact, the main problem in political economy wasn't scarcity, but rather abundance, specifically one of managing abundance.[4] One such individual was Stuart Chase who published a volume entitled, the Economics of Abundance, the idea being that the challenges facing the United States and the World at the time had to do with managing (read: realizing) the potential that had been unleashed by the new power-drive technology that was electric unit drive.

The Neoclassical Rejoinder

Classical price theory was based, in large measure, on two factors, namely labor productivity and the wage. In short, relative prices were a function of relative labor productivity and relative wages. The publication of *Das Kapital* in 1867, which outlined the theoretical bases of wage and price theory, had a salutary effect on the mainstream (read: classical) price theory, forcing it to (i) justify profit, (ii) develop a more complete theory of production and costs and (iii) prove or demonstrate that capitalism was stable and would not collapse in time. In short, provide a response to the radicals.

Justifying Profits

The radicals were adamant: profits were a form of theft as they, roughly one-third of national income, are not earned and thus constitute a form of theft– a form of unmerited or undeserving rent. Not surprisingly, this did not bode well for classical thought, especially in Western democracies based on the rule of law. The owners of capital were seen as truants, as bandits, as robbers.

How did the classics respond? As pointed out in Chapter 3, they simply decreed capital to be productive, complete with a definition and measure of marginal and average productivity. However, as shown in Chapter 2, capital or tools are not, according to classical mechanics, physically productive. In short, they provide mechanical advantage, but are not a source of force-energy per se, and hence, cannot perform work or, simply put, produce. Unfortunately, this fact was lost on the new classical political economists, known heretofore as the neoclassicals.

Nonetheless, the resulting theory – known as neoclassical production theory – would form the basis of neoclassical price theory with its U-shaped marginal and average cost curves. As students will remember from Economics 101, its U-shape owes to the very shape of the marginal productivity of labor function.

A More Complete Theory of Production and Costs

The result was a more complete theory of production and costs, one that was sufficiently general to explain short-run disequilibrium and equilibrium, as well as long-run decreasing, constant and increasing cost industries. Furthermore, it provided a behavioral theory of the firm as consisting of a hypothetical profit-maximizing entrepreneur who chooses output levels such that marginal revenue equals marginal costs, and in so doing, maximizes overall profits. Implicitly, s/he chose quantities of labor and capital that were such that the value of the marginal productivity of each was equal to its price.

The Water-Diamond Paradox

Throughout the early 19th century, a paradox had haunted classical political economy, namely the water-diamond paradox, according to which water, which is essential to life, has a low price, while diamonds, a non-essential luxury good, are sold at exorbitant prices. This led the same classical writers to delve into the whole question of utility, specifically the utility of goods in general.

Just as labor and capital had both total and marginal productivities, goods would have total and marginal utilities, with the latter being defined as the increase in total utility that derives from consuming an extra unit of the good. Applied to water and diamonds, it was argued that goods are priced at the margin. Specifically, water, which is abundant, yields great total utility, but little marginal utility, while diamonds yield low total utility, but high marginal utility. In other words, scarcity is what underlies value.

Neoclassical Price Theory

As pointed out above, classical price theory was as simple as it was straightforward: prices vary according to the labor content of the good in question. And moreover, relative prices vary according to the relative content of labor in goods. A good example is Ricardian trade theory where relative prices are determined by the relative intensities of the labor content in goods.

Clearly, such a view could no longer be invoked in light of the fact that (i) labor's productivity was no longer a constant but rather varied according to the labor input (ii) capital and capital productivity would now need to be factored in, and (iii) value as seen by consumers varied with the quantity consumed.

Ultimately, this led to neoclassical price theory according to which price varies according to a number of factors, including the relevant time framework (i.e. short versus long run). Whereas classical theory ignored the time framework (owing largely to its simplicity), this would no longer be the case as now things like the capital stock and technology could vary. To address this issue, the very short, the short, the long and the very long runs were introduced into the analysis.

When compared to its predecessor (i.e. classical value theory), neoclassical price theory allowed for a number of different pricing strategies over the long run – that is, when the stock of the fixed factor, capital, was flexible. These included industries in which growth led to higher prices, to lower prices or to no change in price, referred to commonly as increasing cost industries, decreasing cost industries and constant cost industries.

The Question of Existence, Uniqueness and Stability

Karl Marx's *Das Capital* contained a bold, not to mention unsettling prediction, namely that over time, the rate of surplus value would increase, leasing ultimately to the breakdown of markets, prices and capitalism in general. In short, more and more wealth would be concentrated in the hands of the capitalists and less and less in the hands of workers. As a result, goods would go unsold, forcing capitalists to adopt new cost-saving technologies, which would further increase the rate of surplus value etc., leading ultimately to the breakdown in the capitalist mode of production.

Set against a backdrop of recurrent crises in the 19th century, this possibility came to haunt classical and neoclassical writers alike. Was capitalism stable? And would shocks, whether on the supply or demand side, lead to a downward spiral, culminating in chaos?

Ultimately, this led a number of writers to examine the question of existence, uniqueness and stability. Perhaps the best known of these were Léon Walras and Vilfredo Pareto of the Lausanne, Switzerland school. Being mathematically trained, they set out to show, using a system of equations and unknowns, the conditions in which a "general equilibrium" would exist, was unique and stable. In other words, find a vector of product prices, wages and profits that would clear the market.

Table 6.1 describes Walras' system of equations. The analysis consisted of defining system-wide demand and supply functions, and the corresponding excess demand functions. Existence of equilibria was defined in terms of a set of prices that would clear all markets (i.e. would eliminate excess demand in all markets. In short, simplicity would become the rule as complexity could only obfuscate matters. Further, all functions would need to be continuous (no breaks) and display convexity.

A by-product of this era was Walras' Law, which stated simply, holds that if *n-1* markets clear, then the *n*th market must also clear. While known as a law, it was in essence a property of matrix algebra.

The Birth of Welfare Analysis

Another by-product of this particularly fertile period in neoclassical price theory was welfare analysis. In short, now that general equilibria could be computed, they could now be compared with an eye to maximizing overall welfare. Perhaps the best-known concept is that of a Pareto optimum, which defines a general outcome such that any one person cannot be made better off without making someone else worse off.

Interest in the welfare aspects of market equilibria was motivated in large part by wealth and income inequality in the late 19th century. For example, in terms of land ownership, French economist Vilfredo Pareto observed that 80 percent of the land was owned by a handful of wealthy citizens, who comprised about 20 percent of the population.

TABLE 6.1 Walras' System of Equations-General Equilibrium

- Individuals supply factor services to factor markets and demand goods from goods markets.
- Firms demand factors from factor markets and supply goods to goods markets.
- Individual demand functions for m goods are of the form $d_a = fa(p_a, p_b, \ldots\ldots p_m, pf_1, pf_2 \ldots\ldots pf_n)$.
- Individual factor supply functions for the n factors will be of the form $sf_1 = f_1(pf_1, pf_2 \ldots\ldots pf_n, p_a, p_b \ldots\ldots p_m)$.

Price Theory in the 19th Century: Summary

As shown, price theory in the 19th century was a combination of pre-industrial ideas regarding prices and relative prices, ideological threats (i.e. Marxism) and classical responses. There can be little doubt that in the absence of non-classical or radical political economists, price theory at the end of the 19th century would have resembled price theory at the beginning, namely the labor theory of value.

Instead, price theory at the end of the century was marked by a number of innovations, including neoclassical distribution theory, neoclassical price theory and the introduction of general equilibrium analysis. As it turned out, the latter would continue to occupy the profession well into the 20th century, especially in the aftermath of the Great Depression when the question of stability and the renewed fear of Marxian-style collapse would rear their heads.

In keeping with the overall theme of this volume, namely the scientific underpinnings of economics, the questions of testing and proof arise. In other words, were any of the myriad hypotheses or price theories presented in the 19th century tested against the facts, against the data? For example, did Alfred Marshall present evidence that the short-run marginal cost curve was downward, then upward sloping? Did he present evidence to the effect that the long-run average cost curve was U-shaped? Or did Karl Marx present evidence to the effect that the rate of surplus value was indeed increasing, or that labor was the only productive factor input?

The answer to all of these questions, unfortunately, is no. Not one of the aforementioned writers attempted to "turn to the data" so to speak. Instead, they relied on logic, cloaked in anecdotes and/or historical facts. Thus, in short, most of that which is referred to as 19th-century price theory, was nothing more than speculation, oftentimes dressed up in mathematics.

How then should this body of work be judged? After all, as pointed out in Chapters 1 and 2, economics is not the only field devoted to understanding wealth-generating material processes. Others include applied physics and process engineering. This raises the question, how does 19th-century price theory measure up to both classical mechanics and thermodynamics? The answer, unfortunately, is not well. By the end of the 19th century, industrial processes in the UK and the United States were being powered by high-pressure steam, with labor and capital acting as organizational (read: non-physically productive) inputs. Hence, it follows that all of classical and neoclassical wage and price theory is based on a set of erroneous assumptions (i.e. that labor and capital are physically productive and thus have non-zero marginal productivities). Since its foundations are compromised, it follows that follows would also be compromised. Nowhere is this more evident in neoclassical distribution theory where the underlying principles are based on the marginal productivities of labor and capital, two concepts that violate basic physics.

This raises the question of why? Why did writers in this period get it so wrong? While the field of physics, from which ironically many of the tools used in neoclassical theory (e.g. Lagrangian, Hamiltonians etc.), was evidence-based, especially the burgeoning field of thermodynamics, economics continued to rely on voluminous narratives, punctuated with anecdotes and numerical examples.[5] The reason, it could be argued, was largely political – that is, with what was at stake. Neoclassical price theory was not a scientific undertaking, the purpose of which was to uncover the laws that govern price, but rather a reaction/response to an existential threat, namely Marxism and all it entailed, especially its policy prescriptions – namely, socialism and communism. This very fact would go on to plague price theory in the 20th century when a new set of challenges would, once again, undermine its validity.

Price Theory: The 20th Century

The 20th century would witness a number of developments that, once again, would serve to undermine the ability of the market mechanism to do its job, so to speak, namely ensure full-employment in a context of sustained growth. Among these was the aftermath of WWI in Great Britain, the Stock Market Crash of 1929, the Great Depression, and the post-WWII period. Specifically, the post-WWI period in Great Britain witnessed the inability of markets, especially the labor market to clear, resulting in unprecedented levels of unemployment (i.e. more than a million unemployed workers). A similar set of issues would appear in the 1930s, when the World economy collapsed amid weak investment, trade wars and questionable macroeconomic policies.

On top of all of this was the emergence in the early 20th-century United States of giant, vertically integrated firms or conglomerates, which circumscribed the market for factors and inputs, coordinating supply lines/chains across space and time. The atomistic market capitalism of the 19th century was replaced by giant firms and managerial capitalism. As business historian Alfred D. Chandler put it, Adam Smith's *invisible hand* of the market was replaced with the *visible hand* of managerial hierarchies, the management or coordination of the activities of large, integrated corporations.[6] The late 19th and early 20th centuries witnessed the emergence of large trusts which controlled key markets, the best examples being John D. Rockefeller's Standard Oil which controlled 90 percent of the US gasoline market and Henry Ford's Ford Motor Corporation which one controlled 90 percent of the US market.

As a consequence, newly minted neoclassical price theory based in large part on the single product, atomistic producer, faced many a challenge and emerged battered and bruised. Clearly, the world of Ricardo, Jevons and Marshall was no longer as was the world of atomicity and competition. In its place would be markets where perfect competition would give way to imperfect competition.

It bears noting that the use of the adjective "imperfect" had nothing to do with science or reality and everything to do with being an intellectual construct. The early 20th century, which coincided with the emergence of "imperfect competition" witnessed an unprecedented increase in the material standard of living, known as modernity. In short, it was anything but a period of imperfection. One could go as far as to argue that what is typically referred to as "imperfect competition" and "imperfect market structures" should be regarded, in actual fact, as being perfect as they led to or were synonymous with and conducive to these historic output and productivity increases.[7]

History of Wage and Price Developments in the 20th Century

Table 6.2 lists the various developments of the early 20th century in so far as prices are concerned. In other words, these are the issues that would, over the course of the century, shape the field. While this had, to a certain extent, been the case in the 19th century, it would become the hallmark of the 20th century, namely a fact-based science.

The first development is the behavior of markets and prices in post-WWII Great Britain. UK prices in general, including wages, had increased by roughly 200 percent in WWI. In short, the government had financed the war effort by selling its securities to the Bank of England, resulting in a classic 'too-much money chasing too-few goods' inflationary scenario. However, as pointed out in Chapter 3, after the war, the government of Robert Baldwin deemed that a return to the gold standard at pre-war parities ($4.86 Pound) would restore Great Britain's position of dominance in the world economy.[8] To accomplish this, prices and wages would have to fall.

Much to the surprise of the government and most observers (including John Maynard Keynes), prices were stubbornly rigid, as were wages. Marshallian "market forces" appeared to be faltering, reintroducing questions regarding the very ability of markets to do their job (i.e., to coordinate and clear). The result was the continued presence of unemployment and stagnation from 1918 well into the late 1920s. Clearly, something was amiss, something about Marshallian reasoning was amiss.

The second development was the alleged failure of prices to fall in the face of the productivity-increasing technological developments in the 1910s and 1920s in the United States. As pointed out in Chapter 3, the widespread adoption of electric unit drive, by increasing machine speeds, increased efficiency and lowered production costs markedly. However, throughout this period, there was an overriding feeling that firms were not passing these savings/cost reductions on to consumers

TABLE 6.2 Major Price-Related Developments of the 20th Century

- Price and wage rigidities in Post-WWI Great Britain
- Wage and price rigidity in the United States during the roaring 1920s
- Price and wage rigidity in the Great Depression
- Non-market-based pricing by large vertically integrated firms
- Profit maximization or managerial prerogatives

in the form of lower prices. Recall that University of Chicago economics professor Thorstein Veblen referred to this as "sabotage." In other words, managers were de facto sabotaging the transition to greater wealth defined by the new process technology. There were, of course, exceptions. One notable exception, however, was industrialist and founder of the Ford Motor Company, Henry Ford, who slashed prices throughout this period and invited his fellow managers to do likewise, an invitation they resoundingly rejected.

In summary, the early 20th century witnessed a number of what could be referred to as market anomalies, anomalies which cast the long shadow of a doubt on the validity of neoclassical price theory – which was, for all intents and purposes, still in its infancy. For some reason(s), markets were not working in the UK and the United States in the 1920s. Conspiracy theories began to appear, the most notable of which was Adolf Berle Jr. and Gardiner Means notion that managers had unlawfully wrestled control of large corporations away from shareholders and were no longer acting as their fiduciary agents, but rather were pursuing their own agenda. In short, private property was under siege.

Price and Wage Setting by Giant Firms

Throughout the early part of the century, the question of price setting by the new, large vertically integrated "giant" firms became an issue in its own right. After all, these large entities, which controlled important sectors of the economy, appeared to behave differently – at least, in comparison with their Marshallian competitive counterparts. For one, they had suppressed virtually all intermediaries in their respective supply chains by combining all stages of value added under one roof. As high volume and speed were of the essence, most had a commanding presence in their respective markets.

Others wondered whether these "giant firms" managed by a new generation of professionals had not changed the very conduct of business in the United States, going from small, owner-managed profit maximizing entities, to ones that were controlled by a set of officers that had usurped control from the owners, namely the shareholders.

What is abundantly clear from this list is the orthogonality of developments in the 20th century and 19th-century price theory. As Keynes would go on to argue, Marshallian economics had become more or less irrelevant, raising the question of whether it had ever been relevant? Could its irrelevance have owed to the fact that it had been born of an ideological debate (radical versus classical political economists) as opposed to a truly scientific one?

As shall be shown, the 20th century witnessed the demise of neoclassical price theory, based on perfect competition, and the rise of imperfect competition, and the emergence of a sub-field of microeconomics known as industrial organization where the emphasis was on understanding firm behavior within specific, well-defined industry structures.

History of Price Theory in the 20th Century

20th-Century Developments

Twentieth-century developments will be broken down into two categories, namely pre-WWII and post-WWII, with the former focusing on the problem of price rigidity and the latter on above-normal profits. The price (and wage) rigidity of the 1920s in Great Britain and the United States prompted a number of responses from both British and American writers, including Joan Robinson and Edward Chamberlin. It is important to point out that most of these contributions pre-date the Great Depression, focusing attention on the price and wage rigidity of the 1920s in Great Britain and incidentally on that in the United States during the 1930s.

CAPSULE: DO FIRMS MAXIMIZE PROFITS?

Downward price stickiness had become an ongoing concern in the 1920s as firms adopted speed-and-efficiency-increasing electric unit drive (see Chapter 3). Adolph A. Berle Jr. Professor of Law at Columbia University was invited by Edwin Gay of Harvard to inquire into the role of corporate structure and control on pricing decisions. Berle then brought Gardiner Means, who was in the process of writing a thesis on administered prices (read: non-market prices), on board. The result was "The Modern Corporation and Private Property, by Berle and Gardiner Means."

Chapter 1, written by Gardiner Means, describes the behavior of the 200 largest US corporations. The rest of the book is devoted to behavior and its legalities. In short, it is argued that managers have usurped control from shareholders, that managers have reneged on their fiduciary obligations – in short, that the veritable owners of these corporations, the shareholders, had been deprived of one of the fundamental property rights, namely control. In short, corporate officers (e.g. CEO, CFO and COO) had hijacked not only the workings of capitalism but also private property.

The second category focuses on post-WWII contributions. Wartime sales, increasing market share and profits of large US corporations are what led ultimately to a shifting of focus away from price and wage rigidity and over to industry concentration, profits and social welfare. In short, the conversion to high-speed electric unit drive increased market concentration throughout the economy à la Ford Motor Company, thus increasing earnings.

Was this a good or bad thing? As corporate officers increased their control à la Berle and Means, did social welfare decrease or increase? As will be shown, for roughly two decades, concentration was seen as welfare decreasing, until the 1970s

TABLE 6.3 Pre-WWII Contributions

- Edward Chamberlin and Joan Robinson's Monopolistic Competition
- Gardiner Means' Administered Prices
- Adolf Berle Jr. and Gardiner Means' Non-profit-Maximizing Corporations
- Paul Sweezy's Kinked Demand Curve
- Hall and Hitch Full-Cost Pricing

when the tide turned in its favor – in short, concentration was seen as a manifestation of more efficient operating methods, lower prices and thus, greater welfare. Which is where the debate stands today – that is, with no declared winner.

As mentioned in Chapter 3, University of Chicago economics professor Thorstein Veblen argued that by not cutting prices, but rather by cutting employment and output in response to technological change (specifically acceleration-based electric unit drive), large corporations sabotaged the transition to the new, higher level of output (GDP). As it turned out, this view permeated much of the 1920s, being the subject of the developments in microeconomics, not the least of which was Joan Robinson and Edward Chamberlin's theory of monopolistic competition, and Gardiner Means extensive work on administered versus market prices. In fact, the pricing behavior of corporations throughout the 1920s is what prompted Columbia University law professor Adolf A. Berle Jr., in conjunction with Gardiner Means, to allege in The Modern Corporation and Private Property, published in 1932, that managers in large public corporations in the post-WWI period had de facto usurped control from shareholders and were no longer acting as the latter's fiduciary agents, casting the long shadow of a doubt on the standard view of profit maximization – and what it entails for behavior. Put differently, pricing decisions were no longer motivated by profit or shareholder value maximization.

The Theory of Monopolistic Competition

This is perhaps the most important development in price theory of the early 20th century. The work of Cambridge economics professor Joan Robinson and Harvard economics professor Edward Chamberlin, it sought to understand pricing behavior when competition occurs among relatively similar firms whose product characteristics confer a form of monopoly power on each. That is, when the assumption of a homogeneous product is replaced with that of a differentiated product, resulting in a certain degree of market or monopoly power on the producers.

While price is above minimum average cost, firms do not earn profits, owing to the fact that entry is not limited, but rather is free – that is, there are the absence of barriers to entry. Firms produce to the left of the point of minimum average cost and thus are alleged to have significant excess capacity. The result was a model that appeared to fit the new reality that was 20th century modernity with its new consumer goods and its rampant product differentiation. A good example of the latter is the automobile industry, which witnessed the arrival of new, large-scale competitors offering a differentiated product.

The problem with monopolistic competition as a theory of price rigidity, however, was with its underlying assumptions, specifically that of market clearing. In other words, prices in monopolistically competitive markets were as variable as in perfect competition. Thus, while it infused a degree of reality into the analysis, it stopped short of providing a credible theory of the price rigidity observed in the 1920s. In other words, it did little in the way of providing the micro-foundations of Keynesian macroeconomic analysis.

The Theory of the Kinked Demand Curve

While the 1930s and 1940s were rich in developments, few were able to provide a credible rationale for sticky prices. Recall that Thorstein Veblen alleged that corporate officers had sabotaged and were sabotaging the transition to the new, higher GDP by holding the line on prices while costs were falling. One such theory was the theory of the kinked demand curve, developed by Marxist Paul Sweezy. The idea was simple, namely that if a firm raises its price, its competitors will not follow; however, if it lowers it, then they will. This creates an indeterminacy, a kink in so far as the firm's marginal revenue curve is concerned. According to Sweezy, unit costs can fluctuate in that "zone" without provoking a variation in price, thus providing a rationalization of the price stickiness observed and described in the 1920s.

The resulting equilibrium provided a plausible rationalization of price rigidity. Cutting one's price would lead competitors to follow suit, thus lowering considerably marginal revenue, forcing the firm to reconsider.

The Theory of Administered Prices

Perhaps one of the most glaring weaknesses of Marshallian price theory (read: perfect competition) was its lack of realism. It reduced firm behavior to a series of fictional curves which intersected where marginal revenue equaled marginal cost, failing to capture what appeared to be the underlying complexity of pricing behavior. For example, what was the relevant time framework? Did markets clear always, every day, every week, every month? Did prices react to hourly, daily, weekly or monthly changes in demand and costs?

By the 1930s, a number of writers, including Columbia University economics professor, Gardiner Means, pointed out that prices in manufacturing and industry in general appeared to be administered – that is, not set by market forces. In a briefing prepared for the US Senate in 1935, he described pricing behavior as either administered or market-based, the former referring to industries in which prices were set by firms and the latter, where prices were set by market forces. Table 6.4 presents a summary of his findings for the ten major industries for the period 1929–1933.

The top five, he argued, were industries where prices were administered, while the bottom five had prices that were determined by market forces.

This was followed by a number of theoretical contributions, the most celebrated of which was the theory of full-cost pricing, put forward by British economists R.L. Hall and C.J. Hitch whose work was the culmination of a large-scale survey of the pricing practices in 38 large British firms.

> *The most striking feature of the answers was the number of firms which apparently do not aim, in their pricing policy, at what appeared to us to be the maximization of profits by the equation of marginal revenue and marginal cost. In a few cases this can be explained by the fact that the entrepreneurs are thinking of long-run profits, and in terms of long-run demand and cost curves, even in the short run, rather than of immediate profits. This is expressed to some extent by the phrase commonly used in describing their policy – "taking goodwill into account." But the larger part of the explanation, we think, is that they are thinking in altogether different terms; that in pricing they try to apply a rule of thumb which we shall call "full cost," and that maximum profits, if they result at all from the application of this rule, do so as an accidental (or possibly evolutionary) by-product.*
>
> *(Hall and Hitch 1939, 18)*

According to their survey results, firms set prices to cover their total costs over the lifetime of the investment (e.g. 20 years). As the early years would see the firm earn losses (owing to the fact that the plant would not operate at full capacity), it had to set price over the life of the investment in order to (i) not price itself out of the market and (ii) cover costs. In other words, the resulting prices would not clear the market at any point in time; however, over the long haul, price would be equal to average unit cost with a normal rate of return on capital. The resulting full-cost

TABLE 6.4 Administered and Market Prices in the Great Depression

	Percentage Drop in Prices	*Percentage Drop in Production*
Agricultural Implements	6	80
Motor Vehicles	16	80
Cement	18	65
Iron and Steel	20	83
Auto Tires	33	70
Textile products	45	30
Food products	49	14
Leather	50	20
Petroleum	56	20
Agricultural Commodities	63	6

Source: Means, G. (1962), 88.

pricing is analogous in many ways to mark-up pricing. In essence, firms mark-up their variable costs by a fraction (percentage), a practice that was found to be commonplace in large manufacturing firms.

Developments in the Post-WWII Period

It is fair to say that the first half of the 20th century was particularly trying for price theory and microeconomics in general. Particularly affected was Marshallian, neoclassical price theory, itself but a decade old (i.e. 1890). Wage and price stickiness in the UK (1920s) and the United States (1930s) had cast more than a shadow of a doubt on the workings of the market, namely its equilibrating nature. Add to this the emergence and growth of large multinational, multiplant, multiproduct, vertically integrated conglomerates, which circumvented the market mechanism in favor of large, multilevel management and control , resulting in increases levels of industry concentration. In short, Marshallian price theory based in large part on atomicity and perfect competition was increasingly irrelevant.

Gone were the days of idyllic atomicity and competition, the days of price-taking behavior, the days of zero profits. Throughout the century, concentration increased as did the number of multiproduct, multiplant and multinational firms, with Henry Ford's Highland Park and River Rouge plants as early examples.

Post-WWII Developments in Price Theory

One of the shortcomings of pricing models in this period was their oversimplification. In short, they reduced a complex problem involving many components and sub-components to a simple *P=marginal revenue=marginal cost* maximization problem. While the majority of goods in the 19th century had been produced by a small, atomistic firm, such was not the case in the early 20th century with the arrival of the multi-good, multi-plant, multi-country firms. In short, the advent of modernity

TABLE 6.5 Large Multinational, Multiplant, Multiproduct, Vertically Integrated Conglomerates

Conglomerate	*Products*
General Electric Corporation	Turbines, public generating equipment, household appliances, electric equipment, medical equipment (and more)
Westinghouse Corporation	Turbines, power-generating equipment, household appliances
Ford Motor Company	Automobiles, Trucks, Agricultural Equipment
General Motors	Automobiles, Trucks, Energy, Household Appliances
Exxon Corporation	Petroleum products, chemicals, alternative fuels
Dupont Chemicals	Chemical Products
Monsanto	Chemical Products, GMOs

increased complexity in a manifold manner. A good example is the automobile industry with its many products, its many plants and its highly complex supply chain.

Consequently, changes in market conditions are not likely to bring about instantaneous variations in price given the inertia that is ubiquitous in the various value chains. If and only if all concerned stand prepared to vary, their price will prices of final goods vary.

While short on empirics, the post-WWII period was a particularly fruitful one for price theory as it witnessed the development of more complex models of behavior, most of which were based on the emerging field of game theory, the latter being largely the result of the work of mathematicians John Von Neumann and Oskar Morgenstern. As pointed out above, interest in oligopoly theory was motivated in large measure by the abnormally high profits of large corporations, especially during WWII when government military expenditure in the United States reached $88 billion, or roughly 45 percent of GDP. Military contractors, which included much of the automotive industry, earned record profits, adding credence to the early 20th-century *Progressive* notion that large corporations behaved anticompetitively, resulting in a decrease in overall welfare.

The emergence of large-scale, multiproduct, multi-country, vertically integrated corporations, combined with Berle and Means' earlier findings regarding behavior, rekindled the debate over the motives underlying firm behavior. Did these large conglomerates maximize profits by setting marginal revenue equal to marginal cost, or was there something else at play? Among the more notable contributions was the work of Herbert Simon, who argued in favor of a theory of decision-making in complex environments – in other words, in large, modern corporations.

Known by various names such as satisficing or bounded rationality, the resulting body of literature attempted to infuse a much-needed dose of realism. The result was myriad theories of firm objectives, from growth maximization, to market-share maximization, to manager compensation maximization, to standard profit-maximization (see Table 6.7). The downside of this literature was (i) its

TABLE 6.6 Post-WWII Contributions

Profit Maximizing versus Satisficing Behavior
Oligopoly models
Cournot
Bertrand
Von Stackelberg
Cartel
Game theory
Static games
Dynamic games
Imperfect information
Structure-conduct-performance framework
Efficient markets framework

TABLE 6.7 Multidimensional Theories of Firm Objectives

Theory	*Author(s)*	*Objective*
Growth Maximization	William Baumol (1959)	Firms appear to maximize growth in lieu of profits.
Managerial Compensation Maximization	Adolf A. Berle and Gardiner Means (1932)	Managers have usurped control from shareholders and pursue their own personal objectives.
Satisficing	Herbert Simon and James March (1958)	Because of their members' bounded rationality and often contradictory goals and perspectives, firms reach decisions that can only be described as satisfactory rather than the best possible outcome.
	Richard Cyert and James March (1963)	In addition to profit, they list objectives for production (including both level and stability of output), stock levels, sales and market share.

sociological bend and (ii) it being non-amenable to mathematical formalization. As such, formalism won out over realism, with the result that little remains of this literature in economics, despite its popularity in business schools. Put differently, simple profit maximization was a more convenient working hypothesis than was satisficing or bounded rationality.

As a result, the theoretical developments in this period were, for the most part, a combination of 19th-century notions of firm behavior and the predictions of game theory. Profit maximization was modeled as a game involving players, strategy spaces and payoffs. A good example is the Cournot oligopoly model where the strategy space is defined over the quantities each firm chooses to produce. It makes the unrealistic (read: irrational) assumption that a firm's choice of output will have no bearing on its competitors' decisions. An equilibrium results in which the firm's output is a function of demand and cost parameters both of the firm and its rivals.

Another similar 19th-century equilibrium is that of Joseph Bertrand, who assumed that firms' play a pricing – as opposed to quantity setting – strategy. In this case, the resulting price is analogous to perfect competition where $p=mc$.[9]

Also noteworthy are two other equilibria, namely the Stackelberg equilibrium and the Cartel equilibrium. The former introduces an asymmetry in the form of an industry leader and a number of followers. The leader comes to dominate the market, while the followers are forced to share that segment of the market that goes unserved. The Cartel equilibrium, as its name implies, has firms sharing the market in a tacit or explicit agreement.

While these models, cast in the language of game theory, provided some key insights into behavior, they failed to shed much, if any light on pricing and output decisions of large corporations. This owed to a number of factors, not the least of which is the fact that they were never tested empirically. This can be attributed to (i) the multi-product nature of most large corporations and (ii) the lack of data. According to *Security and Exchange Commission* rules, firms are obliged to report their consolidated accounting data, not their line-of-business data, making it virtually impossible to test with any accuracy any model of pricing behavior.

However, what did emerge from this body of work was the view that industry concentration in general was welfare reducing, a result that would be formalized in what was perhaps the greatest contribution of the post-WWII period, namely the *Structure-Conduct-Performance* framework.

CAPSULE: EARLY ANTI-MONOPOLY SENTIMENT OR WHY LARGE FIRMS ARE SEEN AS WELFARE DECREASING

The notion that large firms with significant market power (i.e. high concentration rates) are welfare decreasing has an intriguing past, one that crosses many lines, including politics, business and economics. Interestingly, it is decidedly a North American phenomenon, which holds the key to understanding its origins.[10] *For most of its early history, the US economy was characterized by small, local businesses, owing in large measure to the corresponding power-drive technology.*

The advent of the second industrial revolution changed all that as it witnessed the emergence of large, vertically integrated national firms, firms whose market went from the Atlantic to the Pacific (i.e. The Great Atlantic and Pacific Tea Company). While these firms conferred immeasurable gains to consumers, they did not sit well with the political class. After all, US society had been founded on the notions of equality and of flat dominance hierarchies.

The resulting large firms (i.e. monopolies) were seen as fundamentally anti-American and corrupt. By the late 19th/early 20th centuries, a political splinter movement within the Republican party emerged, known as the Progressives. The latter opposed big business interests and argued in favor of competition and regulation. In the 1912 election, unhappy with President Taft's reforms, former Republican president Theodore Roosevelt formed the Progressive Party. The point is that according to the Progressives, concentration and monopoly were deemed to be anti-American, to be corrupt despite the welfare gains that followed from the second industrial revolution. A good example is the Sherman Anti-Trust Act, introduced by Ohio senator John Sherman, that targeted John D. Rockefeller's Standard Oil near monopoly despite the fact that it had lower prices than its competitors.[11]

In short, the anti-concentration bias is as much the result of sociology and politics than it is welfare analysis. The 20th century witnessed repeated examples of how large firms, by lowering costs and introducing new products, actually increased welfare. Many of these, however, earned the wrath of the political class for the power they wielded.

The Structural Theory of Industrial Organization (Mason and Bain)

With the surge of interest in markets that were imperfectly competitive (1930–1945) came the desire on the part of some to impose structure to the debate. Specifically, could markets be categorized and could behavior in the resulting categories be generalized. For example, if an industry consisted of two firms, how could it be described, and secondly, could the behavior of the two firms be described in a meaningful way? Further, could something be said about how behavior varies with industry characteristics? Lastly, was concentration welfare increasing or decreasing?

Enter Harvard economics professor, Edward Mason, who in 1939 presented what can best be described as a general theory of industrial organization, including prices, price-cost margins and overall behavior regarding such things as entry and exit, barriers to entry, and investment. Known as the Structure-Conduct-Performance approach, it maintained that profitability was increasing in industry concentration, while welfare is decreasing. In general, the more an industry is concentrated, the higher is the price-cost margin, the lower is the output, the greater are profits and the lower is consumer surplus (welfare)

This was an important development in the sense that now, the profession had a general theory of pricing behavior across industry structures. Price-cost margins were hypothesized to be increasing in the level of concentration, which itself was increasing in the presence of barriers to entry. A continuum of cases arose, from fictional Marshallian perfect competition to monopoly, with monopolistic competition and oligopoly occupying middle grounds

Oligopoly Theory and Game Theory

In time, the existence of a stable, monotonically increasing relationship between price-cost margins and concentration as argued by Edward Mason and Joseph Bain, however, came under increasing scrutiny. For example, in the case of duopoly, it was shown that if firms play output strategies (i.e. choose the quantity produced), then price-cost margins were indeed decreasing in the number of firms. However, if firms play price strategies, then this result disappears. In short, it became

TABLE 6.8 Market Structures

Perfect Competition
Monopolistic competition
Oligopoly
Cournot
Bertrand
Von Stackelberg
Cartel
Monopoly

increasingly obvious that there was more to industrial organization and policy design than simply counting the number of firms in a given sector.

At roughly the same time, the US military had invested massively in a new field of applied mathematics, known as game theory. With the Cold War in full force, it sought to explore various military strategies, such as mutual nuclear destruction, tit-for-tat bombings etc. Not surprisingly, this promising line of research soon made its way to industrial organization where firm behavior was often cast in military-like terms – that is, playing strategies, having payoffs, engaging in retaliatory behavior etc.

With the wind (i.e. game theory) in its sails, oligopoly theory set out to refine the Mason-Bain structural model. The result was the different strategies and equilibria listed in Table 6.9. Every aspect of firm behavior was examined within the context of game theory. Unfortunately, with every advance in game theory came a whole new realm of possibilities in so far as behavior was concerned. While welcome in most instances, the plethora of results, cases and outcomes cast the long shadow of doubt on the structural approach. Clearly, the level of industry concentration had little-to-no bearing on the outcome. High levels of concentration can be synonymous with high or zero profits.

The Efficient Markets Rejoinder to Mason and Bain

Not only did game theory poke proverbial holes in the Mason-Bain structural approach, so too would a group of economists and jurists at the University of Chicago who maintained that contrary to Edward Mason and Joe S. Bain's views, concentration was synonymous with greater, not lower consumer surplus and welfare. Led by University of California at Los Angeles economics professor Harold Demsetz, their reasoning was based in large measure on the historical

TABLE 6.9 Oligopoly Theory and Strategies

Nash-Cournot Strategies and Equilibria
Nash-Bertrand Strategies and Equilibria
Von Stackelberg Strategies and Equilibria
Cooperative-Cartel Strategies and Equilibria

TABLE 6.10 Game Theory Concepts and Tools

Static Game
Dynamic game
Sequential games
Non-cooperative game
Cooperative game
Stochastic game

record, where companies like Ford, while highly concentrated, provided cheap, affordable automobiles to the United States and the World (Demsetz 1973). Other examples include General Electric and Standard Oil. Put differently, concentration was not the result of attempts on the part of incumbents to bar entry, but rather was the result of their genius. Put differently, big is better, concentration is good as it signals either superior products (i.e. Windows and IOS) and/or lower costs.

Further Proofs of the Existence of Equilibria, Its Uniqueness and Stability

Not surprisingly, the Great Depression rekindled interest in the question of the existence, uniqueness and stability of "general" equilibria – in short, of the long-run viability of the capitalism. Throughout the 1930s, governments and analysts questioned whether Karl Marx had been right all along, namely that the laws of motion of capitalism are such that it will self-destruct.

This led to a push on the part of a number of scholars to prove, beyond all doubt, that market equilibria exist, are unique and stable. Among these were French economist Gérard Debreu who presented an axiomatic proof of existence, uniqueness and stability. This soon became the standard in general equilibrium theory, known commonly as the Arrow-Debreu approach/model/proof.

Whereas Léon Walras and others like Vilfredo Pareto relied on simple proofs (i.e. counting equations and unknowns), the axiomatic approach relied on topology, notably on various fixed-point theorems (Brouwer and Kakutani). Here, mappings were used to prove existence. Uniqueness and stability followed from a set of restrictive assumptions regarding consumer and firm behavior.

Testing the Predictions of Industrial Organization

There can be little doubt. The post-WWII period was an extremely fruitful period in the history of price theory, one that surpassed the late 19th century, which had witnessed the emergence of neoclassical price theory. As pointed out, the introduction of new tools, notably game theory, increased the complexity and breath of the models and predictions.

The question, in so far as the validity of these developments is concerned, is whether they were tested empirically – that is, against the data. And this is where things turn sour, so to speak. First of all, there is the question of the relevant predictions. As pointed out, corporations in the post-WWII period were multiproduct, multiplant, multinational entities, whose decision space was equally complex. Clearly, the world had evolved, but the theory had not. What was needed was a theory of the multiproduct, multiplant, multinational conglomerate, and the data to test it.

This begs the question, if such a theory or theories existed, could it/they be tested? The answer is no. First, the only firm-level data that exist are financial in nature, collected and collated according to the exigencies of the various financial regulatory agencies such as the Securities Exchange Commission. These data are contained in annual financial reports, and moreover are consolidated (i.e. across products, plants and counties) and not by line of business. A good example is the *Compustat* data that are taken from annual reports and contains the most complete data base currently available.

This raises the further question of why? Why are better data not available? The reason can be culled from an example. In 1972, the US Department of Commerce launched a Line of Business data initiative in which it required firms to submit detailed (by produce or line of business) operating data such as price, quantity, costs, etc. The thinking as that such data would allow for the design of better policy, not to mention better analysis.

Fate would have it, however, that the project would abort. Corporations complained that revealing such data would compromise their operations and market position, and secondly, that it was unconstitutional. This was the last such attempt at creating a more complete microeconomic data base at the firm level.

CAPSULE: DO FIRMS MARGINAL COST PRICE?

Neoclassical price theory is founded, in large measure, on optimization (static and dynamic) analysis. Assuming the existence of analytical demand and cost functions, it predicts that firms will set price according to marginal cost. This is commonly known as marginal cost pricing.

One would think that after a century of analysis, there would be evidence that indeed, firms price at marginal cost. However, there just isn't. In the late 1950s, a debate over pricing behavior emerged, one that pitted the theoreticians against the practitioners. The latter, led by John Blair of the, maintained that prices were administered, much in keeping with Gardiner Means' and R.lL. Hall and R.C. Hitch's earlier findings (Blair 1959).

The evidence presented reconfirmed administered prices as the predominant pricing principle. Firms in general were shown to have little information on marginal cost. Did this change anything?

The answer is no, largely on the strength of the argument that while firms were unaware of their marginal cost curve, they behaved as if they did. In other words, profit maximization sufficed for the first-order conditions to hold. Also getting in the way of more realistic pricing models are the implications for the whole of neoclassical analysis. If firms don't marginal cost price, then the upward-sloping supply curve no longer exists, at least not in its current incarnation. In short, marginal cost pricing has more to do with modeling than it does with reality.

Industrial Organization: Ideology or Science?

As shown, the field of price theory in the 20th century experienced unprecedented growth, responding to a number of developments, the most notable of which was the Great Depression. The post-WWII period saw the introduction of game theory and the emergence of the new subfield of industrial organization, a field that provides a richness and complexity that was absent at the end of the 19th century. This then begs the question: Have these developments brought us closer to the ultimate goal of understanding markets and prices? Does our analysis allow us to make predictions, to understand behavior and to design optimal policy? After all, the study of markets and prices is over two centuries old, dating back to Adam Smith's *Wealth of Nations*.

Based on the evidence presented in this chapter, the only plausible answer is no. While the field was infinitely richer tool-and- concept-wise, it continued to be unable to shed light on society's most salient debates. For example, it was (and still is) unable to determine whether concentration is good or bad, or how large, multiproduct, multiplant, multinational conglomerates set prices. As the adage goes, "the proof of the pudding is the eating" and no one is eating. And, despite their sophistication, industrial organization models are conspicuous by their absence in the applied fields of management, international management and marketing.

This then begs the question of why? Why has the profession fared so poorly in what is a key field of economics – in fact, perhaps the most important in market-based economies? Table 6.10 lists a number of possible rationalizations, including the lack of data, the overuse of mathematical optimization models. The fact that firms typically have numerous lines of business, the complexity of supply chains etc. Data has been and continues to be a problem as conglomerates are not obliged by law to publish anything other than the Securities and Exchange Commission-defined consolidated balance sheets and accounts – which are more financial in nature than analytical. This makes analysis exceedingly difficult, given that modern firms are highly complex entities, producing many products, operating complex value chains in a number of countries.

However, perhaps the main reason is the insistence on complex modeling strategies. From the very start, the use of game theory in economics has witnessed an increase in complexity, going from simple, one-shot games to dynamic, sequential Markov games. While this has led to an explosion of work, it has done little to further our understanding of prices – real-world prices. When Cambridge economics

TABLE 6.10 Reasons for the Failure of Price Theory and Industrial Organization

1	Lack of relevant data
2	Firms being increasingly complex (many goods, many plants)
3	Firms not reporting line of business data
4	The false promises of complex modeling – game theory

professor Richard Kahn set out to understand pricing behavior in Great Britain in the 1920s, he started by conducting an extensive survey of UK firms, not by writing down an optimization problem. Despite its simplicity, the results went on to form the basis of the multiplier concept in macroeconomics. This would suggest that more emphasis on survey methods is what is needed today – more so than ever.

CAPSULE: ENERGY-BASED PRICING: A SCIENTIFIC APPROACH TO EXCHANGE?

Perhaps one of the greatest developments in the realm of science over the course of the past three centuries was the progress made in understanding the role played by energy in all things earthy and beyond. As Albert Einstein and others pointed out, energy is everything and everything is energy. Matter is energy, force is energy, mass is energy and vice-versa. It would therefore stand to reason that the cost of any good or service could be expressed in terms of its energy content, and that, in an ideal world, goods and services would trade at ratios that reflect just that, their energy content - sort of labor theory of value where energy replaces labor. In other words, energy is the proverbial "common denominator" of the physical world. Whether measured in joules, calories, kilowatts, horsepower or BTUs, it is the currency of the world around us.

In the 1930s, the Technocrats (see Chapters 3 and 4) were among the first to recognize this, and made it the cornerstone of their thinking. Goods and services would trade at their relative energy content. Energy would replace gold as the monetary standard. In other words, energy certificates (currency) would be issued in an amount equivalent to the total supply of kilowatt-hours. According to Ernst Berndt:

> Scott and the fascinating Technocracy movement he founded proposed that dollars and money be replaced by energy certificates denominated in units such as ergs or joules, equivalent in total amount to the appropriate national net energy budget, which could then be divided equally among all members of the North American Continental Technate.
>
> (Berndt 1982)

Henry Ford, the founder and president of the Ford Motor Company, called for the end of the gold standard and the introduction of an energy standard.

According to Howard Scott, the price (value) of a product is thus energy.

Intrinsic value: How many joules it has cost to make and bring to market
Trade value: For how many equivalent joules it can be traded
Usage value: How many joules can be produced with it

Pleasure value: How much people like it (conversion to entropy joules at 300 K)

> It is the fact that all forms of energy, of whatever sort, may be measured in units of ergs, joules or calories that is of the utmost importance. The solution of the social problems of our time depends upon the recognition of this fact. A dollar may be worth – in buying power – so much today and more or less tomorrow, but a unit of work or heat is the same in 1900, 1929, 1933 or the year 2000.
>
> (Scott et al 1933)

These ideas were further developed in the 1970s.

Price Theory: Timeline Summary

TABLE 6.11 Price Theory: Timeline Summary

Year	*Historical Development*	*Theoretical Development*
Antiquity	Usury	The theory of the just price
1776	Smith's Wealth of Nations	Labor Theory of Value
1815	Ricardian Theory of International Trade	Labor Theory of Value
1867	Marx's Das Kapital	
1871	Jevons' Theory of Political Economy	Marginal-Cost Pricing
1924	Richard Kahn's Pricing Survey	Mark-Up Pricing
1932	Price Rigidity	Theory of Monopolistic Competition
1935	Price Rigidity in Great Depression	Theory of Administered Prices
1939	Price Rigidity in Great Depression	Kinked Demand Curve Analysis

Price Theory: Ideology or Science

Prices are at the very core/heart of a market/exchange economy, and thus of the sub-field of microeconomics. Yet, despite their premier role in the study of markets and economics, the fact remains that the profession today lacks an empirically proven theory of price formation. Students of price theory, both at the undergraduate and graduate levels, are presented with a steady stream of models, concepts and results which are either not testable empirically or have been falsified. As such, an expert in price theory would have little to say or contribute to the workings of a pricing department of a large, multinational firm – a sad, but true situation.

This failure is reflected in the field's limited purview. While industrial organization is replete with theories of pricing behavior, few of these have percolated into the curricula of business schools where mark-up pricing continues to be the overriding

TABLE 6.12 Price Theory: Ideology or Science?

Principle/Hypothesis/Theory	*Ideology or Science*	*Justification*
Labor theory of value	Ideology	VLPW
Utility theory	Ideology	NT
Profit maximization	Ideology	NEMPCON
Principal-agent theory of the firm	Ideology	NT, NEMPCON
Labor marginal productivity	Ideology	VLPW
Capital marginal productivity	Ideology	VLPW
Marginal cost pricing	Ideology	NT, NEMPCON
Perfect competition	Ideology	NEMPCON
Monopolistic competition	Ideology	NEMPCON
Cournot duopoly	Ideology	NT, NEMPCON
Bertrand duopoly	Ideology	NT, NEMPCON
Monopoly	Science	
The theory of lemons	Ideology	NT, NEMPCON

theory. While game theory held out much promise in the 1970s and 1980s, it has been, for all intents and purposes, a bust when it comes to pricing behavior.

This should be seen for what it is, namely a wake-up call. High-level theorizing should perhaps give way to more survey work, much like Richard Kahn in the 1910s and 1920s. After all, economics is an empirical science, one based on facts, not theories, however elegant they may appear.

Summary and Conclusion

That the field be known as price theory and not the science of prices (or price science) is, in our view, telling. As shown here, very little of what constitutes price theory has been tested empirically and found to be true, making for the current situation where undergraduate and graduate students are taught what are unproven theoretical constructs, not science – that is, theories without the evidence. Add to this the shortcomings of the theory (i.e. the Nash game concept only being rational in equilibrium) and you get a field that is top heavy in theory, but bottom light in significant findings. It therefore comes as little surprise that these pricing models and indeed most of industrial organization have not migrated to the corresponding applied fields (e.g. business administration).

Questions for Discussion

1. In what technological setting would the labor theory of value be empirically and scientifically valid? Explain.
2. Do prices only exist in free markets? Why?
3. Is the Theory of Monopolistic Competition a theory of price rigidity? Explain.

4 Has marginal-cost pricing been shown to be empirically valid? State at least one study.
5 List three phenomena that game theory has allowed us to understand.
6 How do market prices differ from administered prices?
7 Outline the basic tenets of Hall and Hitch's theory of full-cost pricing.
8 Why has mark-up pricing come to dominate the debate in non-economic circles – that is, outside of field of economics/industrial organization?
9 How would you go about testing price-setting models in a world of multiproduct, multiplant, and multinational firms?
10 To what extent is competition policy related to Thomas Aquinas' notion of the just price?
11 To what extent are price theory and its offshoot, industrial organization, macro-genic – that is, having its origins in the issues and debates in macroeconomics?
12 Why are the assumptions of the Cournot-Nash model of oligopoly only true in equilibrium?

Appendix: Consumer Theory

This appendix examines the evolution of consumer theory, an integral part of modern-day price theory. It will be shown that with a few exceptions, the modern theory of the consumer dates back to the mid-to-late 19th century and can be attributed in large measure to mid-19th-century classical writers who set out to develop a more comprehensive theory of prices, one that went beyond mere cost considerations to include aggregate preferences. As will be shown, the result was the current theory of the consumer, which is utilitarian in nature, attributing the behavior or *Homo œconomicus* to maximizing an abstract variable construct named *utils*.

Pre-classical Consumer Theory

While consumer theory per se is largely a 19th-century development, history (ancient and modern) is replete with attempts by writers to understand, even formalize what are today referred to as consumer behaviors and the underlying motives. One such example is the work of 18th-century polemist Jeremy Bentham who defined the "principle of utility" as "that principle which approves or disapproves of every action whatsoever, according to the tendency which it appears to have to augment or diminish the happiness of the party whose interest is in question." Being more specific, he outlined a series of "causes of pleasure and pains" underlying utility (see Table 6.13). Included are such things as "pleasures of a good name," "of piety" and "of benevolence."

As Bentham's list indicates, almost anything and everything yields utility. Beyond listing the causes of pleasure and pain, there is no discussion of intensity,

TABLE 6.13 Jeremy Bentham's Pleasures and Pains

The pleasures of sense
The pleasures of wealth
The pleasures of skill
The pleasures of amity
The pleasures of a good name
The pleasures of power
The pleasures of piety
The pleasures of benevolence
The pleasures of malevolence
The pleasures of memory
The pleasures of imagination
The pleasures of expectation
The pleasures dependent on association
The pleasures of relief
The pains of privation
The pains of the senses
The pains of awkwardness
The pains of enmity
The pains of an ill name
The pains of piety
The pains of benevolence
The pains of malevolence
The pains of the memory
The pains of the imagination
The pains of expectation
The pains dependent on association

Source: Bentham (1789).

order and choice. This is also true of early 19th-century writers who failed to go beyond utilitarianism, so to speak.

Neoclassical Consumer Theory

Developments in the field of thermodynamics in the mid-19th century had a profound effect on the classical. The concepts of potential and kinetic energy as well as the relationship between the two were instrumental in the development of marginal analysis in both the study of production and consumption. In a parallel fashion, utility was likened to energy, with *utils* being the equivalents of calories, joules, kwhs and horsepower in physics. Following in the steps of analytical thermodynamics, the consumer's budget was defined to be the equivalent of potential energy. His/her level of satisfaction (or utility) was defined as the equivalent to kinetic energy. Utility would be increasing in the quantity consumed, but at a decreasing rate, not unlike second-law efficiency that was increasing, but at a decreasing rate in technological developments – that is, over time. And so was born, marginal analysis, the cornerstone of modern-say price theory.

While Jevons and Marshall contented themselves with this rewrite of the laws of thermodynamics, others went further, wanting to either infer or impart more structure to the analysis. This was the case of German economist Carl Menger, who introduced the hierarchy of needs – the idea that not all goods are created equal. According to him, individuals have several distinct categories of general needs, which can only be satisfied in succession – a lexicographic ordering of needs.

Hierarchy of Needs

Interestingly, the idea that individuals are more sophisticated than joules or calories dates back to this period. According to Gowdy (1985), the notion of a hierarchy of needs is behind the concept of diminishing marginal utility. He points out:

> Economists, from Menger to Knight, have resorted to examples which imply such a hierarchy in explaining diminishing marginal utility. The shift from diminishing marginal utility to the concept of diminishing marginal rate of substitution was an attempt to move economics from subjective valuation to a behavioralist orientation.
>
> *(Gowdy 1985, 105)*

As early as 1855, a simple need hierarchy was developed by Richard Jennings who classified commodities as being either "primary" or "secondary" (Jennings 1855). Primary commodities are necessities which can confer utility in the absence of secondary commodities or luxuries. Secondary commodities are goods that cannot be enjoyed without primary commodities.

According to Gowdy (1985), Alfred Marshall recognized the notion of a hierarchical conception of human needs, which makes it possible to make interpersonal comparisons of welfare. The hierarchy reveals the order in which needs are satisfied as income increases. In broad terms, at least, this order

Unfortunately, little remains of these advances in modern consumer theory, where for analytical purposes, goods and services are indistinguishably lumped together, with no structure whatsoever.

Rejoinders

The focus of consumer theory on generic goods and services on the one hand, and work effort on the other has, in recent years, led many to widen its purview. Among the addenda are concepts such as altruism, warm-glows, reciprocity, networks, etc. Interestingly, these bear an uncanny resemblance to the many pleasures listed by Jeremy Bentham in the 18th century. Moreover, they point to the presence of a humanistic sub-current in the literature, of attempts to bridge the gap between behavior as modeled in psychology and with models of behavior in economics.

As it currently stands, these two literatures have little in common, to the point that the psychologist would have difficulty reconciling the basic underlying premise of modern consumer behavior with the various behavioral and motivational models in behavioral psychology. This, in combination with a general discontent with the view of *Homo sapiens* in economics, has led a number of scholars to develop more humanistic approaches to behavior, approaches that explore the many different aspects of behavior as it relates to choice.

Notes

1 In this regard, they are analogous to language which is a means of exchanging ideas, not an idea in and of itself.
2 This has to be considered a low estimate as it is not known whether other hominins traded. There is every reason to believe that they did given the physiological similarities with our species.
3 He estimated UK's potential to be 40–100 times its actual level of output.
4 By managing, it should be understood realizing a society's potential level of wealth – typically following power-increasing innovations (e.g. the steam engine, electric unit drive).
5 Optimization theory, specifically Lagrangian and Hamiltonian techniques, originated in thermodynamics, specifically as solutions to the potential-kinetic motion optimization problem in mechanics.
6 Put differently, markets as communication and coordination strategies were being replaced by hierarchical management structures.
7 The adjective "perfect" can be seen as being synonymous with democracy as no one producer has any influence on the price (market power). It has nothing to do with its contribution to overall wealth.
8 Implicit was the view that the UK's fall from grace owed to the breakdown of the gold standard. Only a return to the discipline of the gold standard at what were pre-WWI parities would guarantee a return to glory.
9 The Bertrand model had its origins in a review of Augustin Cournot's Principes mathématiques de la théorie des richesses. It was formalized by Francis Ysidiro Edgeworth.
10 European countries were less obsessed with concentration, given their history of state-sponsored companies. Throughout the early modern period, kings and queens granted enterprising individuals with charters that were essentially disguised monopolies. Examples include the British East India Company, the Hudson's Bay Company etc.
11 Although Roosevelt was known as a trust buster, his ultimate goal was not the destruction of big business but its regulation. For him, the concentration of industry in ever fewer hands represented not just a threat to fair markets but also to democracy as wealthy industrialists consolidated power in their own hands. He turned to the Sherman Anti-trust Act to challenge business monopolies, bringing suit against the Northern Securities Company (a railroad trust) in 1902. The Justice Department initiated 42 additional anti-trust cases during his presidency. During Roosevelt's second term, regulating business became increasingly important. Roosevelt had always believed big business was an inevitable economic development; regulation was a means to level the playing field and provide the "square deal" to citizens, as Roosevelt had promised in his re-election campaign. He supported laws like the 1906 Hepburn Act, which regulated the railroads, and the same year's Pure Food and Drug and Meat Inspection Acts, which controlled the drug and food industries (https://www.gilderlehrman.org/history-resources/essays/square-deal-theodore-roosevelt-and-themes-progressive-reform).

References

Baumol, W. (1959) *Business behavior, value and growth*, New York: Macmillan.

Bentham, J. (1789) *An Introduction to the Principles of Morals and Legislation*, Oxford: Clarendon Press.

Berndt, E. (1982) *From technocracy to net energy analysis: engineers, economists and recurring energy theories of value, Working papers 1353–82*, Massachusetts Institute of Technology (MIT), Sloan School of Management.

Berle, A.A. Jr. and G. Means. (1932) *The Modern Corporation and Private Property*, New York: Transactions Publishers.

Blair, J.M. (1959) Administered Prices: A Phenomenon in Search of a Theory, *The American Economic Review,* 49(2), Papers and Proceedings pp. 431–450.

Boyd, W. (2018) Just Price, Public Utility, and the Long History of Economic Regulation in America, *Yale Journal of Regulation,* 35, 721–777.

Cyert, R. and J. March (1963) *A behavioral theory of the firm*, New York: Wiley-Blackwell.

Demsetz, H. (1973) Industry Structure Market Rivalry and Public Policy, *The Journal of Law and Economics*, 16(1), pp. 1–9.

Gowdy, J. (1985) Utility Theory and Agrarian Societies, *International Journal of Social Economics*, 12, pp. 104–117.

Hall, R.L. and C.J. Hitch. (1939) Price Theory and Business Behavior, *Oxford Economic Papers*, 2, pp. 12–45.

Jayabalan, K. (2019) Thomas Aquinas on the Just Price. Public Discourse, *A Journal of the Witherspoon Institute*. https://www.thepublicdiscourse.com/2019/03/49361/.

Jennings, R. (1855) *Natural Elements of Political Economy*, Austus Kelley, Fairfield, 1969.

Jevons, W.S. (1871) *The Theory of Political Economy*, London: Macmillan and Co.

Marshall, Alfred. (1890) *Principles of Economics*, London: Macmilllan.

Marx, K. (1867) *Das Kapital*, Verlag von Otto Meisner.

Mason, E. (1939) Monopoly in Law and Economics, *Yale Law Jou*rnal, 31–49.

Means, G. (1962) *The Corporate Revolution in America, Economic Reality vs. Economic Theory*, New York: Crowell-Collier.

Ricardo, D. (1817) *The Principles of Political Economy and Taxation*, New York: Everyman's Library, 1966.

Scott, H. et al. (1933) *Introduction to Technocracy*, New York: The John Day Company.

Simon, H. and J. Marsh (1958) *Organizations, New York*, NY: Wiley.

7

INTERNATIONAL TRADE THEORY

Introduction

Trade be it local, regional, national or international is as old as our species. From time immemorial, *Homo sapiens* have traded raw materials, food and finished products. Large-scale organized trade, based on specialization and exchange, began with the emergence of large-scale empires thousands of years ago (e.g. Mesopotamia, Egypt, Persia). For roughly eight millennia, trade occurred within such empires, including the Roman, Holy Roman, Byzantine, Persian, French, British, Spanish and Portuguese empires. By the mid-19th century, new institutions emerged, specifically the emergence of free-trade, bringing with it the beginning of the end of the monopoly of empires. In other words, large-scale trade could now occur outside of traditional empires. This period, however, was short-lived as by the start of the 20th century, yet another new form of trade institution emerged, namely the transnational or multinational firm, which, in many regards, was a form of private empire, designed to consolidate under one roof, all stages of production and distribution, from the mining of raw materials to the sale and financing of the final good, not to mention, of overseeing the trade of goods and services across countries.

This chapter examines both the history of trade as well as the history of trade theory. It shows how the latter both contributed to and reacted to the many changes that occurred over the past three centuries. However, as will become clear, the debate over free trade had less to do with the much-celebrated principle of the gains from trade that is a cornerstone of trade theory, than it did to the question of making a successful transition to new, higher equilibrium growth paths defined by new process technologies. More specifically, it will be shown that Adam Smith's support for free trade had more to do with extending the British market so as to favor specialization (i.e. adoption of the steam engine) than it did with increasing the gains

DOI: 10.4324/9781003527060-7

from trade to British consumers. Interestingly, many contemporary international trade agreements (e.g. multilateral and bilateral) are premised on the ability of trade to foster economic growth (i.e. the North American Free Trade Agreement).

What You Will Learn in This Chapter

In this chapter, you will:

- Long-distance (interregional and international) trade is as old as our species, tool making, raw materials.
- There are two general types of trade, vertical and horizontal, the latter referring to trade in finished goods (goods for goods) and the former to trade in value added (raw materials for value added).
- Trade has been and continues to be overridingly vertical in nature. Finished goods are rarely traded against finished goods.
- Trade institutions include empires and multinational firms, the former being public networks and the latter, private networks
- Most of the world's trade today is vertical in nature and occurs within the context of multinational firms.
- Early writings on trade (Adam Smith and David Ricardo) were forms of propaganda, aimed not at increasing welfare (standard gains from trade) but in eliminating impediments to growth.
- The factor content theory of trade predates Eli Heckscher and Bertil Ohlin's work in the 1920s and 1930s.
- Ricardian trade theory has not been tested.
- Heckscher-Ohlin trade theory has been repeatedly rejected by the data.
- Economies of Scale/Increasing Returns to Scale (Krugman models) theories of trade have never been tested.
- Trade statistics, being collected by and for revenue purposes, fail to provide an accurate picture of a country's actual trade and comparative advantage.
- The WTO-OECD has recently embarked on an ambitious program of trade-in-value-added data, offering a more accurate portrait of international trade.

By the End of This Chapter, You Should Understand

- That early trade theory was more about fostering growth than about generating gains from trade.
- That world trade has been and continues to be predominantly vertical in nature
- That trade theory, by focusing on horizontal trade, is mostly irrelevant empirically, despite being a worthwhile exercise in general equilibrium analysis. In short, countries do not trade goods, they trade value added.

- That Harvard Business School professor Michael Porter's notion of *competitive advantage of nations* was a response to the failure of conventional trade theory to yield any useful predictions and related policy measures.
- That despite the claims of the WTO, World Bank and IMF trade cannot increase growth rates.
- That trade theory has been, over the years, the near-exclusive domain of the UK and the United States, countries that dominated world trade in the 19th and 20th centuries, respectively.

A Brief History of International Trade

The focus of this chapter will be on the modern era, that is, from the late 18th century to the present. However, it is worthwhile to examine briefly the history of trade prior to the industrial era. This includes the emergence of large-scale trading networks in the Neolithic era (i.e. Mesopotamia), and the evolution, over time, of hierarchical trade networks.

Large-scale trading networks appeared in the late Neolithic era and were, in large measure, a response to resource exhaustion and scarcity. City-states in the Tigres and Euphrates valley were faced with a vexing problem, namely resource scarcity owing to over exploitation and scarcity in general. This led many of them to turn to foreign lands in search of natural resources and the development of trading networks and empires. In short, the trading network mimicked a value chain, with resources being imported and finished products being exported. Such was the logic of virtually all large-scale trading empires (see Table 7.1). In short, for over eight millennia, international trade was (i) largely vertical in nature and (ii) organized around the state or state-sponsored institutions (e.g. chartered companies). In virtually all empires, trade between the center/metropole and the periphery/colony was vertical in nature. Second, it was coordinated and overseen by the state. This was achieved either directly or via the issuance of permits or charters for the conduct of trade. The point is that at no time in history was trade organized around private merchants operating in free, open markets. A good example is international trade in the Roman Empire, where raw materials were imported from its various colonies, and trade was conducted under the auspices of Rome and involved royal merchants – that is, those chosen by the authorities.

While trade was not free, the empires listed in Table 7.1 flourished, achieving new heights in material civilization. Trade was decidedly vertical in nature, with little to no horizontal trade. An example of this is provided in Table 7.2, where the imports and exports of in the Egyptian Empire are listed.

The 19th Century

As shown in Chapters 3–6, the 19th century witnessed the dawning of a new era, the era of large-scale industry against a backdrop of what were mercantile

TABLE 7.1 Pre-industrial Trade Empires (Networks)

Sumer and the First Empires
The Assyrian
The Acheminde
Athens and the Greek World
Alexander the Great
The Mauryan Empire
The Chinese Empire Under the Han
The Roman Empire
The Justinian Empire
The Sassanide Empire
The Empire of the Omeyyades
The Tang Chinese Empire
The Abbassides Empire
Charlemagne's Empire
The Byzantine Empire
The Seldjoukide Empire

Source: Chaliland and Rageau (1993), 67.

TABLE 7.2 Trade Patterns in Ancient Egypt

Imports	*Exports*
Timber from Syria and Lebanon	Yarns
Arsenic and Copper from Cyprus	Fine Linens
Tin from Asia and Europe	Glass Bottles
Lapus Lazuli from Afghanistan	Vases
Obsidian from Abyssinia	Embroidered Work
Medicinal Plants from Africa-Middle East	Paper
	Potter's Wheels
	Weaver's Looms
	Pullies
	Valves

Source: Chaliland and Rageau (1993), 78.

empires (Spanish, Portuguese, French, British). Foremost among these new industrial nations was Great Britain whose conversion to Watt-Boulton steam power increased process speeds as shown in Chapter 3, thus increasing output and wealth. Problems soon appeared, the most important of which was sourcing raw materials. As had been in the case in Mesopotamian city-states, the UK's ability to transform raw materials exceeded its endowments, notably of cotton, silk, wool, linen and food.

Furthermore, problems in the 13 Colonies had led to the American War of Independence, thus depriving the UK of a precious feedstock, notably cotton. Cotton and silk, both of which cannot be grown in Britain, were keys to British industrialization, without which its trade not to mention its wealth would be severely compromised. After all, her advantage lay not in cotton and silk textiles per se, but rather in transforming imported raw cotton and silk.

The Role of Foreign Markets in British Industrialization

As Adam Smith made abundantly clear in the *Wealth of Nations*, specialization is determined by the "extent of the market" by which it should be understood, the transition to the industrial economy defined by Boulton-Watt steam engine-powered material processes was determined by market (demand) conditions. Without expanding markets, there was little incentive on the part of British industrialists to adopt the new, more productive technology.

Trade Theory

Throughout the early 19th century, Great Britain faced a number of challenges, ranging from extending the market, to food shortages, to the sourcing of raw materials, notably cotton. In the past, these challenges would have given rise to colonial expeditions abroad aimed at securing new sources of raw materials – a story as old as time. Whenever a people or country found itself lacking in a key raw material, it resorted, in most instances, to colonization (read: military intervention) with an eye to acquiring the sought-after raw material.

Great Britain in the early 19th century was no different. If it were to thrive, it would need to increase imports of food and other feedstocks, notably cotton. However, adding to its woes was the growing view, among former and potential colonies, that supplying raw materials to Britain would counter-productive as it would condemn it to a life of servitude, preventing it from industrializing – in short of emulating Great Britain and the other industrializing nations. Such was the case in the former 13 Colonies, where the Founding Fathers, specifically Alexander Hamilton, favored a policy of import substitution, aimed at reducing dependency on imports of manufactured goods (specifically, from Great Britain) and industrializing the fledgling democracy.

Clearly, the UK's future appeared uncertain, despite great advances in its potential (i.e. the steam engine). On the one hand, it could attempt to retake the 13 Colonies by force as was the tradition in mercantilism. However, this would be problematic as it would involve taking up arms against what were, in actual fact, former British nationals.

An alternative was to trade openly and freely with the United States, without any formal political ties. In short, to trade freely outside of the nation-state context. It was against this background that was born the notion and concept of free trade – that is, trade free of government oversight. Free trade would allow Great Britain to import food (thus lowering food prices and salaries), secure adequate supplies of key feedstocks (cotton and silk) and expand the market for its exports, without having to govern "colonies."

The problem it faced, however, was with growing foreign resistance. As Great Britain thrived, its neighbors and indeed all European nations, became increasingly wary of its intentions. In their eyes, it sought first and foremost to become the workshop of the world, to dominate global manufacturing. And as pointed out, this involved importing raw materials and exporting finished goods, thus compromising the manufacturing sectors of its trading partners.[1]

19th-Century Trade Theory: Convincing the Doubters

As shown, the stakes were high for Great Britain. Its success depending on ensuring a growing supply of feedstocks from abroad, especially the Americas – and, according to Adam Smith, of extending the market. However, its success was increasingly compromised by foreign nations wanting to industrialize and enjoy a similar standard of living.

Enter David Ricardo, a financier by trade, who set out to convince foreign nations of the gains from trade, gains that would be shared between both Great Britain and its trading partners. Up until then, trade theory consisted of a series of obvious propositions. For example, if a country had no iron ore, gains could be had by importing it. Or, if a country was particularly inefficient in the production of a particular good, then gains could be had by importing it. This is now known as the concept of absolute advantage. More specifically, a country will export goods for which it has an absolute advantage and import those for which it has an absolute disadvantage.

The problem Ricardo and indeed Great Britain faced, in so far as trade was concerned, was the fact that industrialization (read: the use of steam-based power drive) had conferred an absolute advantage on virtually all sectors of the economy.

TABLE 7.3 Ricardo's Numerical Example

Country	*Wheat*		*Wine*	
	Cost Per Unit in Man Hours		*Cost per Unit in Man Hours*	
England	15		30	
Portugal	10		15	
Country		*Production*		
	Before Trade	*Before Trade*	*After Trade*	*After Trade*
	Wheat	*Wine*	*Wheat*	*Wine*
England	8	5	18	0
Portugal	9	6	0	12
Total	17	11	18	12

Source: Ricardo, D. (1817), 234.

In other words, productivity in all sectors and industries in Great Britain was greater in all sectors than in France, Spain, Italy, Portugal and the United States. Were any of these countries to engage in open and free trade with Great Britain, its manufacturing sector would be compromised, if not eliminated altogether. The price of UK textiles, iron goods, and consumer goods (glass, etc.) was significantly lower than in all other countries.

Enter the concept of comparative advantage. Using a carefully conceived-of numerical example involving Portugal and England and wheat and wine, he was able to demonstrate mathematically that despite the fact that Portugal had an absolute advantage in both wine and cloth relative to Great Britain, it was still advantageous for Portugal to specialize in wine, and Great Britain in cloth (see Table 7.3) This numerical example, while trivial, was nonetheless a theoretical and analytical breakthrough as it marked the beginning of what can be referred to as embryonic general equilibrium analysis – that is, the study of more than one sector of the economy.

It is important to keep in mind that David Ricardo did not set out to revolutionize political economy as his purpose was more practical than it was scientific (see Table 7.4). Free trade or open trade was the key to prosperity as it (i) would allow for the importation of cheap corn (ii) would extend the market, thus accelerating specialization and (iii) provide the necessary feedstocks in the textiles sector (i.e. cotton and silk).

Its somewhat trivial nature owed to the fact that science was not foremost in his mind. After all, it starts and finishes with classical production theory, which holds

TABLE 7.4 Sundry Observations on Free Trade in the UK

- Halevy described Ricardo as the theorist of the "great English manufacturers who dreamt of making the economic conquest of the world." The weapon that the would-be conquerors intended to employ was an international free trade, justified by the doctrine of comparative advantage; the form of this projected economic dominance was to be a trading system established upon England's leading position in industrial production. The view that a freer trade would facilitate the perpetuation of England's industrial dominance was foreshadowed by Josiah Tucker, a mercantilist, who had become convinced that free trade was in British national interest. That this substantially mercantilist goal of making England the Workshop of the World, a goal largely set by the economists, was widely accepted in surveying the parliamentary debates, which led to the abolition of the corn laws (Semmel 1980, 9).
- One Whig, speaking before the House of Commons during the Corn Law debate of 1846, described free trade as the beneficent principle by which 'foreign nations would become valuable Colonies to us, without imposing on us the responsibility of governing them (Semmel 1980, 8).
- We must find new lands from which we can easily obtain raw materials and at the same time exploit the cheap slave labor that is available from the natives of the colonies. The colonies would also provide a dumping ground for the surplus goods produced in our factories (Semmel 1980, 10).

that labor is the only physically productive factor input. This comes as a bit of a surprise as Ricardo and his contemporaries were writing at a time when labor had been reduced to a supervisory role, no longer providing force/energy. Put differently, labor was no longer physically productive, yet the notion of labor productivity stood at the center of the analysis.

CAPSULE: FRIEDRICH LIST AND IMPORT SUBSTITUTION

Import substitution, or the policy whereby a country attempts to substitute domestically produced goods/services for imported ones, has a long history in international trade. Throughout the 17th century, the British imposed heavy duties on imports from the Continent, France and Italy in particular. The idea was to create conditions favorable to the emergence and growth of equivalent British industries.

The Founding Fathers of the United States had similar ambitions, vis-a-vis British imports in the late 18th/early 19th century. The Federalist party advocated high external tariffs in order to protect domestic industry. Subsequent governments raised tariffs on imports throughout the 19th century.

Its success in fostering a nascent American industrial sector caught the eye of German political economist Friedrich List, who traveled to the United States to observe it first-hand. This would lead ultimately to the first systematic treatment of import substitution in the literature.

Trade Theory Stasis

Surprisingly, Ricardian trade theory in its original form held sway for over a century. There were, for all intents and purposes, no refinements, no tests, no extensions. Which is rather odd, given the increasingly important role international trade played throughout the century. In fact, the only innovation came from a German anti-free trade theorist by the name of Friedrich List, who elaborated what has since become known as the infant industry argument. In other words, there exist grounds on which to condone tariffs, namely to encourage new industries, or all of manufacturing in general.

CAPSULE: RICARDIAN COMPARATIVE ADVANTAGE AS A POLITICAL INSTRUMENT

In 1846, the government of Robert Peel revoked the Corn Laws and in the process adopted free trade whereby the UK government stood prepared to sign free trade agreements with its potential trading partners. That is, it was prepared to trade without the traditional colonial administration. That is not to say, however, that they abandoned colonialism, but rather that they now operated on two levels, free trade and colonial, whichever was more profitable.

Despite its generalized nature, the UK's decision to adopt free trade was based on its desire to trade openly with the US. The American Revolution had severely hampered its access to cotton, the lifeline of its textiles industry. Hence, throughout the 19th century, its diplomats made numerous overtures to successive US governments, pleading the advantages of free and open trade. To buttress their argument, they would oftentimes invoke the Ricardian concept of comparative advantage to allay fears that the nascent United States would revert to a mere source of raw materials.

Such was the nature of the debate over trade in the late 19th century, with Great Britain advocating free-trade and countries like the United States and Canada staunchly defending its increasingly protectionist policies. Great Britain's main argument – form of propaganda – was Ricardian trade theory with its unambiguous gains from trade, while the US's main argument was the theory of protection as outlined by German political economist Fredrich List.

It is important to keep in mind that while Great Britain abolished/revoked the Corn Laws in 1846, it did not abolish the Commonwealth, its formal and former trading network. For example, it retained most of its colonies with the exception of those for which it no longer had a commercial interest (i.e. Canada), but strengthened its ties with Commonwealth nations. Only in the latter part of the 20th century did it formally abolish all (nearly all) of its former colonial ties. Thus, clearly from a theoretical point of view, it did not condone wholeheartedly the notion of free trade. Rather, it would be fair to say that free trade was a second-best solution when the first-best one was not available – as was the case with US-UK trade.

Trade in the 20th Century

The 20th century witnessed nothing short of a revolution in the world of international trade, from the emergence of the United States as the premier trading nation overtaking Great Britain, to the emergence of myriad new products which together defined modernity, to the emergence of a trade-related institution, namely the multinational firm – an institution that would come to dominate world trade. All of this against a backdrop of what was a propaganda-motivate theory of trade (i.e. Ricardian) that was a century old. The extremely high throughput material processes, powered by high-speed electric motors, of the early 20th century stood in stark contrast with the underpinnings of classical production theory with labor as the only physically productive factor.

In little time, it became increasingly apparent that Ricardian trade theory was redundant. That time came at the end of WWI, when the world's trading system had been decimated as the result of (i) war, (ii) the breakdown of the gold standard and (iii) competitive devaluations mostly on the part of European nations.

As is well known, the United States and Canada emerged from WWI relatively unscathed, not being a theater of war. Such was not the case in Europe and elsewhere where governments, in an attempt at restarting their economies, engaged in a number of anti-competitive trade-related policies including devaluing their currencies and imposing tariffs. It was in the midst of this topsy-turvy situation that the United States, wanting to guard against unfair trade practices, established the *International Trade Commission* with the specific mandate of identifying such practices and imposing countervailing trade measures.

Other countries did likewise. One such country was Sweden, which toyed with the idea of imposing tariffs on its imports. As it turned out, this would lead, eventually, to an important development in trade theory, namely the Heckscher-Ohlin theory of international trade. Eli Heckscher, its main architect, set out to examine the effect of tariffs on both wages and profits in Sweden. Ricardian classical production theory, being devoid of capital, was abandoned, in favor of neoclassical production theory. This allowed Heckscher and his student Bertil Ohlin of the Stockholm School of Economics to elaborate a theory of trade based on relative factor proportions, one that was amenable to testing and to policy evaluation.

The post-WWII period witnessed the continued domination of the United States in world trade. The technological advances of the 1920s and 1930s, combined with massive foreign direct investment (i.e. US multinational firms) made the United States the premier trading nation. Given that European and Japanese industry had been devastated by the War, the post-WWII period saw US multinational firms establish themselves on all continents.

This was not without consequences as many countries, wanting to encourage the growth of domestic industry, adopted a series of trade restrictions, known collectively as import substitution or conversely the infant industry principle. The latter has a history in trade theory that goes back in time to Friedrich List, who in the mid-19th century, wrote extensively of the virtues of protection, especially as a means encouraging domestic production (List 1837).

One such nation was Canada whose manufacturing sector was dominated by US branch plants. From 1945 to roughly 1975, successive Canadian governments enacted policies that not only discouraged imports from the United States but also more importantly restricted foreign investment. In 1973, the government of Pierre Trudeau enacted the Foreign Investment Review Act, which, as its name implies, created an agency to oversee foreign – typically United States – foreign direct investment in the Canadian economy. In 1981, in the midst of the second energy crisis, it went even further, enacting the National Energy Program which nationalized a number of foreign oil companies (creating Petro-Canada) and made foreign investment in the oil-energy sector prohibitively costly.

Canada was not alone. Countries like Mexico, Argentina, India, Australia and others adopted import-substitution policies with the hope of jump-starting their manufacturing sector. The problem, however, was with the chosen means, namely tariffs on imported manufactures. In a world in which dominant firms can export either goods (merchandise trade) or plants (foreign direct investment), many of these policies enjoyed limited success as US firms simply got around or put differently jumped over the tariff walls by building branch plants in the countries in question.

Trade in the Post-Productivity Era

The Productivity Slowdown of the 1970s, described in detail in Chapter 2, had an indelible effect on world trade. As pointed out, many countries and supranational institutions (WTO, IMF' World Bank) came to believe (unsupported by the science) that economic growth (GDP and productivity) was an increasing function of market openness. In other words, economic growth was increasing in the extent to which a country subscribed to free and open trade (read: unrestricted trade in either goods or plants). This manifested itself in the signing of a number of free trade agreements (NAFTA), and a push for greater economic integration in common markets (e.g. the European Union).

This period also witnessed the breakdown of the Warsaw Pact and a new era in Chinese foreign policy, one based on openness to the West. These developments, not surprisingly, were trade increasing. The level of world trade increased markedly throughout this period. US, European and Japanese multinational firms invested heavily in these former communist countries.

From a historical point of view, this was decidedly a new era. As pointed out above, Adam Smith's argument in favor of free trade was based on his adage "specialization is determined by the extent of the market" and the stated desire to make a successful transition to the new higher equilibrium growth path in response to the new power-drive technology that was the steam engine (atmospheric and reciprocating). Now, free trade would not allow a country to exploit an existing process technology, it would result in the development of new process technologies and in so doing, restore growth rates to their post-WWII, pre-Productivity Slowdown levels.

As shall be shown in the next section, most of these developments had little basis in science – that is, in the international trade literature. The problem, for the most part, resided in the zero-sum nature of trade liberalization in so far as employment was concerned and, second, the absence of any theory or evidence of free-trade as being innovation and thus productivity increasing.

20th-Century Trade Theory

As pointed out in the introduction to this chapter, 20th-century trade theory began with Eli Heckscher's attempt at analyzing the effect of a tariff on capital- and labor-intensive goods (Heckscher, 1919). To do so would require a more complete model of production, one that included explicitly, the capital input. Ultimately, this would be achieved by incorporating neoclassical production theory (described in the previous chapter) in addition to a number of additional concepts and assumptions into classical trade theory.

Unlike David Ricardo, Heckscher was not only a trained scholar but also an avid student of economic history. In fact, his doctoral thesis was on the history of mercantilism. This would ultimately have an impact on what would become the Heckscher-Ohlin model in the form of relative factor proportions. Specifically, as pointed out above, the basis of trade in mercantilism was resources and hence, resource endowments. By assuming that technology was essentially free and thus symmetric (unlike Ricardo), Heckscher elaborated a model of international trade based on factor endowments, factor intensities and factor-price equalization, known as the Heckscher-Ohlin (H-O) model of international trade (Ohlin, 1935).

According to the predictions of the model, countries that were relatively well-endowed in capital would specialize in capital-intensive goods which they would export. Countries that were relatively well-endowed in labor would specialize in labor-intensive goods which would then be exported.

The gist of the model is quite straightforward. In a world of differing relative factor proportions, factor prices will vary across countries, leading to factor movements across borders (labor and capital). However, in the H-O framework, factors are assumed to be immobile across countries. Nonetheless, factor price equalization is achieved via product markets, specifically product prices. As the latter are equalized across countries, factor payments fall into line. This is known as the factor price equalization theorem. In short, factor market equilibrium is achieved via product market equilibrium – in short, by the presence of an integrated world market. A country's abundant factor is made available to the world via exports of the good(s), which utilize the abundant factor. Thus, while factors do not cross borders, factors embodied in products do. Put differently, a country does not export its factor inputs directly; rather, it does so via its exports.

Heckscher-Ohlin Crosses the Atlantic

As shown in the previous section, the United States emerged from WWI as the preeminent trading nation in the world, a status that was only reinforced by WWII. Not only was it the number one exporter of goods, but it also became the premier exporter of its firms, known as multinational or transnational firms. Furthermore, by the end of WWII, any and all political opposition to open and free trade in the United States had been quelled as the Republicans, the champions of protectionism, now openly embraced free trade.

Ironically, the nation that single-handedly invented import-substitution and protection in the 19th century had become, via its involvement in drafting the General Agreement on Tariffs and Trade (GATT), the champion of free and open trade. Not surprisingly, this change reverberated in academic circles in the form of a renewed interest in international trade.[2] How was the US's new-found status to be understood? How was its trade position to be seen? How had it come to dominate world trade?

The baton, so to speak, was handed to a number of academics, including Paul Samuelson and Charles Kindleberger at MIT, and Wolfgang Stopler at the University of Michigan. And the result was a more comprehensive version of Eli Heckscher and Bertil Ohlin's factor proportions-based theory of international trade. In short, US exports of manufactures owed to its relative endowment of capital, and its imports, to its relative disadvantage in so far as its relative labor endowment was concerned. In short, the United States exported its capital endowment to the rest of the world (ROW) via its exports, and imported labor from the ROW via its imports.

CAPSULE: THE EARLY HISTORY OF THE FACTOR PROPORTIONS APPROACH TO INTERNATIONAL TRADE

The Heckscher-Ohlin Approach to international trade is based on factor proportions, relative factor proportions. Was this novel at the time, or were there precedents? As it turns out, the notion that trade was based on relative factor proportions has a long history in political economy. This being said, let us turn to the question of paternity, proper. Bertil Ohlin himself attributed it to French works, specifically to the writings of Jean-Charles Léonard Simonde de Sismondi who in De la Richesse Commerciale that the comparative abundance of capital and labour in different countries determines their territorial specialisation as between industries requiring relatively much labour and those requiring relatively much capital.

The point is that given its intuitive nature, it is not surprising that factor proportions as a theory of international trade would have a long history, one that extends back in time.

The Heckscher-Ohlin Theory of International Trade Gets Tested

No sooner had the ink dried on the Heckscher-Ohlin-Samuelson view of the US trade position did the opportunity to put it to the test presented itself. Armed with input-output and trade data, Wassily Leontief, a newly appointed professor at Harvard, set out to test what was a simple proposition, namely that US exports ought to be more capital intensive than its imports. To do so, he combined industry-level trade data with factor proportions data to construct an index of factor intensity. In short, this consisted of a weighted average of industry/sector factor proportions, the weights being based on an industry/sector's contribution to overall exports and imports.

His results are presented in Table 7.5, where the capital-labor ratio of exports in 1953 stood at $13.99 per man year, while that of imports, at $18.18. This result

TABLE 7.5 Domestic Capital and Labor Requirements Per Million Dollars of US Exports and of Competitive Import Replacements (of Average 1947 Composition)

	Exports	*Import Replacements*
Capital (dollars in 1947 prices)	2,550,780	3,091,339
Labor (man years)	182,313	170,004

Source: Leontief (1953), 346.

was counter-intuitive, earning it the title of paradox, the Leontief Paradox: the US exports were more labor intensive than its imports. In other words, the richest nation on earth (i.e. the United States) was importing capital and exporting labor, its scarce factor. Not surprisingly, this led to a long and acrimonious debate between its defenders and detractors.

The final word on Heckscher-Ohlin as an account of international trade came in 1987 when Harry Bowen, Edward Leamer and Leo Sveikauskas published the findings of the most exhaustive test of the model, involving ten factor inputs and 64 countries. Table 7.6 presents a sample of their findings. Positive entries indicate that the country is a net exporter of the factor and vice-versa. Developed countries were found to export labor, while importing capital, against all expectations. Developing countries were shown to do the reverse.

The upshot was devastating: the Heckscher-Ohlin-Vanek multi-country, multi-factor, multi-good version of the simple 2x2x2 model could do no better in explaining the direction of world trade than a simple coin toss. In other words, when compared to the country's share of the worldwide endowment, it correctly predicted the direction of trade in half the cases.[3] Moreover, the Leontief Paradox was found to abound in the leading industrialized nations. Countries like Great Britain, Switzerland, Austria, France, Italy and others were found to export labor-intensive goods and import capital-intensive goods.

Vertical versus Horizontal Comparative Advantage

We submit that one of the problems with trade theory from Ricardo to Heckscher-Ohlin has to do with its basic assumption, namely that a country's comparative advantage is horizontal in nature – that countries produce goods for which they have a comparative advantage and then trade with other countries for others goods. The goods in question are wholly produced in the country in question, and thus have no foreign components.

It turns out that this assumption is violated not only by trade today but also throughout history. As pointed out earlier, international trade has, since time immemorial, been vertical in nature, often involving imported natural resources. For example, Great Britain did not have a comparative advantage in textiles in the 19th century. Rather, it had a comparative advantage in transforming imported cotton, silk and wool. Traditional trade theory ignores this fundamental fact.

TABLE 7.6 Bowen-Leamer-Sveikauskas' Ratio of Adjusted Net Trade in Factor to National Endowment Data (Sub-sample)

Country	*Capital*	*Labor*	*Prof/Tech*	*Manager*
Argentina	1.32	−0.30	−1.64	−2.60
Australia	−3.77	−0.41	−2.95	−1.79
Austria	−2.03	3.01	2.74	5.64
Bene-Lux	−2.36	1.81	0.88	1.82
Brazil	−5.54	−0.27	−0.85	−0.49C
Canada	1.82	−3.49	−3.40	−2.23
Denmark	−4.89	5.82	2.37	8.70
Finland	4.69	2.14	0.49	4.22
France	−4.07	0.82	0.70	1.17
Germany	−1.05	−0.43	1.01	1.34
Greece	−5.50	2.93	4.48	14.85
Hong Kong	−46.06	4.52	5.24	3.68
Ireland	−1.93	6.73	4.49	13.84
Italy	−7.03	0.74	1.25	4.67
Japan	−5.47	0.10	0.44	0.48

Source: Bowen, Leamer and Sveikauskas (1987), 802.

Theoretical Alternatives: The Theory of the Multinational Firm

In light of the growing realization that conventional trade theory was ill-suited to describe and explain current trade patterns, a number of alternatives have since emerged. One such alternative is the theory of the multinational firm (MNF), which goes back half-a-century to the pioneering work of Canadian Stephen Hymer (circa 1960). While conventional models assume either perfect or monopolistic competition, it is a well-known fact that world trade today and in the post-WWII period is/was dominated by large, multinational conglomerates (roughly 2/3 of world trade), whose tentacles reach out to the four corners of the world.[4] In short, MNFs are corporations that control (own and manage) their supply chains and are present in most Western industrialized nations.

Hymer, in his 1960 PhD dissertation written at MIT, set out to understand the workings of transnational corporations (Hymer, 1976). The result was the OLI, organization, location and internationalization approach, with organization referring to the firm's intangible asset, location to the decision whether to export or produce locally, and internalization, to whether to license production to a local firm or to invest directly.

Unlike conventional trade models, the OLI approach is a partial equilibrium one, that is, abstracting from the general equilibrium aspects of trade. It has endured the test of time and data, being the core model in international management. Further, it has been tested against the data and found to be a relatively accurate description of multinational firm activity.

Other Theoretical Innovations

Other alternatives to the general equilibrium-based theory of international trade include the *Differentiated Product-Economies of Scale Approach* of Columbia University economics professor and Nobel Laureate Paul Krugman, the technological asymmetry model of Marc Melitz and the burgeoning field of trade in value added.

In the 1970s, Max Corden, an Australian economist, turned the standard Heckscher-Ohlin approach to trade on its head by pointing out that most of world trade (roughly 70 percent) occurred between industrialized nations with similar factor endowments, a datum that runs contrary to its predictions. Moreover, a good part of this trade involved a phenomenon known as cross-hauling, which consists of trade involving similar goods (e.g. automobiles, beer, cigarettes, fashion). In other words, countries were importing and exporting similar although differentiated products.

Paul Krugman was one of the first to address this question within the context of a world in which preferences were of the Dixit-Stiglitz variety. In a nutshell, aggregate utility is assumed to be increasing in the variety of goods available to consumers. He then was able to show that with non-convex costs, the opening up of trade increased the number of varieties available to consumers, thus increasing overall welfare.

In a similar vein, Harvard University economics professor Marc Melitz examined the effects of trade liberalization on firm behavior in a world in which technological asymmetries abound. Taking his cue from the data, which show that not all firms export, and those that do are typically large, he generated a closed-economy equilibrium with asymmetric firms. Trade is then liberalized and the effects on the industry are examined.

Another major development in the study of trade was provided by Harvard Business School professor Michael Porter who, dissatisfied with mainstream trade theory, introduced the concept of the "competitive advantage of nations." Among his motives was bringing more of a policy angle to the field. In short, classical and neoclassical trade theory provides little by way of policy instruments, other than the traditional policy tools (e.g. tariffs, subsidies, quotas). But how could governments either create or foster a comparative advantage? For example, how could a country whose electronics sector is threatened by foreign competition strengthen the sector?

Unfortunately, traditional trade theory offers little by way of policy instruments. Ricardian theory simply assumes the existence of a cost-and technology-related comparative advantage, Heckscher-Ohlin theory ignores technological asymmetries altogether, while Melitz-style models assume it to be purely random.

Recall that in the wake of the Productivity Slowdown, free trade or freer trade was one of the key policy instruments chosen to increase growth. The United States and Canada signed the US-Canada Free Trade Agreement in 1988, Europe moved to deepen its integration with a common currency in 1992 (Treaty of Maastricht) and numerous other countries put the finishing touches on multilateral and bilateral trade agreements.

In short, the demand for hands-on trade policy was at a peak – in fact, a historic high. Michael Porter responded with the notion of competitive advantage, which he defined in terms of four generic strategies, namely cost leadership, differentiation, cost focus and differentiation focus.

Last but not least is what could be called a quiet revolution in the study of trade, namely the study of trade not in traditional goods and services, but in value added. Countries, firms and plants rarely export goods that are produced entirely under one roof, within a single firm, or within one geographical region. Instead, they produce and export value added. For example, Great Britain in the 19th century did not export textiles, but rather value added to the raw materials (cotton and silk) imported from abroad. Today's global supply chains are testimonies to the increasing prevalence of trade in value added.

The OECD and WTO recently embarked on an ambitious plan to move the collection of trade data away from the current customs-based total value approach, which is built around total value entering and leaving a country to a value-added approach where imported are netted out of exports. The underlying view is that such data eliminate any biases and provide, as such, a more accurate view of a country's trade position and comparative advantage.

It is hoped that with the publication of TiVA data, the testing and design of trade theories will be improved. As it now stands, most empirical work is based on what are inaccurate/biased value of final output data.

Trade as an Engine of Growth

As pointed out, the post-Productivity Slowdown era witnessed a number of important policy developments, one of which was the belief that openness to trade was growth increasing, or conversely, economic growth was increasing in a country's openness to trade as manifested by adherence of the WTO, the signing of free trade and investment agreements, and economic integration. Anne Krueger, chief economists at the IMF, is quoted as saying: "It is straightforward to demonstrate empirically the superior growth performance of countries with 'outer-oriented' trade strategies" (Krueger 1998, 513).

The evidence, however, is anything but conclusive. Table 7.7 presents the evidence, specifically the results of a whole string of studies on the question of openness and growth. As it turned out, one of the main problems in this literature is the measure of openness (Column 2), some of which are more problematic than others. All in all, the earlier studies found a positive relationship between the two.

This finding, however, was challenged by Ricardo Rodriguez and Dani Rodrik who pointed to a number of inconsistencies and flaws in virtually all empirical studies, concluding that there is no solid, steadfast evidence that growth in increasing in openness. In fact, one could argue that causality may run in reverse, namely

TABLE 7.7 Openness and Growth: Empirical Studies

Author(s)	*Measure(s) of Openness*	*Findings*
Dollar (1992),	Exchange Rate Distortion and Variability	Weak Support
Sachs and Warner (1995)	Binary 0–1 variable is country meets one of a number of criteria	Support
Edwards (1998)	Amalgam of measures used in previous studies	Weak Support
Rodriguez and Rodrik (2000)	Previous measures	Rejected

TABLE 7.8 International Trade: Timeline Summary

Year	*Historical Development*	*Theoretical Development*
1817	Corn Laws and Need to Extend Markets	Ricardian Trade Theory
1854	Import Substitution in the United States and Germany	List's Theory of Optimal Protection
1919	Post-WWI Beggar-Thy-Neighbor Policies	Eli Heckscher and Bertil Ohlin's Factor Proportions Theory of Trade
1955	Leontief Input-Output Tables and Trade Data	The Leontief Paradox
1960	Dominance of Multinational Firms	Stephen Hymer's O-L-I Theory of Transnational Firms
1977	Two-Way Trade, Crosshauling	Paul Krugman's Imperfect-Competition-Economies of Scale Trade Theory
1987	Complete Data Set	Harry Bowen, Edward Leamer and Leo Sveikauskas' Refutation of H-O Trade Theory
1985	Increased Demand for Trade Policy Instruments	Michael Porter's Competitive Advantage Theory

TABLE 7.9 International Trade Theory: Ideology or Science?

Principle/Hypothesis/Theory	*Ideology or Science*	*Justification*
Ricardian Trade Theory	Ideology	NT, NEMPCON
Heckscher-Ohlin Trade Theory	Ideology	NEMPCON
Krugman Differentiated Product Trade Theory	Ideology	NT
Melitz Trade Theory	Ideology	NT
Hymer OLI Theory of the Multinational Firm	Science	EMPCON
Porter's Competitive Advantage	Ideology	NT
Openness and Growth	Ideology	NEMPCON

that greater growth fosters greater openness as countries are forced to import more and more raw materials and intermediate goods.

That the evidence is inconclusive should not come as a surprise as the hypothesis itself is, for the most part, inductive, not having a basis in any known model or theory of trade. Clearly, the historical evidence is mixed. For example, in a counter-factual way, the post-WWII period, which witnessed the multiplication of import substitution policies in lesser-developed countries was one of record high growth in the West. The post-Productivity Slowdown push for freer trade has not restored the high growth rates of yore.

The study of trade is as old as economics itself, having been a key part of Adam Smith's *Wealth of Nations*. Yet, some two centuries later, the profession is still without a proven theory of international trade. As with other fields, this was not on account of not trying. Theories have abounded, especially in the latter part of the 20th century. One such theory is the existence of a positive relationship between trade and growth. However, this has been all for naught as most have been disproven or are either not testable.

Needless to say, this is extremely disconcerting as trade and trade policy have, over the course of the last four decades, been an integral part of public policy. Countries have radically overhauled their trade policies in the hope of stimulating growth, but seemingly to no avail. Free-trade has been a bust growth wise, as evidenced by on-going low growth rates. However, this is not surprising as there was and continues to be no scientific evidence which shows trade to systematically increase growth rates

Summary and Conclusion

International trade policies, especially free trade agreements, have been, over the past four decades, a key element in policy at the local, regional, national and international levels. In a quest to restore growth to its post-WWII levels (see Chapter 3), countries have turned to free or freer trade as one of the key policy instruments. Ironically, all of the hundreds of regional trade agreements and myriad multilateral trade agreements have been achieved without as much as a solid theoretical or scientific basis. Not one theory of trade has been proven scientifically and second, there is no conclusive proof that trade is growth-increasing.

This explains the rise of alternate views of trade and trade policy such as Harvard Business School's Michael Porter's concept of competitive advantage. Clearly, mainstream trade theory has come up empty, opening the way for a whole new generation of trade gurus.

The future, however, looks promising if only because the WTO and the OECD have recognized openly that trade is not for the most part horizontal in nature, but vertical and that the relevant data or stylized facts pertain to vertical trade or value added. Countries and regions don't export goods, they export value added. Hopefully, this key realization will open the way to new, more promising approaches to trade and trade policy.

Questions for Discussion

1 Is world trade mostly vertical or horizontal in nature? Has this always been the case or is this a recent phenomenon?
2 Why did Ricardo, in his numerical example, give Portugal an absolute advantage over Great Britain in both cloth and wine?
3 Was David Ricardo a trade theorist?
4 Why was the United States staunchly opposed to free trade in the 19th century?
5 Was the Ricardian model of international trade ever tested?
6 What event(s) led Eli Heckscher to venture into the international trade field?
7 What is the Leontief Paradox?
8 Is there today a scientific theory of international trade? Explain.
9 Does the presence of multinational firms violate the assumptions of Heckscher-Ohlin trade theory? Why?
10 What does traditional trade theory say about the relationship between trade liberalization and economic growth?

Directions for Future Research

1 An empirically consistent model of international trade (based on value-added data and technological asymmetries)
2 A detailed taxonomy of vertical comparative advantage (upstream and downstream)
3 An empirically consistent model of international trade with multinational firms.
4 A complete history (including causes) of the multinationalization of the world economy.
5 Integrating comparative with competitive advantage

Notes

1 This is analogous the current rise of China as the workshop of the world at the expense of other industrialized G7 nations.
2 Interestingly, the Wharton School of Business at the University of Pennsylvania was founded-financed by St Louis merchant Joseph Wharton with the proviso that all students would be schooled in the virtues of high external tariffs.
3 In essence, the direction of factor trade was compared with the country's output adjusted share of the worldwide endowment. For example, if a country had more of a factor than predicted by its place in world trade, then it should be a net exporter, and vice versa.
4 Miroudot, S., and D. Rigo (2021). "Multinational Production and Investment Provisions in Preferential Trade Agreements," *Journal of Economic Geography*, 00, 1–34.

References

Bowen, H., E. Leamer and L. Sveikauskas. (1987) Multicountry, Multifactor Tests of Factor Abundance, *American Economic Review*, 77(5), pp. 791–809.
Chaliland, G. and J.P. Rageau. (1993) *Atlas des empires*. Paris: Payot.

Dollar, D. (1992) Outward-Oriented Developing Economies Really Do Grow More Rapidly: Evidence from 95 LDCs, 1976–1985, *Economic Development and Cultural Change*, 40(3), pp. 523–544.

Edwards, S. (1998) Openness, Productivity and Growth: What Do We Really Know? *The Economic Journal*, 108, pp. 383–397.

Hecksher, E. (1919) The Effects of Foreign Trade on the Distribution of Income, *Ekonomisk Tidskriff*, pp. 497–512.

Hymer, S. (1976) *The International Operations of National Firms: A Study of Direct Foreign Investment*, Vol. 21. Cambridge, MA: MIT Press.

Krueger, A. (1998) Why Trade Liberalization Is Good For Growth, *The Economic Journal*, 108, pp. 1513–1521.

Leontief, W. (1953) Domestic Production and Foreign Trade; The American Capital Position Re-Examined, *Proceedings of the American Philosophical Society*, 97(4), pp. 332–349.

List, F. (1837) *The Natural System of Political Economy*, London: F. Cass.

Ohlin, B. (1935) *Interregional and International Trade*, Cambridge, MA: Harvard University Press.

Porter, M. (1985) *Competitive Advantage, Creating and Sustaining Superior Performance*, New York: Free Press

Ricardo, D. (1817) *The Principles of Political Economy and Taxation*, New York: Everyman's Library, 1965.

Rodriguez, F. and D. Rodrik. (2000) *Trade Policy and Economic Growth: A Skeptic's Guide to the Cross-National Evidence in Bernanke,* B.S. and K. Rogoff, eds. NBER Macroeconomics Annual 2000, Cambridge, MA: MIT Press.

Sachs, J. and A. Warner. (1995) Economic Reform and the Process of Global Integration, *Brookings Papers on Economic Activity,* pp. 1–118.

Semmel, B. (1980) *The Rise of Free Trade Imperialism*, Cambridge: Cambridge University Press.

8

MODERN ECONOMIC THOUGHT

Ideology or Science? A Summary

In this chapter, a summary of this volume's scientific findings by field is presented. Specifically, the results reported at the end of each chapter are combined in a whole, defining the scientificity of the discipline. It is worthwhile to recall that by science, it should be understood principles, which are (i) consistent with the laws of the physical world (CWLPW) (ii) testable (TEST) and (iii) found to be empirically consistent (EMPCON) – that is, have been validated repeatedly – more than once – by the data. Consequently, principles that violate the laws of the physical world (VLPW) are not testable NT, and/or have been disproven NEMPCON, are deemed to be ideology.

It is important to point out that science and the scientific method were the only two criteria used throughout the volume. While the results are shown to be somewhat damning of the overall corpus of economic thought in each of the five fields, they should be seen as an important step, and a useful one at that, in the Kuhnian quest for understanding and knowledge in the field of economics.

Growth Theory: Ideology or Science?

As Table 8.1 indicates, the bulk of growth theory is non-scientific, largely as a result of the fact that most theories/models are based on assumptions which violate the laws of the physical world (VLPW), notably the fact that labor and capital are assumed to be physically productive. Unfortunately, faulty first principles are the grounds that lead us to invalidate this field altogether. This holds true of classical, Marxian and neoclassical approaches. Not helping matters is the fact that most of the post-productivity slowdown work, including the contributions of Nobel laureates, are not testable in their original form.

This is an extremely unfortunate situation as production theory and its dynamic equivalent, growth theory, lie at the very base of each of the four other fields

DOI: 10.4324/9781003527060-8

TABLE 8.1 Growth Theory: Ideology or Science?

Principle/Hypothesis/Theory	*Ideology or Science*	*Justification*
Classical production theory	Ideology	VLPW, NT
Neoclassical production theory	Ideology	VLPW, NEMPCON
KLEMS production model	Ideology	VLPW
Harrod-Domar	Ideology	VLPW
Solow-Swan	Ideology	VLPW, NT
Neoclassical growth model	Ideology	VLPW, NT
Romer *Ak* Model	Ideology	VLPW, NT
Schumpeterian growth	Ideology	VLPW, NT
Bourgeois dignity industrial revolution (McCloskey)	Ideology	NT
Republic of letters industrial revolution (Mokyr)	Ideology	NT

examined in this volume. Nothing can be right in economics until the profession gets wealth, its creation and its growth right. While this is a sobering though after some 250 years of study, it needs to be raised.

This failure can be attributed to, among other factors, the total disregard for applied physics and process engineering over the past two centuries. As we were able to show, standard production theory operates in a parallel universe with laws of its own (law of diminishing marginal productivity of labor and capital), laws that violate the known laws of the physical world. Growth theory has been reduced to labor, capital and a residual. As the first two are not physically productive, and the third is a residual, it stands to reason that growth theory explains virtually nothing. Put differently, the core theory of growth consists of two non-productive factor inputs and a residual.

Distribution Theory: Ideology or Science?

The state of knowledge in the field of income distribution is one best described by the adage, *if the foundation isn't solid, the whole structure will eventually collapse.* In other words, because production theory is, for the most part, non-scientific, it stands to reason that distribution theory, specifically neoclassical distribution theory, cannot be anything but non-scientific. The idea that wages are based on/reflect the value of labor's marginal physical product in a world in which labor is not physically productive is preposterous. Ibid for capital.

This critique also applies to the surplus-value approach according to which labor is the source of all value. Clearly, radical distribution theory, best associated with the writings of Karl Marx, was and remains scientifically invalid. At the time of writing (i.e. 1867) of *Das Kapital*, labor had been reduced, for the most part, to a supervisory or operative role in machinery-dominated material processes.

In short, there is little one can salvage in distribution theory other than the lessons learned. Further, the only credible theory of income distribution would start

TABLE 8.2 Distribution Theory: Ideology or Science?

Principle/Hypothesis/Theory	*Ideology or Science*	*Justification*
Wage fund	Ideology	NT
Surplus value	Ideology	NT
Neoclassical distribution theory	Ideology	VLPW

TABLE 8.3 Macroeconomics: Ideology or Science?

Principle/Hypothesis/Theory	*Ideology or Science*	*Justification*
Say's Law	Ideology	NT
Quantity theory of money	Tautology	
Real Bills Doctrine	Ideology	NT
Stock Market Bubble (1929)	Ideology	NEMPCON
Animal spirits	Ideology	NT
Monetary theory of the Great Depression	Ideology	NEMPCON
Secular stagnation	Ideology	NEMPCON
Real business cycle theory of the Great Depression	Ideology	NT
Real business cycle theory	Ideology	NT
Unit root hypothesis	Science	EMPCON

with the affirmation that energy and energy alone is productive, making for a situation in which payments made to labor and capital would be apportioned from the earnings of energy – energy rents. As earnings would not be based on any metric (i.e. physical productivity), it stands to reason that bargaining power would figure prominently in such a theory.

Macroeconomics: Ideology or Science

Macroeconomics put economics on the map, so to speak. The Great Depression transformed what was a fledging social science into a premier scientific discipline. So, it comes as somewhat of a surprise, not to mention deception, that virtually all of macroeconomics is non-scientific in the sense that it is either not testable, or has been found to be false. Other than mere tautologies such as the quantity theory of money or macroeconomic accounting, there is very little in the way of solid science in macro. For example, Real Business Cycle theory is not testable, given the absence of a theory of real shocks (aggregate). As such, shocks are residuals, much like in growth theory. Which explains, to a certain degree, the continued existence of schools of thought or ideologies (e.g. Real Business Cycles, Neo-Keynesian, Monetarist and Radical).

The fact that events that took place decades ago are still not understood with any certainty reflects poorly on the field. Among these are the Stock Market Boom and

Crash of 1929, the Great Depression, the Productivity Slowdown and the Financial Meltdown of 2008.

Price Theory: Ideology or Science

Prices are at the very core/heart of a market/exchange economy, and thus of the sub-field of microeconomics. Yet, despite their premier role in the study of markets and economics, the fact remains that the profession today lacks an empirically proven theory of price formation. Students of price theory, both at the undergraduate and graduate levels, are fed a steady stream of models, concepts, and results which are either not testable empirically or have been falsified. An expert in price theory would have little to say or contribute to the workings of a pricing department of a large, multinational firm – a sad, but true situation.

This failure is reflected in the field's limited purview. While industrial organization is replete with theories of pricing behavior, few of these have percolated into the curricula of business schools where mark-up pricing is the overriding theory. While game theory held out much promise in the 1970s and 1980s, it has been, for all intents and purposes, a bust when it comes to pricing behavior.

This should be seen for what it is, namely a wake-up call. High-level theorizing should perhaps give way to more survey work, much like Richard Kahn in the 1910s and 1920s. After all, economics is an empirical science, one based on facts, not theories, however elegant they may appear.

International Trade: Ideology or Science

The study of trade is as old as economics itself, having been a key part of Adam Smith's *Wealth of Nations*. Yet, some two centuries later, the profession is still without a proven theory of international trade. As with other fields, this was not on

TABLE 8.4 Price Theory: Ideology or Science?

Principle/Hypothesis/Theory	*Ideology or Science*	*Justification*
Labor theory of value	Ideology	VLPW
Utility theory	Ideology	NT
Profit maximization	Ideology	NEMPCON
Principal-agent theory of the firm	Ideology	NT, NEMPCON
Labor marginal productivity	Ideology	VLPW
Capital marginal productivity	Ideology	VLPW
Marginal cost pricing	Ideology	NT, NEMPCON
Perfect competition	Ideology	NEMPCON
Monopolistic competition	Ideology	NEMPCON
Cournot duopoly	Ideology	NT, NEMPCON
Bertrand duopoly	Ideology	NT, NEMPCON
Monopoly	Science	

TABLE 8.5 International Trade: Ideology or Science?

Principle/Hypothesis/Theory	*Ideology or Science*	*Justification*
Ricardian trade theory	Ideology	NT, NEMPCON
Heckscher-Ohlin Trade Theory	Ideology	NEMPCON
Krugman differentiated product trade theory	Ideology	NT
Melitz trade theory	Ideology	NT
Hymer-Dunning OLI Theory of the multinational firm	Science	EMPCON

account of not trying. Theories have abounded, especially in the latter part of the 20th century. However, this has been all for naught as most have been disproven or are either not testable.

Needless to say, this is extremely disconcerting as trade and trade policy have, over the course of the last four decades, been an integral part of public policy. Countries have overhauled their trade policies in the hope of stimulating growth, but to no avail. Free-trade has been a bust, as evidenced by on-going low growth rates. However, this is not surprising as there was and continues to be no scientific evidence which shows trade to systematically increase growth rates.

Laws of Economics versus Laws of Science

These findings point to the presence of an important cleavage in economics as a whole, namely one between what are regarded as the "laws" of economics and those of science. Put differently, the profession has, over the course of the last two centuries, formulated a number of "laws," which are fundamental to the analysis in the five fields surveyed here.[1] Referring to Table 8.6, these are the law of diminishing marginal product of labor, the law of diminishing marginal product of capital, the law of diminishing marginal utility, the law of diminishing marginal utility, the law of increasing costs, and the law of demand and supply.

This raises the obvious question of whether they are consistent with the laws of science. The analysis presented in the previous five chapters casts serious doubt over their scientific validity, to the point that each essentially violates the laws of science. For example, because labor in an industrial setting is essentially a

TABLE 8.6 Laws of Economics and Laws of Science

Law of Economics	*Law of Science*
Marginal product of labor	Labor is a supervisory input
Marginal product of capital	Capital is not physically productive
Law of diminishing marginal utility	No equivalent in behavioral psychology
Law of demand and supply	Tautology
Law of increasing cost	Law of kinetics?

supervisory input, overseeing the workings of machines, it is not physically productive and thus cannot seen as being productive, nor having a marginal product. The same holds for capital, which, according to classical mechanics, provides mechanical advantage, but is not physically productive.

It goes without saying that these findings are disturbing, to the point of being downright depressing for the future of the profession. While thermodynamics, a field also born of the steam engine, stands today as an integral part of physics, economics is fraught with contradictions and half-truths.

It could be argued that the failure of economics in general to explain phenomena, whether it be growth, income distribution, the business cycle, prices or the gains from trade stems, in large measure, from a set of questionable first principles.

It is important to point out that this is not the first time its scientific validity has been questioned, has been doubted. Interestingly, in most cases, the questioning or doubt has come from scholars from outsiders, scholars from applied physics to engineering. Unfortunately, these well-intended incursions were summarily dismissed as a form of intellectual quackery.

Note

1 Another way of looking at this is to distinguish between the laws of moral philosophy (i.e. economics) as they apply to the natural world (i.e. studied by natural philosophers), and the laws of science proper.

9

NOBELS

Ideology or Science?

In this chapter, the contributions of the 55 Nobel Prizes in economics (1969–2024) are examined critically. This involves determining whether the work for which they were awarded is scientific in nature, by which it should be understood, consistent with the laws of nature and the scientific method. Given that the Nobel committee awards prizes for the development of analytical tools and methods in the fields of physics, chemistry and medicine, an additional criterion (to those used in the previous chapter) will be added, namely the development of tools and methods (DTM).

As can be seen, the large majority of contributions leading to the awarding of a Nobel Prize (Bank of Sweden Prize in Economics in honor of Alfred Nobel) were not and are not scientific either because they are not consistent with the laws of the physical world, are not testable or not confirmed by the data. Take, for example, Paul Romer's 2018 prize for his contribution on ideas and growth. As shown in Chapter 3, the Romer *Ak* model violates the laws of physics as it assumes that both labor and capital are physically productive, leaving the residual, which the profession attributes to ideas, without however providing any evidence. A similar rationale can be applied to Robert Solow's 1987 prize for his contributions to economic growth. Again, his theory violates basic mechanics, leaving the residual as the only legitimate (?) factor. Another example is Paul Krugman's work on differentiated products and scale economies. While intuitively appealing, it has never been tested and found to be accurate.

Of those prizes deemed to be scientific, most are based on the DTM, hence not truly scientific. A good example is Claudia Goldin's 2023 prize for documenting the wage gap for women. We added this criterion to those in the previous chapter to render the analysis consistent with that of the various Nobel committees (physics, chemistry, medicine). While these tools and methods play an important role in the

DOI: 10.4324/9781003527060-9

TABLE 9.1 Nobel Prize Recipients, Their Contributions and Science

Year	*Recipient*	*Country*	*Contribution*	*Ideology or Science*	*Justification*
1969	Ragnar Frisch; Jan Tinbergen	Norway	Work in econometrics	Science	DTM
1970	Paul Samuelson	US	Work in scientific analysis of economic theory	Ideology	VLPW, NT
1971	Simon Kuznets	US	Extensive research on the economic growth of nations	Ideology	NT
1972	Kenneth J. Arrow; Sir John R. Hicks	US; UK	Contributions to general economic equilibrium theory and welfare theory	Ideology	VLPW
1973	Wassily Leontief	US	Input-output analysis	Science	DTM
1974	Friedrich von Hayek; Gunnar Myrdal	UK	Pioneering analysis of the interdependence of economic, social, and institutional phenomena	Ideology	NT
1975	Leonid Vitalyevich Kantorovich; Tjalling C. Koopmans	USSR	Contributions to the theory of optimum allocation of resources	Science	DTM
1976	Milton Friedman	US	Consumption analysis, monetary theory, and economic stabilization	Ideology	NEMPCON
1977	James Edward Meade; Bertil Ohlin	UK; Sweden	Contributions to the theory of international trade	Ideology	NT
1978	Herbert Alexander Simon	US	Decision-making processes in economic organizations	Ideology	NT
1979	Sir Arthur Lewis; Theodore William Schultz	UK; US	Analyses of economic processes in developing nations	Ideology	NT
1980	Lawrence Robert Klein	US	Development and analysis of empirical models of business fluctuations	Ideology	NT
1981	James Tobin	US	Portfolio selection theory of investment	Science	DTM

(*Continued*)

TABLE 9.1 (Continued)

Year	*Recipient*	*Country*	*Contribution*	*Ideology or Science*	*Justification*
1982	George J. Stigler	US	Economic effects of governmental regulation	Ideology	NT
1983	Gerard Debreu	US	Mathematical proof of supply-and-demand theory	Ideology	NT
1984	Sir Richard Stone	UK	Development of a national income accounting system	Science	DTM
1985	Franco Modigliani	US	Analyses of household savings and financial markets	Science	EMPCON
1986	James M. Buchanan	US	Public-choice theory bridging economics and political science	Ideology	NT
1987	Robert Merton Solow	US	Contributions to the theory of economic growth	Ideology	VLPW, NT
1988	Maurice Allais	France	Contributions to the theory of markets and efficient use of resources	Ideology	NT
1989	Trygve Haavelmo	Norway	Development of statistical techniques for economic forecasting	Science	DTM
1990	Harry M. Markowitz; Merton H. Miller; William F. Sharpe	US	Study of financial markets and investment decision-making	Ideology	NT
1991	Ronald Coase	US	Application of economic principles to the study of law	Ideology	NT
1992	Gary S. Becker	US	Application of economic theory to social sciences	Ideology	VLPW
1993	Robert William Fogel; Douglass C. North	US	Contributions to economic history	Science	EMPCON
1994	John C. Harsanyi; John F. Nash; Reinhard Selten	US	Development of game theory	Science	DTM

(*Continued*)

TABLE 9.1 (Continued)

Year	*Recipient*	*Country*	*Contribution*	*Ideology or Science*	*Justification*
1995	Robert E. Lucas, Jr.	US	Incorporation of rational expectations in macroeconomic theory	Ideology	NEMPCON
1996	James A. Mirrlees; William Vickery	UK	Contributions to the theory of incentives under conditions of asymmetric information	Ideology	NT
1997	Robert C. Merton; Myron S. Scholes	US	Method for determining the value of stock options and other derivatives	Ideology	NEMPCON
1998	Amartya Sen	India	Contributions to welfare economics	Ideology	NT
1999	Robert A. Mundell	Canada	Analysis of optimum currency areas and of policy under different exchange-rate regimes	Ideology	NT
2000	James J. Heckman; Daniel L. McFaden	US	Development of methods of statistical analysis of individual and household behaviour	Science	DTM
2001	George A. Akerlof; Michael Spence	US	Analysis of markets with asymmetric information	Ideology	NEMPCON
2002	Joseph E. Stiglitz; Daniel Kahneman	US	Analysis of markets with asymmetric information	Ideology	NT
2002	Vernon L. Smith	US	Establishment of laboratory experiments as a tool in empirical economic analysis	Science	DTM
2003	Robert F. Engle; Clive W.J. Granger	US; UK	Development of techniques for the analysis of time series data	Science	DTM

(*Continued*)

TABLE 9.1 (Continued)

Year	*Recipient*	*Country*	*Contribution*	*Ideology or Science*	*Justification*
2004	Finn E. Kydland; Edward C. Prescott	Norway; US	Contributions to dynamic macroeconomics	Ideology	NT
2005	Robert J. Aumann; Thomas C. Schelling	Israel; US	Contributions to game-theory analysis	Science	DTM
2006	Edmund S. Phelps	US	Analysis of intertemporal trade-offs in macroeconomic policy	Science	DTM
2007	Leonid Hurwicz; Eric S. Maskin; Roger B. Myerson	US	Work that laid the foundations of mechanism design theory	Ideology	NT
2008	Paul Krugman	US	Analysis of trade patterns and location of economic activity	Ideology	NT
2009	Oliver E. Williamson; Elinor Ostrom	US	Analysis of economic governance, especially the boundaries of the firm	Ideology	NT
2010	Peter A. Diamond; Dale T. Mortenson; Christopher A. Pissarides	US; Cyprus; UK	Analysis of markets with search frictions	Ideology	NT
2011	Thomas J. Sargent; Christopher A. Sims	US	Empirical research on cause and effect in the macroeconomy	Science	DTM
2012	Alvin E. Roth; Lloyd S. Shapley	US	Work on market design and matching theory	Ideology	NT
2013	Eugene F. Fama; Lars P. Hansen; Robert J. Shiller	US	Empirical analysis of asset prices	Ideology	NEMPCON
2014	Jean Tirole	France	Analysis of market power and regulation	Ideology	NT
2015	Angus S. Deaton	UK	Analysis of consumption, poverty, and welfare	Ideology	NT

(*Continued*)

TABLE 9.1 (Continued)

Year	*Recipient*	*Country*	*Contribution*	*Ideology or Science*	*Justification*
2016	Oliver Hart; Bengt Holmström	UK; Finland	Contributions to contract theory	Ideology	NT
2017	Richard Thaler	US	Contributions to behavioral economics	Science	EMPCON
2018	William D. Nordhaus; Paul M. Romer	US	Integration of climate change into long-run macroeconomic analysis	Ideology	NT
2019	Abhijit Banerjee; Esther Duflo; Michael Kremer	US; France; US	Experimental approach to alleviating global poverty	Ideology	NT
2020	Paul Milgrom; Robert B. Wilson	US.	Improvements to auction theory and inventions of new auction formats	Ideology	NT
2021	Joshua Angrist; David Card; Guido Imbens	US; Israel; Canada	Methodological contributions to the analysis of causal relationships	Science	DTM
2022	Ben Bernanke; Douglas Diamond; Philip Dybvig	US	Research on banks and financial crises	Ideology	NEMPCON
2023	Claudia Golden	US	For tracking American women's labor participation over centuries, evolution of wage gap	Science	DTM
2024	Daron Acemoglu; Simon Johnson; James Robinson	Turkey; US; US; US	For studies of how institutions are formed and affect prosperity	Ideology	NEMPCON

field today, they have failed to solve some, if not most, of the on-going issues and puzzles in economics.

This leads us to conclude that the Nobel in economics bears little in common with those in the other scientific fields where the contributions are truly pathbreaking and scientific in the Popperian sense. The awarding committees in these fields (physics, chemistry, and medicine) reward major findings that have gone on to change our understanding of the universe. The findings in question have been shown to be empirically accurate, on a repeated basis. Such, however, is not the case in economics where few contributions (in fact, none) have solved some of the puzzles or mysteries in economics. For example, despite 55 prizes, we still do not understand the Great Depression, the Stock Market Boom and Crash of 1929, the Productivity Slowdown and the Financial Crisis of 2008. Robert Solow was awarded a prize for what was a restatement of the neoclassical growth theory and the information paradox. It goes without saying that prizes in other fields have not been and could not have been awarded on similar grounds.

10

DIRECTIONS FOR FUTURE RESEARCH

As pointed out in Introduction, the study of economic thought should not only provide the student with an understanding of the events that shaped the thinking in each of the five fields examined here but also provide a blueprint of sorts for future research. In other words, based on the history of the field and the current state of knowledge, on the trials and tribulations in each of the fields, what needs to be done.

The following is admittedly a subjective guide to where future research should go. It is based on the exigencies of science and of the scientific method.

Running through each one of the five fields examined in this book is the need for a more scientific framework for the understanding of material processes. This is not surprising, given its foundational nature as the starting point for all others. As pointed out in Introduction, if the foundation isn't solid, then there are risks that the rest of the structure will collapse.

In many regards, these directions for future research were hinted at by a number of observers over the course of the past two centuries. In many cases, the source was from outside the profession, a good example of which was the Technocrats in the 1920s and 1930s who were, for the most part, engineers. Another is 1921 Nobel laureate Frederick Soddy who was a chemist turned economist.

This, however, can only be achieved with a greater openness on the part of the profession to cooperating with other related fields. A good example is in the field of economic growth, where in the aftermath of the Productivity Slowdown, the profession turned inward in search of answers to what were clearly matters and issues outside of its purview, notably technological change and the actual Solow residuals. At no point in time, over the past five decades, did the profession reach out to production engineers for answers or clues.

DOI: 10.4324/9781003527060-10

TABLE 10.1 Directions for Future Research

Field	*Directions*
Growth Theory	Formalizations of growth that are consistent with the universal laws that govern material processes.
	This entails more emphasis on the laws of mechanics, thermodynamics and kinetics as well as a deeper understanding of the organization of material processes.
	Work in closer collaboration with production engineers.
	Promote the idea of consilience across fields that study material processes.
Income Distribution	In dire need of a scientifically correct model of material processes.
	Dispense with the invalid concept of marginal productivity, except for energy.
	See modern-day workers as lower-level managers (of machines).
	Place more emphasis on bargaining.
Macroeconomics	Place more emphasis on understanding epoch-defining events like the Great Depression and the Financial Meltdown.
	Focus on the multidimensional nature of macroeconomic equilibria, adding such things as visions and expectations and the variable/fixed national income distinction.
Price Theory	Focus on the need for data.
	In the tradition of Richard Kahn and Hall and Hitch, make more place for survey methods and case studies.
	Acknowledge the multiproduct, multi-plant, multi-national nature of the modern industry.
	Concentrate on pricing decisions over the course of firm's expected lifetime as opposed to at a single point in time.
International Trade	Focus on TiVA, trade-in-value-added.
	Acknowledge the predominantly vertical nature of trade.
	More case studies.
	More emphasis on general equilibrium models of trade.

It is important to remind ourselves that the field of economics is one that is primarily concerned with the material processes that underlie wealth creation. Hence, by definition, it falls in the domain of natural philosophy, not moral philosophy. Yet, the profession that was dominated and continues to be dominated by moral philosophers has resisted and continues to resist any and all dialogue with the tributary fields of applied physics/engineering and psychology.

11

HISTORY OF ECONOMIC THOUGHT

Fun Facts

1 Adam Smith's *Wealth of Nations* was first and foremost a critique, a critique of the inability of a for-profit economy to make the transition to specialization (higher growth). This he attributed to the extent of market, specifically, the fact that markets were limited. This explains his support for free trade, which would extend markets and thus allow Great Britain to take advantage of the steam engine.
2 Most of the early advocates of laisser-faire and free markets were Calvinists (e.g. Adam Smith, Jean-Baptiste Say). According to Calvin, the hand of God operated on an individual (distributed), not a hierarchical level (i.e. Popism).
3 David Ricardo was not an economist, but rather a financier with a flair for polemics. His theory of international trade was just that, a theory. No evidence was ever provided. His career was short-lived and he died before Great Britain, under Robert Peel, adopted free trade in 1846.
4 Both Karl Marx and Jean Charles Léonard Simonde de Sismondi emigrated to Great Britain with the express purpose of studying the industrial revolution.
5 Robert Owen, one of the foremost critics of the for-profit economy and social reformer, was himself a successful industrialist, owning the New Lanark Mills in New Lanark, Scotland.
6 Alfred Marshall, the proverbial father of neoclassical economics, began his career as a classical economist (also true of all neo or new classical economists).
7 John Maynard Keynes was not a trained economist, not having had studied (either at the undergraduate or graduate levels) the field. It is said that he enrolled in one economics course but did not write the mid-term exam.
8 The University of Chicago was financed in large measure by the John D. Rockefeller, founder and president of Standard Oil, which had been the target of the

DOI: 10.4324/9781003527060-11

Sherman Antitrust Act of 1890, leading to its eventual break-up. It is said that its decidedly free-market bend owes to this.

9 The National Bureau of Economic Research and the Brooking Institution were founded in response to allegations that profits as a share of national income had increased markedly in the 1910s and 1920s.

10 The Cobb-Douglas production function along with its estimates of labor and capital's output elasticities were not developed with production theory in mind, but rather with distribution theory.

11 The Lagrangian and Hamiltonian optimization techniques originated in late 19th-century physics, more specifically in the fields of classical mechanics and thermodynamics. In thermodynamics, the budget in economics is potential energy, while the utility function is kinetic energy, with the Lagrangian multiplier being the rate at which potential energy is converted into kinetic energy.

12 Frederick Soddy, the Nobel Prize recipient in Chemistry 1921 for his work with Ernest Rutherford on the transmutation of elements, devoted the latter part of his career to economics, specifically to reformulating the laws of production and distribution.

13 The 2006 Nobel Peace Prize was awarded to Muhammed Yunus and the Grameen Bank for work on microcredit and its role in economic development.

14 While Nobel Prizes in physics, chemistry and medicine are often interchangeable, economics prizes are generally not.

15 Both Herbert Hoover and Franklin D. Roosevelt staunchly opposed government expenditure in the depths of the Great Depression.

16 On November 5, 2008, not quite two months after the Lehman Brothers bankruptcy and the Western economy's descent to the abyss, Queen Elizabeth II inaugurated a new building at the London School of Economics. Referring to the financial crisis, she asked the professors: "Why did nobody forecast it?" The faculty was caught off guard.

12

THE GENEALOGY OF ECONOMIC THOUGHT

This chapter starts with a bold assertion, namely that contemporary economic thought owes, in most part, to the inability of market economies to make a smooth transition from one equilibrium growth path to another higher one in response to what were largely energy-based shocks. That is, it all started/evolved with new or improved power-drive technologies that increase potential rated capacity, thus opening up a gap between actual and potential output.

The 19th Century

I realize that this is a bold statement. So, let me explain. Early classical thought, as Adam Smith so deftly put it, was about the "nature and causes of the wealth of nations," more specifically about the role steam power-driven machinery played in specialization and productivity growth.[1] However, the transition was not instantaneous, but rather protracted owing to a constraint that he referred to as the "extent of the market." The latter acted as a constraint in the conversion. Other impediments include chartered monopolies and the absence of fully functioning credit markets.

These same concerns would reappear at the beginning of the 19th century, raising questions about income distribution and prices in the failed transition. Robert Owen, Thomas Malthus and Simonde de Sismondi all pointed to the failure of wage income to rise in step with productivity. Thus was born the field of income distribution, which literally took off with radical economics (i.e. Engels and Marx).

Another related issue was price adjustment. Could the price mechanism ensure the transition? Would prices fall in response to technological change? Or would firms simply reduce the demand for labor in response to technological change as

DOI: 10.4324/9781003527060-12

Engels and Marx argued, and Thorstein Veblen would go on to reiterate in the early 20th century (i.e. sabotage).

Put differently, running through all these developments were the disequilibria brought about by power drive-based innovations. In a counter-factual way, if the latter were to be removed from the equation, then you get the status quo of the British economy in the 17th century, no Adam Smith, no David Ricardo, no Karl Marx and no Alfred Marshall.

The 20th Century

As shown in the previous chapters, developments in the 20th century paralleled those of the 19th century both in cause and effect. The 20th century witnessed the development of a new power-driven technology in the form of electric unit drive, raising the question of successful transitions again. Both income distribution and price theory would, once again, be in the spotlight. Charles Cobb and Paul Douglas' empirical work on the neoclassical production was motivated by distribution concerns – notably that wages had not kept up with productivity. Various developments in price theory (hereafter industrial organization) owed to the failure of prices to seemingly fall in response to cost-reducing technological change, monopolistic competition and the kinked demand curve being two examples.

Again, remove the relevant power drive-based innovation (i.e. electric unit drive) and you get the economic thought of the late 19th century and the US economy of the 19th century.

The Birth of Communism

Karl Marx's blueprint for a communist-based economy and society was also the result of the failed transitions in response to technological change. His macroeconomic model of cycles and the eventual demise of capitalism was based on future failed transitions, the weight of which would lead to the collapse of capitalism.

Ironically, the rise of the Soviet Union, the earliest manifestation of radical thought, was the result of the failure of pre-Bolshevik society to adopt the new power-drive technology that was transforming the world, namely electric unit drive and electricity in general. As Lenin so aptly put it, socialism was about electrification and soviet governance.

> *You will hear the report of the State Electrification Commission, which was set up in conformity with the decision of the All-Russia Central Executive Committee of February 7, 1920. On February 21, the Presidium of the Supreme Council of the National Economy signed the final ordinance determining the composition of the commission, and a number of leading experts and workers, mainly from the Supreme Council of the National Economy, over a hundred of them, and also from the People's Commissariat of Railroads and the People's*

Commissariat of Agriculture, are devoting their entire energy to this work. We have before us the results of the work of the State Commission for the Electrification of Russia in the shape of this small volume which will be distributed to you today or tomorrow.174 I trust you will not be scared by this little volume. I think I shall have no difficulty in convincing you of the particular importance of this book. In my opinion it is the second program of our Party. We have a Party program which has been excellently explained by Comrades Preobrazhenskii and Bukharin in the form of a book which is less voluminous, but extremely useful. That is the political program; it is an enumeration of our objectives, an explanation of the relations between classes and masses.

(Lenin 1920, 15)

The Power Surge Analogy

In conclusion, the rise of economics in its many incarnations can be seen, metaphorically speaking, as a response to the power surges of the 19th and 20th centuries – that is, steam power-based and electric unit drive-based technology shocks, surges that were overwhelming and which tripped the breakers, metaphorically speaking, shutting down – at least partially – sectors of the economy, raising the issues of income distribution, price adjustment and macroeconomics.

Take away these two power surges and you get a 17th-century world, essentially, a poor world, and of course, no economics – and, no thermodynamics.

Descendants by Field

Growth Theory

Growth theory was first and foremost about a power surge in the form of the steam engine. As pointed out in Chapter 2, the moral philosophers at the time – and later – had difficulty understanding both the essence and fallout of this new power-drive technology. This would also be true of the 20th century when electric unit drive revolutionized material processes, accelerating throughput rates for most of the century.

Income Distribution

Early interest in the functional distribution of income came on the heels of the productivity gains that resulted from the conversion to steam-powered material processes. Specifically, the debate revolved around the question of whether wages and income had increased commensurately with productivity, or had the owners of capital appropriated all of the gains? The National Bureau of Economic Research and the Brookings Institution, two think tanks, were created in large measure to address these questions.

Macroeconomics

It was no coincidence that the birth of macroeconomics coincided with the introduction of new power-drive technologies. All aspects of classical proto-macroeconomics pertained to the downturns that seemed to proceed technology shocks, the 1820s and 1830s being a case in point. This was also true of the Great Depression, which followed the conversion to electric unit drive.

Prior to the introduction of new, power-drive technologies, economic performance ebbs and flowed, changing in response to the agricultural cycle, wars and calamities.

Price Theory

While the question of prices has a history dating back to ancient Greece and Rome, price theory in its present incarnation owes to the questions raised by the new power-drive technology that was steam power. How would prices be set in a world in which labor was no longer productive? How would wages be set?

The radicals predicted that technological change and the ensuing cycle would spell the end of capitalism. Neoclassicals responded in the negative arguing that capitalism could adjust without collapsing, that stable and unique general equilibria existed.

The second industrial revolution in the early 20th century and its shortcomings rekindled a century-old debate, namely how were prices set and why they appeared to be sticky? This gave rise to a new type of price theory in the form of industrial organization, which dealt with the behavior of large, vertically integrated, highly concentrated (due to the power-driven technology) corporations. Technology had changed the fundamentals. What was left was understanding the behavior of these behemoths.

International Trade

While the current trade literature is about understanding both the causes of and implications of trade, this was not always the case. Adam Smith, for example, viewed trade as an instrument to increase the "extent of the market" and in the process, increase specialization and ultimately growth in the UK. David Ricardo's contributions to trade were premised on the twin objectives of extending the market for UK products and lowering the cost of foodstuffs, the effect of which would be to reduce the pressure on wages. While his defense of the concept of comparative – as opposed to absolute – advantage was based on the gains from trade, the veritable gains from trade were growth-related, not unlike the current view of trade as an engine of economic growth.

Summary and Conclusion

To summarize, most of that which constitutes contemporary economic analysis can be traced back in time to its proverbial Y-Chromosome Adam, namely energy- and power-drive-related shocks.[2] Classical and neoclassical analysis, as well as Marxian analysis (radical), have their roots in the power-drive technologies of the 19th and 20th centuries. In a counterfactual sense, remove these technologies from the picture, and it will, for all intents and purposes, disappear, as will the UK of the 19th century and the United States of the 20th century.

While this conclusion will appear to be far-fetched to most students of economics, it is consistent with our understanding of the physical world. Increasing energy consumption manifesting itself in the form of greater and greater material process speeds made the West what it is, as well as fostering a science of wealth known as economics. Remove it from the equation and you get the "economic thought" of the ancient Greek and Roman moral philosophers.

Notes

1 The only new/novel element among Smith's three causes of productivity growth (Chapter 1) was machinery, fire-powered machinery. The other two (learning and lower down-time) were well known at the time.
2 Y-Chromosome Adam is the earliest expression of modern human DNA, hence the origins of *Homo sapiens sapiens*. Researchers estimate that he actually existed between 163,000 and 260,000 years ago.

Reference

Lenin, V. (1920) *Report on the World of the Council of People's Commissars*. December 22, 1920. Polnoe sobranie sochinenii, 5th ed., Moscow, 1975–1979, Vol. 36, pp. 15–16.

13

SUMMARY AND CONCLUSIONS

Before concluding, it is important to restate the initial purpose of this book, namely of providing a critical approach to the history of economic thought. By critical, it should be understood scientific, or in other words, consistent with the known laws of the universe and empirically valid – not falsified. This stands in stark contrast with most history of economic thought textbooks that are reverential in nature.

The results, as shown in the previous chapter, are devastatingly and disturbingly negative, with little-to-no scientific content. In short, we are forced to face the reality of it all, namely that the bulk of economic thought is a form of ideology, having little to no basis in science. And it all starts with the cornerstone and keystone of the field, namely production theory which was shown to violate the most elementary laws of physics. Clearly, if the very foundation upon which the discipline is based on is mis-specified or just plain wrong, nothing else can be right. Which is exactly where the field finds itself today.

Some will undoubtedly seek to discredit these conclusions, arguing that it is a veiled attack on mainstream economics by a left-wing radical. However, I want to reassure the reader of the contrary. Chapters 3 and 4 were equally critical of Karl Marx's *Labor Theory of Value*, arguing that it too was based on a complete misunderstanding of material processes in the industrial age, a fact that we contend Marx was quite aware of. In fact, it could be argued that the edifice of Marxist thought, the idea of surplus value, was a ruse of sorts, an ideology intended to spawn a new social and economic order, but one that had no basis in science or fact.

No, the highly critical approach is intended to do one thing, namely raise awareness and hopefully, steer the discipline on to a more solid scientific footing. The steam engine was, for the most part, responsible for birth of thermodynamics and of political economy. While the former went on to develop a sets of fundamental laws (i.e. the laws of thermodynamics) and today stands as one of the cornerstones

DOI: 10.4324/9781003527060-13

of science in general, economics has staggered and stumbled, with a theory of wealth-creating material processes that violates both classical mechanics and thermodynamics.

It is important to point out that this is not a critique of the mathematicalization or formalization of economics, but rather a critique of the underlying axioms – that is, of its starting points. Mathematics is not a science, but a tool. Logic cannot, by itself, lead to truth. False or refuted axioms cannot, regardless of the chosen tool, yield truth, no matter how hard one tries.

How We Got Here?

The tables in Chapter 8 are disquieting, to say the least. Little in the five fields of modern economics examined in this volume has a basis in science and most is impressionistic at best. Enigmas abound, and attempts to resolve them have oftentimes led to a new set of enigmas etcetera.

This raises the question, how did we get it so wrong? Why has a profession that counts hundreds of thousands of graduate degrees and thousands of departments and research centers been reduced to little more than a collection of ideologies? Why is economics orthogonal to its tributary fields? Why is there little exchange between the latter and the mainstream? Were there not warning signs? Canaries in the proverbial mine shaft?

These are interesting and important questions to which we have no definitive answers. One could suggest a number of possible reasons, including the fact that the discipline has been and continues to be dominated by moral philosophers (as opposed to natural philosophers), to the dynamics of ideology and knowledge, and lastly, to the sheer size of the profession. In all belief systems based on ideology, there is an unwritten rule/requirement of adherence. A graduate degree in economics signals (i) having acquired a set of results/beliefs and (ii) a willingness on the part of students to uphold these beliefs. The heightened formalization of what are, in essence, simple concepts increases the cost, thus making adherence almost a foregone conclusion. Put it differently, who in their right mind would devote 5–7 years of their lives to the acquisition of a set of beliefs that they then turn around and reject them? It's a little like realizing after a decade of marriage that your spouse is a psychopath. Hard to admit and accept.

This being said, there is hope for the future. Unlike Adam Smith and Alfred Marshall, today's scholar has access to a wealth of information, such as the physics of material processes. In short, the science of wealth has to be rewritten with the laws of the universe in mind, shedding its 19th-century heuristic, moral philosophy-based foundations. This book is not the first to make such a claim, Frederick Soddy and the Technocrats having done so over a century ago. It is, however, the first to show why and where science has a fundamental role to play in the very corpus of economics.

INDEX

Note: **Bold** page numbers refer to tables and page numbers followed by "n" denote endnotes.

FSC
www.fsc.org
MIX
Papier | Fördert gute Waldnutzung
FSC® C083411

Kolibri 360 GmbH
Ferdinand-Jühlke-Straße 7
99095 Erfurt, Deutschland
produktsicherheit@kolibri360.de